IT'S
NOT
OK
TO
FEEL
BLUE
and other lies

IT'S NOT OK TO FEEL BLUE

and other lies

INSPIRATIONAL PEOPLE OPEN UP
ABOUT THEIR MENTAL HEALTH

CURATED BY

scarlett curtis

PENGUIN BOOKS

PENGUIN BOOKS

UK | USA | Canada | Ireland | Australia
India | New Zealand | South Africa

Penguin Books is part of the Penguin Random House group of companies
whose addresses can be found at global.penguinrandomhouse.com.

www.penguin.co.uk   www.puffin.co.uk   www.ladybird.co.uk

Penguin
Random House
UK

First published 2019

001

Contents

IT'S OK TO SHOUT

IT'S OK TO BE VULNERABLE

IT'S OK TO ASK FOR HELP

IT WILL BE OK

LAST WORDS

TRIGGER WARNING

BY

Scarlett Curtis

JOURNALIST, ACTIVIST

This book is intense.

Words and images can be powerful. The entire reason we've created this book is because we believe that words have the power to comfort, provoke, and create feeling. Words and images can be used for good, but they can also, through no fault of the writer or creator, cause extreme pain. One of the most intense panic attacks of my life happened while I was watching a play of George Orwell's *1984*. It was a beautiful, powerful production but the experience of seeing someone being tortured and gaslighted on stage for thirty minutes was a little too much for my brain to handle at the time. I should have known better (I mean, it was *1984* FFS) but I didn't quite think it through and since then I've tried to be a little more careful with the content I consume.

People like to argue that trigger warnings are a new phenomenon, a symptom of an overly emotional generation who need comfort blankets and handholding. In fact, the concept of trigger warnings began in the sixties when PTSD, then known as 'shell shock', emerged as a medical condition to diagnose soldiers suffering with symptoms of trauma after the Vietnam War. Around the same time, feminist activists began to develop a language around 'trigger warnings' and 'safe spaces' to help women who had been sexually abused avoid re-experiencing symptoms such as flashbacks and intrusive thoughts.

Today, trigger warnings are used to protect vulnerable people from content that might re-traumatize them. There aren't that many things I get very angry about in this world (I tend to be quite a passive person) but the criticism of trigger warnings is something that makes me see red, blow smoke out of my ears and transform into a feminist hulk. If you think a trigger warning is an inconvenience, that it in some way 'disrupts' the purity of art, I'd like you to think, for just a minute, about how much more of an inconvenience it is to have to worry that you're going to be plunged back into the worst moment of your life every time you read a book, watch the news or go to the cinema. To be triggered is not to be whiny or 'precious'; it is to be shot in the gut with a memory too painful for your body to withstand. To be triggered is to be flung back in time without any tools available to pull yourself back out.

Some days, engaging with a piece of art that reminds you of your trauma can be a beautiful thing; it can make you feel less alone, and there is a specific kind of beauty that only comes from seeing your experiences reflected back at you. But other days it can be too much to handle; you might be tired, a bit upset, or simply not in the mood. On days like that it's OK to close the book, switch off the TV, leave the cinema.

If you've ever found yourself getting frustrated at a trigger warning, if you've ever said to yourself, 'God, people are just too sensitive these days,' if you've ever rolled your eyes at PC language or tutted at someone's careful use of pronouns, I'd like to say one thing: please shut up for a minute. Trigger warnings are not a symptom of an oversensitive society.

THEY ARE A MUCH-NEEDED SIGN THAT OUR CULTURE IS FINALLY CATCHING UP TO **THE REAL AND URGENT NEEDS OF THOSE WHO SUFFER FROM TRAUMA OR PTSD**.

So, this book is intense. Some bits are funny, some bits are joyful, some bits are sad, some bits are heartbreaking; all the pieces are about mental health in some way. We've tried to use the pages of this book to highlight the good and the bad of being a human, but there are pieces in here that might be hard to read. We hope this trigger warning helps you navigate this book.

ABOVE ALL,
TAKE YOUR TIME,
REMEMBER TO BREATHE.
AND I HOPE,
MORE THAN ANYTHING,
THAT YOU GET SOMETHING
YOU NEED FROM THESE
EXTRAORDINARY STORIES.

IT'S OK NOT TO BE OK

IT'S OK NOT TO BE OK

BY

Scarlett Curtis

JOURNALIST, ACTIVIST

I was first told that I was 'crazy' when I was seventeen years old. It's not the best or most PC word, but it's the word that I adopted because at the time it was all I knew: I was 'crazy' and I was 'broken'.

My experience with mental health has ticked a lot of 'crazy person' boxes. I spent two years of my life barely able to leave my bedroom without having a panic attack. I spent a year in and out of rehab. I've tried every drug, seen every therapist, had multiple panic attacks in toilet cubicles on trains, had someone open the door of said toilet cubicle (how on earth do you lock those circular doors?), and cried more tears than I ever thought was humanly possible (it's why I drink so much water: to make up for it).

At twenty-one years old – after struggling for four painful years to try to grasp on to some slim branch that would pull me out of the dark, dark hole I plunged deeper into every day – I sat on my bed in a puddle of tears and came to a painful, inevitable realization. My life was not going to be the life I had thought it was going to be. It was not going to be a life of unfettered joy, happily dealing with work and marriage and children without worry; instead it was going to be a life of attempting, every single day, to fight the demons in my head and make it out of bed.

I had glimpsed my future and, while it was nothing like the drawing of my 'grown-up' self that I had doodled on craft paper as a seven-year-old, I slowly began to accept that my brain had betrayed me and this was my life now.

When I was diagnosed (with depression, anxiety and PTSD – all the fun ones!) I honestly thought that I was the only person in the world who had ever had a mental health problem. I would scour the internet searching for stories of people who were going through the same thing as me, and every tweet or blog post that I found felt like a lifeline.

I wasn't alone – I know that now. According to MQ's website (a mental health research charity): 50% of mental health problems that adults experience are established before the age of fifteen, and more than half of young people link mental illness with alienation and isolation; 56% believe that anyone their age diagnosed with a mental illness would be treated differently, and 55% believe they would lose friends; 51% of young people feel embarrassed about mental illness. In addition, other research has found that a third of young people worry that admitting to a problem could affect their job prospects. In England, women are more likely than men to have a common mental health problem and are almost twice as likely to be diagnosed with an anxiety disorder. Suicide is a leading cause of death among people aged twenty to thirty-four and is the single biggest killer of men aged under forty-five. In 2015, 75% of all UK suicides were male.

There are two distinct parts to the experience of having

any kind of issue with your mental health. First there's the physiological/neurological part – something happening in your brain that stops it from working like it should. The treatment for this part is complicated and nuanced and different for everyone. This book can't fix that part, but hopefully it might be able to shine a light on some of the options that are out there and on the people who are doing incredible research in this area.

Then there's the second part: the psychological, emotional part. There's the shame: the shame that society makes people feel for having a 'broken' brain, which isn't dictated by serotonin or genetics. The shame is on society, on all of us. We caused it and we must fix it. The shame is the thing that stops you asking for help; it's the thing that makes you mutter, 'I'm fine,' when asked how you are. The shame is the part that twists and turns inside you until it becomes an aching, rotting mass – too painful for one person to carry and too toxic to be explained.

THE SHAME IS ONE OF THE THINGS THAT CAN KILL.

THE SHAME IS ONE OF THE THINGS THAT THIS BOOK HOPES TO FIX.

When I was twenty-one I started to accept that my life wasn't going to turn out quite the way I'd hoped it might. Three years, 100 therapy sessions, 5 different medications, 50 breakdowns, 98 panic attacks and too many tears later, I still feel exactly the same way. Mental health will always be a part of my life. My brain will always be a wild, rogue, overgrown garden that I spend each day trying to tame into something fit for inhabiting. I will struggle with my 'broken' brain for the rest of my life, but I've slowly started to realize something that has turned this acceptance into something worthy of celebration: IT'S OK.

My mental health is OK. It's OK to be not OK. It's OK to cry. It's OK to be angry. It's OK to ask for help. It's OK to stay in bed. It's OK to find it funny. It's OK to not want to talk about it. It's OK to go to therapy. It's OK to take medication. It's OK to be human.

We all have a mental health – just like we have physical health. I don't think I quite realized the extent to which that statement is true until I read the contributions in this book. This book is many things, but more than anything it's a love letter to humanity.

So, this book is not just a book – it is a SHOUT, a scream into the void that lets everyone know they are not alone. This book is a safety net, showing young people that what they're going through isn't something to be afraid of. My hope is that

"

IT'S OK TO BE NOT OK.
IT'S OK TO CRY.
IT'S OK TO BE ANGRY.
IT'S OK TO ASK FOR HELP.
IT'S OK TO STAY IN BED.
IT'S OK TO FIND IT FUNNY.
IT'S OK TO NOT WANT
TO TALK ABOUT IT.
IT'S OK TO GO TO THERAPY.
IT'S OK TO TAKE MEDICATION.
IT'S OK TO BE HUMAN.

"

it will speak to those who've been suffering for years and those who just don't quite feel right. It's a guide to the friends and family of someone who is going through a tough time and a piece of cold hard evidence to show that having a mental health problem doesn't have to define your life. More than anything, this book is a puzzle piece of the global movement that is working to dismantle the shame around mental illness and to tell everyone going through something that they are not alone.

It's not a textbook; it's not been written by lots of professional psychiatrists. It is personal, and there is real power in people sharing their personal stories.

This book is being published to raise money for our amazing charity partner **Shout**. Born from the Heads Together campaign, **Shout** is the first twenty-four-hour crisis text line. As someone who used a suicide hotline on the worst day of my life, I wholeheartedly believe that the work they are doing couldn't be more necessary. Penguin and I created this book to support **Shout**'s incredible work, but we also created it in the hope that it would help in some small way to ensure that fewer people get to that point – the point where they want to give up, the point where they feel so alone that an anonymous call is their last hope.

Finally, this book is for me. The day that the human race discovers how to time travel (a girl can dream, OK?) I'll do just one thing: I'm going back in time to meet myself at sixteen. I'll wear a disguise (that girl's already going through enough) and I'll hand this book to that broken shell of a human – because that girl, who felt so alone, so hopeless, so worthless and so ashamed, needs this book more than anyone I know. And I know that it would have helped her. I hope it helps you too.

BEFORE
YOU ASK FOR
EVERYTHING

BY

Sam Smith

SINGER, SONGWRITER

Before you ask for everything,
Can I tell you where I've been?
Can I talk to you about my life and the saddest things
    I've seen?

You see, now I'm stood upon this stage,
Singing for you all,
You seem to think you've worked me out,
You're such a know-it-all.

I'm not a poet,
I'm not a linguist,
So the rhyme in this is simple,
But the voice you hear is the kid in me
Who still gets growing pains and pimples.

Yesterday I walked off stage,
I found it hard to breathe.
I cancelled all of my commitments,
And flew home over the seas.

See lately I've been feeling low,
A darkness keeps me blue –
I've always felt it deep inside,
Successfully kept it all from you.

But now I'm bursting at the seams,
My chest is getting tight –
I think there's something wrong with me:
My days now feel like night.

It's made me question regrettably
How much I want to live.
I'm embarrassed, ashamed and petrified,
I have so much more to give.

So I'll stop the show,
Put down the drink,
Throw poison down the sink.
I'll turn away from what I love,
I'll pray, I'll cry, I'll think.

My mum will whisper, 'You're OK,'
My dad will kiss my head,
My sisters keep me laughing
Till I'm safe and warm in bed.

My friends will try to empathize,
Their efforts fill me up
With joy and pain and gratitude
I'll slowly feel enough.

I LOOK AROUND AND REALIZE SO MANY FEEL LIKE ME,
SO MANY PEOPLE GET THIS LOW AND FEEL ANXIETY.

The only thing that helps me is the ability to talk,
To write my feelings down like this,
On blackboards drowned in chalk.

I wonder if I didn't have this outlet that I do,
What do you think would be of me?
Would I be here now with you?

These questions go unanswered –
This life is so insane
I guess I have to live with all this self-inflicted pain.

So goodbye for now,
I'm sorry if this poem was too sad.
Before you ask for everything,
Remember,
Like you,
I'm fucking mad.

SO MANY NIGHTS

BY

GIRLI

SINGER, SONGWRITER

So many nights

Spent trapped in conversation with myself.

Paralysed by the deafening volume of thoughts ricocheting
off the walls inside my head

Curled up in the foetal position on my bedroom floor

Wondering what's wrong with me

Wondering why I can't just be wild and free and young like
I'm supposed to be.

What malfunctioned in my brain to stop me enjoying the
present as it is?

I'm always grasping

Grasping for the future, for an outcome, for answers.

At the same time, I'm always running away.

I'll drive hours out of the city to where there's fields as far as
the eye can see to find peace

Only to arrive and realize that the loudness has followed
me there

Because the loudness was inside me.

Some days are fine.

Some days are sublime.

Some days I feel so ecstatically at one with the flow of life

That I can't understand why

I would ever feel anxious or depressed or isolated or low.

But some days I lose myself.

I lose the happy-go-lucky, winning-at-life, excited, creative girl.

Some days she's replaced by grey

Fuzzy grey with a side of self-doubt, self-hatred, an anxious
buzzing that something's not right.

Some days I feel like *What's the fucking point?*

This happens a lot on days with no structure or plans.

My obsessive compulsive disorder makes it hard for me to
'go with the flow' or relax.

So I keep myself busy, to feel like I have purpose

Useless busyness, filling time to distract myself from asking
'What am I actually doing?'

Sometimes my neurotic planning and moving and organizing
is productive. Sometimes it's the reason I make shit
happen and get shit done.

It's hard when that happens because when destructive
behaviour reaps good results it feeds into the lie you tell
yourself that you should keep behaving like that, even
though it makes you miserable.

BUT HERE'S SOMETHING YOU DIDN'T EXPECT: **I LOVE MYSELF**.

Most of the time I forget that, but I really do.

I have a deep love and understanding of myself.

Just most of the time I can't see it underneath all the other
shit, the self-doubt, self-imposed stress, confusion, panic,
obsessive thoughts.

Social media WORSENS my mental health. No question. But
it is so linked to my job. It's my tool, my platform to
spread my music and talk to my fans. This is the hardest
thing to wrap my head around. How to have a healthy
relationship with something that effectively measures my
worth in numbers.

How successful and popular and great and worthwhile are
you based on HOW MANY FOLLOWERS you have and
HOW MANY LIKES on your pictures? It's a nightmare
for an obsessive, anxious person like me.

But mental health to me, like physical health, can be worked
on and improved and strengthened over time. It just
takes more effort to understand what works for you. I'm
learning to nurture my mind, learn more about it, accept
it and love it.

I have a therapist. I see her every week.

I take antidepressants every day. This doesn't work for
everyone, but it's helped me to cope with everything a
little bit better than before.

I try to exercise a few times a week. Whenever I forget to do this, my mental health deteriorates. When I remember, my mind clears, I feel calmer. But I have to make sure I'm doing it to make myself feel better, not to feed a self-hatred of my body. I have struggled with anorexia and body dysmorphia in the past, and so I have to constantly evaluate my relationship with food and exercise to make sure I'm making decisions based on what is best for me, not based on whether I feel like I look ugly that day. It needs to come from a place of positive self-love, not negativity. How you look after your body is so linked to your mental well-being.

I take a day off and leave the city almost every week. Nature and travel are very important to me.

Making sure to do things for you, things that have no other purpose than to make you happy in that moment, is very important.

Meditate. I forget this one so often. But it fucking helps.

My journey to understand my mind is an ongoing one. Like training a naughty puppy, I'm having to backtrack and rewrite a lot of bad brain habits. It'll take a lifetime.

The most important thing I've learned is: *Be kind to yourself.*

Don't get angry because you feel a certain way and can't help it. Instead sit with what you're feeling. Try to understand where it's coming from and try to reason with it. Everything passes. Eventually.

"
THE MOST
IMPORTANT
THING I'VE
LEARNED IS:
**BE KIND
TO YOURSELF**.
"

SILVER LINING

BY

Fearne Cotton

BROADCASTER, AUTHOR

There is a big, fat silver lining to the depressive episodes I have experienced. It is chunky and bright, like a silver trail left by a black, cumbersome and ugly slug. That shining silver lining has saved me in many ways and also propelled my life and career into completely uncharted waters.

The unexpected good bit, the liberation after harsh shackles, is trying to help other people. Carrying on a conversation that has been started by mavericks in the modern world such as Stephen Fry. Opening up and telling my own story to give others solace and comfort, feeling empathy so potent it cannot be ignored. Of course I hadn't expected any of this. I'm not sure what my hopes were when I first penned my book about dealing with depression, *Happy*; I was simply trying to write myself out of a hole.

Each time I punched at my laptop keys, a little weight lifted. Each time I honoured the words that were spilling out of me like hot lava, the less heat they actually held: **I just had to get it out**.

At best, I thought people would find the book mildly interesting. So many assumptions had been made about who I was, and I knew I was about to change all that. Yet deep down I feared everyone would judge me further and not really understand.

The generosity and connection I have experienced since writing my first book still blows me away now – so thank you if you were one of the brilliant and brave people who came up and tapped me on the shoulder in Sainsbury's to tell me you got something from reading it. Thank you if you have taken the time to write me a letter or tweet me a response. Each moment of connection reaffirms to me that I must keep doing what I'm doing.

When you're on the telly (and I've been on the telly for a long time), people obviously make assumptions about you. I do this too, even though I know about the smoke and mirrors, and how life can be warped to appear bigger, brighter and better on our screens. We all also make assumptions from looking at social media, which has become a beautifully connective medium in which to discuss topics, yet also a destructive and toxic tool with which to compare ourselves to others.

People have assumed from my first appearance on TV at the age of fifteen that I am bubbly all the time, like some sort of demented cartoon character who constantly sucks on lollipops while grinning inanely. Perhaps they assumed that because I did live radio every day during my twenties, I was always switched on, alert, happy and hanging out with pop stars in my free time. Maybe people looked on my social media and assumed I had it all sorted, that I was coping.

These small slivers of myself that were presented on TV, through the radio or even online were and still are, of course, only tiny grains of sand in the grand scheme of things.

In reality, I have always had a completely different life outside work. Parents, a brother, friends, now a family of my own, and of course tidal waves of uncontrollable circumstance that at times have floored me. Being on the TV does not make you immune to life. Life is simply too big, too beautiful, too brutal to be diluted or tamed by a job. I count my lucky stars every day that I have a job I actually like. And every day I feel incredibly lucky to have a family to lean into when needed. And of course I am beyond fortunate to be able to buy food, have a roof over my head and clothe my children. Believe me when I say I'm not the sort of person who lets this sort of thing pass me by.

I AM GRATEFUL, YET IT IS STILL POSSIBLE **TO BE SUFFOCATED BY CIRCUMSTANCE AND DEBILITATED BY DEMONS**.

We all know this, deep down: how many incredible, legendary talents have we seen take their own life? People who shone so brightly they were blinding with their skill and charisma. True creatives and brains who surpassed what was deemed normal to be at the top of their game. I'm in no way comparing myself to these people or putting myself in the same bracket; I'm merely using these beautiful lost souls to demonstrate how fame, success and adoration are clearly not enough. Those heady accolades may have positive feelings attached to them, but they're not what anchor us. They're not rooted in the deep bits that keep us ticking over and balanced.

A while back I fell into a black hole and, even when straining my eyes for the light, just couldn't see it. I was stuck. Rigidly fixed in a pit of despair. Self-loathing, shame and paranoia all close by, smothering my every move.

It took great friends, medication and a whole new perspective on life to get me out of it, but it has led me to something great. I'm not cured, better forever or living happily ever after, but I'm more aware. I know I don't want to go there again and I have a few more tools in my arsenal to make sure I don't. There are no guarantees, but I know so much more today and have started an honest conversation that will stop me from keeping it all a secret as I did before. An indestructible spider's web of people who I know understand me, who will not judge me, and who want to hear my authentic story and in turn tell their own.

DEPRESSION DOES NOT MEAN YOU HAVE TO BE ON YOUR OWN. IT DOESN'T MEAN THERE IS NO LIGHT AT ALL; WE JUST CAN'T SEE IT.

There will be people around you, good souls wanting to help. Even when it seems impossible to open our mouths to let out the grief and despair – the weight of it feels insurmountable – we *must*.

That silver lining just keeps shining brighter for me. The conversation is getting bigger globally, I'm meeting more and more incredible people who are willing to be vulnerable and authentic, and I feel more connected than ever.

YOU ARE ENTITLED TO YOUR EMOTIONS

BY

Michelle Elman

AUTHOR

Growing up, I didn't realize I had a mental health. People don't talk to you about your mental health when there is so much wrong with your physical health. Or, at least, fifteen years ago they didn't. Now, we have evolved ever so slightly and, if you are hospitalized for as long as I was, you'll probably be asked more frequently (and more compassionately) about your mental health, but, back then, it was just me and my butchered body.

Before the age of twenty, I went through fifteen surgeries for a brain tumour, punctured intestines, an obstructed bowel, a cyst in my brain and a condition called hydrocephalus, and yet I was never asked how I felt about any of this until just before my twelfth operation. Although I wasn't so much asked as prodded with the question 'Are you scared of dying?' needless to say I didn't have the best reaction, and what ended up happening is that I internalized all my emotions. During my teens, I couldn't have told you what I felt because I felt nothing. I couldn't have even told you what I thought because I was too scared to vocalize my worst thought – that I believed my surgeries were my fault. And all this was made worse by the fact that I had physical reminders of my most traumatic memories scarred on to my stomach forever, so every time I looked in the mirror I was reminded of the past that I could never escape.

All this would only come out when I was twenty years old,

in my final year of my university degree, when I was diagnosed with PTSD. For the first time in a decade I felt every single emotion I should have felt over the course of those fifteen surgeries. Dragging myself to the first therapy appointment was the hardest thing I have ever had to do, and admitting I needed help felt like a kick to the gut, combined with shame, that logically and rationally I knew made no sense. After all, I was training to become a psychologist myself! While that never ended up happening . . .

I HAVE BEEN ABLE TO **TURN ALL THIS ADVERSITY INTO SOMETHING THAT EMPOWERS ME** AND THAT HAS FUELLED MY CAREER TO CREATE CHANGE IN THE WORLD.

It was the reason why I started my campaign Scarred Not Scared and gave people with similar experiences a place to talk about both their physical scars and their emotional scars.

It has been five years since I have experienced a symptom of my PTSD but, as the saying goes, 'a smooth sea never made a skilled sailor'. So here are my top tips, having weathered quite a few mental health shitstorms:

1. We all have a mental health.

Good mental health takes constant attention and maintenance. If you let your positive habits and routines slip, your mental health will too.

2. There is no such thing as a negative emotion.

From a young age we are taught that there are negative emotions (anger, sadness, guilt, fear and shame) and positive ones (happiness), but this is not truc. All emotions are good and they tell you important information: like anger might tell you when your boundaries are being crossed. The emotion itself is not wrong, but how you express that emotion may be.

3. Your problems are real, with or without a diagnosis.

You do not need a diagnosis for your symptoms to be valid and your emotions to be important.

4. It is not your fault, but it is your responsibility.

You are not to blame for any of the shit things that happen in your life. You did not deserve it. No one deserves it and there is nothing you could have done differently to prevent it from happening. (Even if your brain tries to convince you otherwise.) It is, however, your responsibility to change how you react, because you are the only person who can and you are the person it is affecting the most.

5. Get rid of toxic relationships.

When you are experiencing a low point in your life, you may find that you attract people with a saviour complex. This sort of dynamic often thrives on you being a 'fuck-up'. I don't believe in toxic people, but there are toxic dynamics that have an impact on your mental health. Cutting those people out might seem mean, but if you have to be perceived as a bad person in order to take care of your mental health, so be it. Have no guilt about making yourself your top priority.

6. You have to go through your emotions, not around them.

People get told to process their emotions a lot but are never taught how to do so. Find the place in your body where an emotion sits, and get to know it. How big is it? Does it feel warm? Does it feel heavy? Does it have a shape or does it have foggy edges? The longer you feel it, the more you will notice it warp and change shape. It may even get more painful but if you feel it long enough it will eventually disappear. Every time you do this, you will realize your emotions aren't as scary as you thought and if you can last that pain, then you can do it next time too!

7. Anxiety is fear in the future.

The unconscious mind doesn't know the difference between real and imagined. That's why when you imagine biting into a lemon your body reacts to it anyway, even without the lemon being present. That's exactly what happens when people get travel anxiety, for example; their unconscious mind is physically reacting to a car crash without it happening. The story they are telling themself and the pictures they are playing in their mind are what is scaring them. If this happens to you, stay in the moment and watch the anxiety diminish. Remember that a thought always precedes a feeling, and it's the thought that is the problem, not the feeling.

8. Set boundaries.

Boundaries are simply what is and isn't an acceptable way for people to treat you. Using phrases like 'Do not speak to me like that' or 'I won't accept being treated like this' is important for protecting your mental health. We need to release our fear of wanting to be liked, in order to embrace our need to be respected. If you are scared of enforcing a boundary with a specific person, that's the person you need to set up that boundary with most. Allow them to have whatever reaction they need to have. You are not responsible for caretaking their emotions.

BLANK 33

BY

ACTOR, SINGER, SONGWRITER

I've spent a lot of my life working alongside some incredible as well as incredibly anxious people. Having worked in the mental health sector for a little bit now, I've got a much better understanding of how things work and what measures need to be taken to manage particular struggles. This includes measures I've also had to implement myself to deal with some wonderfully personalized forms of anxiety and depression, even though I'm really, really good at distracting myself and have basically weaponized being funny.

BUT

before I knew this, working alongside/living with/loving someone anxious was really fucking difficult in itself. By anxious, I don't mean normal anxiety like *Whoops I missed the bus*; I mean generalized, sometimes debilitating anxiety like *Am I going to die tomorrow?* and *Why aren't I happy all the time?* At times, this internalized tension would find its way into social interaction and occasionally come across as arrogant, rude or nonchalant. If you're supersensitive like me and definitely take everything personally, it can hurt. Sometimes we then react to that pain as a response to our own until we're all just wounded children poking each other in the eye complaining about sustained eye contact. However, a pure part of me, and indeed us, understands that the best way to handle these situations is through empathy, compassion and effort, so I wrote a poem in my head that I've titled:

'Why are you being such a dickhead I thought we were friends this is pissing me off'

I hope you like it.

I've written this with an incredibly close friend in mind, who I love and adore. Also, I thought this up and have genuinely never written it down before so apologies if it's a load of shit.

I tried to recognize
Cognitive functioning wise
The cogs behind his eyes
The reason so many partners got lost inside
Wondering
Why do you never smile?
Why don't you ever cry?
The answers were always
Pride
Jealousy
The suggestion that he was never kind
But it was never, mind – right?
Like, maybe he doesn't have his mind right

But we feel so sensitive and confined by

The fact that the sense we're using

Is our eyesight

But there's a flaw to the level of insight

And on that floor is someone laid on their back

Meddling with their insides still

We roll our eyes to the ceiling

So surprised by the lack of desire

Inside of a human being

LIKE IF HE CAN'T EVEN COMMUNICATE

HOW HUMAN IS HE BEING?

But it's difficult to see a feeling

And even when we

See how someone's feeling

We base our decision on what we're hearing

When they're speaking

And this whole time they're just praying

That this weight is going to lift

And no matter how many buttons we press

They're still waiting for a lift
And even when we're pushing weights in the gym
People rarely chew the fat when getting thin
And always watching weight will rarely
Change the way you think.

I saw a meme online recently that said
STOP MAKING STUPID PEOPLE FAMOUS

I thought, *FAIR ENOUGH*

But wanted to respond with one saying
STOP PUTTING IMAGE ON A PEDESTAL

'Cause if we all stopped using Kim Kardashian emojis
Then there might be a reality show
About medic school

BUT STILL WE'RE ALL
SUSCEPTIBLE
TO FEARS OF NOT BEING
ACCEPTABLE

Questioning ourselves if we're not socially presentable

It's a very difficult obstacle to hurdle

We take things so personally

It's often hard to be personable

But all I'm saying is

Before doubting the very essence

Of a person's core

Just know that

By hurting you

They've almost certainly

Hurt themselves some more.

FABULOUS
AND FUCKED UP

BY

Professor
Tanya Byron

CONSULTANT CLINICAL PSYCHOLOGIST,
WRITER, JOURNALIST, BROADCASTER

I am a clinical psychologist and I love my job. In fact I think I have the most privileged job of anyone I know: every day in my clinics, I get to meet extraordinary people who have courageously decided to tackle their mental health difficulties. To be with someone at probably the most vulnerable time of their life; to have their trust that, together, we can help them find a way through the darkness and back into the light is a privilege I never take for granted.

As I write this, I think about the many incredible people I have worked with over my many clinical years. There're those who have experienced abuse and trauma and come to me either still reeling from their recent experiences or many, many years later when the pressure of locking it all down becomes impossible to sustain; those for whom an unseen sudden life event shatters everything they thought they knew about themselves and their lives; those with legacies from childhood that they can't shake off.

Although their problems are varied and different, one thing is always the same: the sense of shame they all bring when they first ask for help. Indeed, before we even get to the difficulties they struggle with, I spend time helping everyone I meet to understand that there is no shame. Would they be ashamed if they were consulting a physician about a physical difficulty that was having an impact on their life? No. Well, bodies get tired, worn out, sometimes break, and so do minds. I tell them that they are normal.

We all know that, despite physical health outcomes being the best they have ever been in the developed world, mental health outcomes are the worst. We live longer but also more miserably. How has this happened? Even after thirty years of clinical practice, my heart races and I despair as I look into the eyes of a child who wants to be dead. Suicide is now the biggest killer of men aged between nineteen and forty-four. The UK have the highest rates of self-harm in Europe. Instances of depression in teenagers have increased by 70% in the past twenty-five years. Alcohol, drugs and food have become increasingly popular coping mechanisms. Why are we so unhappy?

We live in a fast-paced world where there is a constant drip-feed of tragedy via the many platforms that offer us up-to-the-second news. Children are raised in captivity as we panic about safety and reduce their opportunities to be free range, take risks and learn about themselves and the world.

"

I SPEND TIME HELPING EVERYONE I MEET TO UNDERSTAND THAT **THERE IS NO SHAME** ... BODIES GET TIRED, WORN OUT, SOMETIMES BREAK, AND SO DO MINDS. **I TELL THEM THAT THEY ARE NORMAL.**

"

Education is built around targets and testing, and we fetishize IQ over EQ (emotional intelligence). Making mistakes, failing, is never an option. Success is measured materially, not emotionally. Aging is devalued as wrinkles are eradicated. We live in a constant state of hypervigilance, fear and anger. So much anger.

What is most striking about all this – to me, anyway – is that the increased rates of fear, anger, self-loathing and depression that I and my many brilliant colleagues see every day are coming at a time when we are more psychologically minded, self-helped, mindful, meditative, medicated than ever before. We know how to do more to feel better, and yet we feel worse. How can this be?

I think that, at the age of fifty-two, after one period of clinical depression (the cumulative effect of the murder of my grandmother, crippling postnatal depression and the sudden and unexpected early death of my beloved father) and thirty years of clinical practice, I now get it. I get the problem. The problem is, we don't know how to be unhappy. In my clinical world we call that 'lacking the capacity for distress tolerance'.

Being miserable is not the same as being depressed. Being stressed and afraid is not the same as having an anxiety disorder. Have we all got a bit confused? In our quest to live happy, productive lives, have we forgotten that it is normal to have periods when we feel low, afraid, unhappy? When we feel low, do we then spiral into something darker as we loathe ourselves for our vulnerability and hate ourselves for not being on top of our game? Despite knowing that minds, like bodies, can break, have we decided that, if ours does, we've failed at being human? Is that part of the shame we feel when we ask for help with mental health difficulties? We are ashamed because we think that somehow we have failed.

I get that. I didn't like being clinically depressed. In fact I hated it. I felt so unhappy I couldn't stand it but, even worse, I couldn't stand myself for feeling so unhappy. I didn't want to see the depression that was staring me in the face. I couldn't accept that I, a mental health practitioner, could become unwell. I knew about this stuff, I treated people with depression, it shouldn't happen to me. Thankfully my arrogant denial was pierced by those around me who didn't see my illness as a failure but as an illness. With the love and support of my amazing husband, I accepted that I needed treatment. I realized that, after years of telling those I treated to feel no shame, I had to tell myself the same thing. And I did, and with therapy and medicine my depression lifted and I returned to the light.

Before my depression I was good at my job; after my depression I am so much better at it. I get it.

So how did I get it? It was my husband who helped me get it when I was depressed:

'Tan,' my husband said, 'you are fabulous, you really are. I love you. You are fabulous, but you are also fucked up and at the moment that part of you has taken over. Let's get you the help to find the balance again.'

Fabulous and fucked up. Absolutely right. That's what we all are. It's called being human. Let's celebrate that, not fear it. And let's never, ever feel ashamed when the challenges of life become too overwhelming and the fucked-up part gets into the driving seat. That is called being normal.

" FABULOUS AND FUCKED UP. ABSOLUTELY RIGHT. THAT'S WHAT WE ALL ARE. IT'S CALLED BEING HUMAN. **LET'S CELEBRATE THAT, NOT FEAR IT.** "

MORE THAN A GAME

BY

Claire Stancliffe

FOOTBALL PLAYER, DEAFLYMPIAN MEDALLIST

Football really is more than just a game. For me, it's a lifeline. A chance for me to escape the pressures of being in the hearing world. It's incredibly hard being deaf in a hearing world. I work with children in schools; if I mishear a child or cannot understand them, I beat myself up. I feel that I've let that child down. Going to football training in the evening or playing a match is my release. My way of coping.

In July 2017, I suffered a very serious knee injury while representing my country at the Deaflympics, the biggest deaf sporting event in the world. Upon my return to the UK (after two flights with a five-hour stopover), a trip to my GP led to me being sent to A&E. An emergency MRI was needed but I couldn't have it done due to my cochlear implant. I had to wait to be referred to my implant centre for an MRI, which took seven weeks. Seven long, painful weeks of feeling helpless, useless, a burden.

Soon after, I received the devastating news: I had ruptured my ACL along with plenty of other damage to ligaments, cartilage and bone contusions. Three months after the injury, I still couldn't walk normally but luckily I had reconstruction surgery privately. It took another three to four months to learn how to walk correctly and a further two months before I could start jogging. The rehabilitation from ACL reconstruction is brutal and you will only truly understand it if you have been through it yourself. It's a huge physical and mental battle.

The day I finally returned to football training, it felt like a huge, heavy black cloud had been lifted off my shoulders. I felt a lot happier, but that fear of re-injury still stays with me.

We take little things for granted, such as being able to walk properly, sit normally, go up and down the stairs, make and carry our own meals, get in and out of the car, drive, sleep – all basic tasks and activities that I was unable to do. Not being able to work was a particular struggle; I have a job I love, so I see it more as a hobby. There are people who cannot do all these things permanently, and I have no idea how they cope.

I also really struggled with the realization that one day I won't be an athlete any more. No more car shares to games with team-mates. No more being covered in bruises after a game. No more pre-match routines. Team-mates becoming distant, as I won't see them or be involved in training. The one thing that I rely on to relieve stress and provide an escape from the hearing world won't be there any more. The one thing that changed my life will be gone and become just a memory. That's hard to accept and something I will not accept . . . yet.

Through a lot of hard work and even a second surgical procedure, I've managed to return to international football. It's been an incredible learning journey where I've had to reassess my future. Football is obviously a very important part of me and there will be a day when I need to hang my boots up. So what will I do after that? I will need something to replace playing to give me that release from everyday life. I have a few things in mind, but for now I'm going to enjoy playing again.

For those going through serious injury, it's important to realize that it's OK to have a bad day. Bad days are part of the rehab process.

CELEBRATE EVERY SMALL BIT OF PROGRESS AND **NEVER COMPARE YOURSELF TO ANYONE ELSE**. EVERYONE'S RECOVERY IS DIFFERENT AND UNIQUE.

WE CAN BE HEROES

BY

Travon Free

COMEDIAN, ACTOR, WRITER

The mind is a terrible thing to waste. The mind is a terrible thing. The mind is. The mind is a beautiful thing to change. The mind is a beautiful thing. The mind is.

In the quest to find myself, I have found truth in all of these things. As a black man in America and the world at large, there are days, weeks and sometimes months when my mind volleys between feeling like a terrible and a beautiful thing.

And the health of your mind can forever feel like a question. As if your perception of reality is one lifelong gaslighting. Is this real? Do I feel this? Is this real? Do I actually feel this? All the while not realizing the casual stress that the minds encased in blackness endure on a minute-to-minute basis. Wearing away at the very fabric of your soul until the final perfect thread is pulled, and there you are. Becoming unravelled. For the entire world to see. Angry is what they'll call you. Violent. Bitter. They will call you everything but what you actually are.

STOLEN. BROKEN. BEAUTIFUL. COMPLEX. **HUMAN.**

It is with this occasionally terrible, occasionally beautiful mind that I have embarked on a lifelong mission to learn to love myself in every possible way and then every impossible way. And, in doing so, learning to limit the chaos and the noise that would want to drive my ever-changing mind into the ground. Because our inclination is to reject the terrible and protect the beautiful, but there is a wisdom and education in both. All the while, the mind just is. Donning whatever dress we wake up and decide to put on it that day.

This is the truest beauty of the mind.

It doesn't have to wear the pain, sadness, grief, despair, anxiety or depression it wore yesterday or the day before or the week, month or year before. Because a mind is a beautiful thing to change. The difficulty sometimes is knowing that change is possible. Feeling like it's possible. Knowing that when you can't get your mind's dress, pants or shoes off, there is someone who can help.

THERE IS SOMEONE WHO CAN HELP. THERE IS SOMEONE WHO CAN HELP.

THERE IS SOMEONE WHO
CAN HELP. HELP YOU.
HELP ME. HELP US.
THERE IS SOMEONE.
THERE IS.
BECAUSE THE MIND IS AN
AWFUL THING TO LOSE.

And in the end we can only be what we are and what we
have become, wavering from day to day, and the mind in all
its malleability will just continue to be. A beautifully terrible
thing. But it's only by being armed with this knowledge that
we can win.

And we can be free. We can be happy. We can be OK. We can
be fine. We can survive.

We can be heroes.

SAY OUT LOUD

BY

Dawn O'Porter

WRITER

Scarlett asked me to contribute to this book and I agreed immediately, but it's taken me the best part of five months to work out what to write about. I have thought about it every single day since then. I am now around twelve hours away from the deadline, and still utterly stumped. 'Write anything you want about mental health.' That's all the brief said. Why is that *so* hard?

Leading up to the moment where I decided to submit this brain-fart of an article, I have written everything from a haiku on grief to an essay on sexual shame. I thought those things were important.

Losing my mum as a kid means that grief, or some version of not knowing what the fuck just happened, presented itself to me at the age of seven. I try not to go on about it, but I seem to mention it at least once every single day. I'm forty now. I guess I have to admit that it's as much a part of me as my skeleton. Nonetheless, my haiku didn't feel right for this book. Too depressing.

So then I wrote the essay on sexual shame, and how almost everyone I know suffers from some level of it – whether it was promiscuity at college, a one-night stand that took a kinky turn, or being a straight-up virgin. Sexual shame is a constant part of our culture, and I thought that was worth writing about. But I'm not sending it to Scarlett because I didn't have a conclusion other than: 'Don't worry about it. Don't beat yourself up.' But, as I'm sure you'll agree, that's hardly the motivational slogan of the century, is it? Although I must say, if you suffer from sexual shame, please know that you really shouldn't worry about it, and that you mustn't beat yourself up. We all have something. It's OK. Nonetheless, I deleted that piece as well. Too generic.

Another piece I toyed with was a poem about how talking about myself saved me from losing myself when I was in my twenties. I started to open up about losing my mum and would pin anyone who would listen against a wall and make them listen to my story. Annoying for them; life-changing for me. But no matter how I worded the piece, I thought it made me sound like a narcissistic arsehole (maybe I was), so I deleted that one too. Too self-centred.

I then wrote a few lines about the anxiety I suffered after having my second kid. How I had Hollywood-blockbuster-level visualizations of jumbo jets landing on my car, sharks attacking me in swimming pools, gunmen mowing me down in supermarkets. A constant fear of the death of my kids, of my husband, or of myself – all the while denying it was happening and insisting I was fine. But as I started to write about it, I realized that the conversation I had to have with myself required more than a few paragraphs in a book; it was one I needed more time to calibrate. So I gave up on that too. Too confessional.

But that's the problem, isn't it? Feeling like things are too depressing to say out loud, too generic to bother anyone with, too self-centred to admit to, too confessional to be comfortable sharing. It's no joke when people say it:

MENTAL HEALTH
IS REALLY HARD TO TALK ABOUT.

I learned that during this process. Me deleting pages of thoughts is what too many people do to their feelings every day. We brush stuff under the carpet, decide we don't want to give it the attention it almost definitely needs. But we can't just delete our thoughts like a Word document. We need to talk more, listen more, share and understand more. Otherwise loneliness and fear will overtake us, and we'll become socially reclusive, living entirely through our online personas, too afraid of our real selves to live our real lives. Terrified of our truth. Desperate, and alone.

Too dramatic?

Maybe. Maybe not.

While we ponder that, I'm going back to my trash folder.

A lot of my feelings are in there and I have to get back to them. I'm not going to pretend they don't exist. I'm not going to deny myself the joy of an existence where I've got it all off my chest. Life, after all, is far too short.

" WE NEED TO **TALK MORE, LISTEN MORE, SHARE AND UNDERSTAND MORE**. "

A WEEK
IN THE LIFE
OF A
MADWOMAN

BY

Ella Purnell

ACTOR

MONDAY

I wake up bright and early. Crack of dawn. (Kinda.) I'm well rested and fabulous. Birds are chirping! The sun is shining! For a moment, I even forget about the patriarchy! My flicks are equal. I'm wearing the new white shoes that make me look far more trendy than I really am. Frankly, I'm adorable. All is right with the world. It's like a goddamn Disney film. Mondays are my bitch and life is worth living. This is MY week. I am pumped, and I am READY, because everything is good. Yep, you heard me. Allllllll is right. Everything. Eeeeverything. Kinda. Except, well. Yeah. There she is.

Good morning to you too, Karen. *

It was my therapist's idea to name the intrusive thoughts. And it was with her help that I learned how to very politely but firmly tell the newly christened Karen to fuck off. As my therapist very reasonably points out, I wouldn't let anyone else treat me that way, so why let myself do it? I'll admit, naming and shaming the abuser has helped somewhat, but it's still *really* bloody exhausting having to battle with your own mind every single day.

*Karen: a massive cunt.
Not the kind of cunt I can punch in the face. An invisible cunt who is literally just a voice in my head telling me that I am shit. All the time. Like, seriously, all the time. She doesn't go away, and she hurts my feelings in all kinds of wonderfully creative ways. (It's kind of like moving back in with your parents again, except worse, and your parents are, like, inside you.)
Yep.
I'll leave you with that.

Today's battle lasts six hours, one panic attack and thirty unread emails. I am defeated. (She's really put in an extra shift today, so it's only fair.) Turns out, Mondays really aren't my bitch. By the time I'm home, my flicks are sweated off, my white shoes are grey shoes, and I've lost two jobs and an earring. My mind is in overdrive. I'm exhausted. I try to end the day with my usual night-time routine of herbal tea and a good book, but I spill the fucking tea. It's the final straw. It's agony. I'm a drama queen. I'm clumsy. An idiot. I hate my brain and my camomile-scented self.

Fuck off, Karen.

TUESDAY

I leave therapy feeling lighter.

Mainly because my wallet is now empty. Hurrah! Depressed AND broke! I take out a second mortgage on the house. I consider taking up gambling. I remember I do not have a mortgage at all, or a house. I remember that I am a millennial, I am lazy, and bReXiT, and will in fact NEVER own a house, because I am addicted to my iPhone. I remember I don't understand how taxes work, and cry on the bus.

I spend large parts of my day feeling anxious and panicked about absolutely nothing at all. *I can't. stop. thinking.* I get frustrated that I am like this. I get frustrated that I do not know why I am like this. I get frustrated that nobody else seems to be like this.

I get frustrated, but I have to interrupt the thought pattern. I remember to be gentle with myself. I cancel plans with friends, because right now I think I need me more than they do. I feel guilty about it, but I must take care of myself, and my friends will understand. Or I'll die alone. Either way, ice cream!

Somebody asks me about the scars on my arms and I don't want to make them uncomfortable, so I cheerfully reassure them that all is well, and dutifully repeat that I'm fine, but they should see the other guy.

WEDNESDAY

I wake up and immediately remember that time an ex-boyfriend told me he'd never have got involved with me in the first place if he'd known I had this much baggage. I thank Karen for this wonderful start to the day, and then remember that the same ex is literally allergic to celery, and for some reason this is hilarious. I love my brain. I realize I have overslept. I hate my brain. I make a mental note to cry later but right now I am late for work.

I try to say nice things to myself before I leave. A little on-the-go pick-me-up. The only compliment I can think of is that I have a really nice bum. I'm not sure that this is how it works, but it seems to do the trick. I feel like a new woman, and wink at myself in the mirror.

I am in the middle of unloading the dishwasher when I'm suddenly filled with an overwhelming sense of despair. I question the meaning of life. I question whether my parents would have preferred a son. I question whether fidget spinners are still a thing. I remember I need to go to the post office. I remember the horror of starting my period in the middle of the Year Eight school disco. I am terrified that side fringes might come back in fashion. I wonder who the fuck I am supposed to be. I wonder if my father was right and I should have chosen Geography for GCSE instead of Religious Studies. Am I doing the right thing with my life? Do cats have knees?! Was that email too passive-aggressive??? Will an asteroid explode into the Earth?!?! I forget how I'm related to my cousin and panic-call my mum in tears, screaming, 'HOW DO COUSINS WORK?' Everyone is very concerned.

THURSDAY

I wake up feeling stressed and overwhelmed. I'm mean for no reason. I have too much to do and no time to do it. Why is it so hard for me to say no?! My brain feels like one big scrambled mess that I can't pick apart. I write down a list of things that are worrying me. My list is seven pages long. I want to throw up.

I focus on breathing. I remember my old Tumblr username, 'this too shall pass', and try to apply a thirteen-year-old's philosophy to my current situation. I prioritize my list and write solutions to problems. Then I write down three things that I am grateful for. I don't want to, but I tell myself I have to. This miraculously works every time.

I allow myself to feel proud of this tiny self-soothing act. I remember that self-care is something I have to practise. I remember that mental well-being is something I have to maintain and attend to consistently, however much I don't feel I need to in the moment. I remember to be kind to myself and forgive myself for the past. I remember I am still healing, and give myself permission to have good days and bad days.

I wonder why it's so much easier to make time for other people than for myself. I wonder why my brain always seems to

"THEN I WRITE DOWN THREE THINGS THAT I AM GRATEFUL FOR. I DON'T WANT TO, BUT I TELL MYSELF I HAVE TO. **THIS MIRACULOUSLY WORKS EVERY TIME.**"

focus on the bad things more than the good. I wonder why it's so hard to treat myself like someone I love.

I dedicate the rest of the day to myself. I take a walk outside. I appreciate the colour of the sky and the shape of the clouds. I take all my vitamins. I buy myself a new candle from my favourite shop. I wash my bedsheets. I take the bins out. I order chicken ramen (basically a hug in a bowl, don't argue with me), and watch my favourite show. I lie in the bath for hours and feel guilty about the amount of water I'm wasting. I do a facemask and cut my toenails. I listen to an inspirational podcast and write down some goals. I vow to take a social media break, be a better feminist, and call my nan more. I book some yoga classes and Marie Kondo the shit out of my underwear.

Self-care works, and I do feel better.

FRIDAY

I get myself into an Instagram hole. You know the kind.

Everyone else's 'feel-good Fridays' threaten to uproot my entire existence because I'm THAT insecure, and I hate myself for falling into the trap. I scroll endlessly, wishing I could stop, and blaming my thumbs for having a mind of their own, and my stomach for not being as flat as hers, and WHY did I cut my hair?!?!? Wait – what the fuck am I actually doing?! Where am I going?!! I'm not good enough! I'm not working hard enough! Who am I! Am I going to spend the rest of my life being chased by the crippling fear that one day very, very soon I am going to get caught, and everyone is going to figure out that I'm *really, actually, not-very-good!!!!*

I can't do anything right. I look at my scars and am disgusted. I'm ashamed of my broken, fragile self. I shout at my mum on the phone, and immediately feel guilty. I know I'm not really angry at her. I'm angry at myself. I'm angry at Karen. I'm angry at everything. I'm angry that all the scented candles and downward dogs in the world couldn't cure depression. I'm angry that I can't be one of those beautiful, effortlessly cool women you see in the movies. I'm angry that those kinds of women don't actually exist, and we all think they do. I'm angry that I feel ashamed of the way my brain is. I'm angry that society has made it this way. I'm angry that we don't talk about mental health enough. I'm angry about the cuts to funding for mental health services. I'm angry that my younger brother feels like he can't cry in front of people. I'm angry that people look at my arms and judge me. I'm angry about all the times I've been called 'too emotional', 'too complicated', 'broken', 'crazy'.

I know that I'm only angry because I'm sad. I wish I could just cry instead.

Five hours and two panic attacks later, I have made a sort of duvet burrito of myself. I don't think I will ever leave this soft and feathery pillow prison. From now on I will take all my meetings from the safety of this very damp and pathetic pity party. All will be right with the world once again.

I'm not angry any more. I'm just sad. And I know this sadness won't ever go away. And I'm OK with that. I'd just like the rest of the world to be OK with that too.

SATURDAY

I am immediately drunk. (I am British, after all.)

I spend the day with my best friend and laugh so hard I go to the loo and check for abs.

She reminds me that I am not a burden and helps me take off the mask I wear that makes me look strong. I realize that the mask has been really fucking heavy, and I let myself cry. I remember that it's OK to ask for help and let people in.

She tells me about her week and it makes me almost wee myself and I think *IT'S NOT JUST ME!* and I love her more than anyone has loved anything before. I am touched by the way my heart feels things in extremes and I remember how weird and wonderful brains are. I feel grateful and happy to have one like mine. I would rather feel everything at once than nothing at all.

I REALIZE THAT THIS IS WHAT LIFE IS ABOUT.
FINDING BEAUTY IN THE LITTLE THINGS. LIVING IN THE MOMENT.

Being vulnerable, and open, and kissing our friends' faces, and filling ourselves with melted-cheese toasties, and being kind to one another. I wouldn't be able to appreciate the joys of today if I hadn't let myself feel the downs of yesterday. Cheesy, but true. We are lucky if we choose to be.

It's a journey, and we are constantly evolving. And it's all worth it. And it's all beautiful.

And, in the end, it's all valid.

SUNDAY

Three things I am grateful for:

1. I am grateful for my pain, for giving me the understanding and sensitivity to recognize pain in others, and the empathy to help whoever may need it.

2. I am grateful for my overactive imagination, for always making me laugh, always keeping me creative, always being curious about the world, and always having such a unique perspective on life.

3. I am grateful for Karen, for teaching me that I am stronger than I think. For encouraging me to reflect and grow. And for giving me the opportunity to forgive myself, be proud of myself, and remind myself every day that *I am a good person*, worthy of love and respect.

I try to end the day with my usual night-time routine of herbal tea and a good book, but I spill the fucking tea. I laugh at my clumsiness because, frankly, it is hilarious, and I am great.

I make another cup of tea.

Look at me go.

MENTAL
& HEALTH

BY

Sharon Chalkin Feldstein

FOUNDER OF EXPERT MANAGEMENT,
CO-FOUNDER AND CEO OF YOURMOMCARES,
ENTREPRENEUR, COSTUME DESIGNER,
FASHION STYLIST

Illustrator: Gracie Warwick, @got.legs

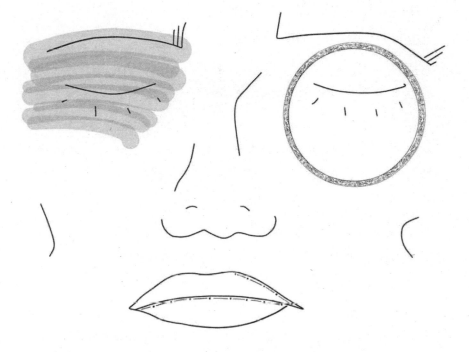

CHAPTER ONE – WAKING UP

Mental said, 'I don't want to get out of bed. I don't feel well.'

Health said, 'But I'll miss my bus and be late for school.'

Mental said, 'OK, I'll get up.'

CHAPTER TWO – SCHOOL

Mental said, 'I'm anxious and feel invisible.'

Health said, 'I'm OK. I'm not alone. I have friends.'

Mental said, 'But my friends don't always get me.'

CHAPTER THREE – LUNCH

Mental said, 'Lunchtime makes me nervous.
    I never know who to sit with.'

Health said, 'I think I'll sit with Jane. I like her.'

Mental said, 'But what if I say something stupid?'

CHAPTER FOUR – BUS HOME

Mental sighed and said, 'I have so much homework,
    but what's the point?'

Health said, 'But I do feel good sometimes and I know
    my family loves me.'

Mental said, 'But this isn't working.'

CHAPTER FIVE – GOING TO BED

Mental said, 'I sometimes wish I wouldn't wake up.'

Health said, 'Sometimes is not always.'

Mental said, 'I need help.'

I personally believe that when there's life, there is hope. We must bring hope into kids' heads, bedrooms, homes, schools, places of worship, and so on. I co-founded YourMomCares with other celebrity and influencer mothers to band together for kids' mental health.

WE ARE CHANGING THE DIALOGUE FROM **MENTAL ILLNESS TO MENTAL WELLNESS** TO ENSURE THAT THE STORY ENDS **WELL**.

SAYING GOODBYE

BY

COMMUNICATOR, WRITER, STRATEGIST

The editor said the contribution could be anything I fancied, as long as it was mental health related . . . so I am going for a eulogy. I hope that's OK. I know that death is a sad subject, but it can be inspiring too – at least, the lives we eulogize can be. I want you to meet my brother, Donald. His illness, not mine, is the real reason I campaign for better mental health services and understanding. And I miss him every day.

Donald Lachlan Cameron Campbell, born Keighley, Yorkshire, 3 May 1954. With names like that, was he ever not going to be a piper? Was he ever not going to join the Scots Guards? Was he ever not going to live most of his life in Glasgow, a city he said was home to 'the greatest people on earth, Alastair' in an accent so strong people doubted that we really were brothers.

I start with a thank you. To Glasgow University. For understanding that it is possible to have a severe mental illness and do a good job well. Donald worked in the security team, mainly in the library, where he would often tell students, 'See that carpet under your desk? That's where you put your feet! . . . Good lad. Now keep them there.' Oh, he liked having authority. But what he *loved* was his role as the university principal's piper. He played at hundreds of ceremonies and graduations. At his farewell party, retiring early because of his breathing problems, exacerbated by a lifetime of antipsychotics, he announced proudly that among the tens of thousands of students he piped out: 'I did seven thousand, two hundred doctors.' 'Yep,' I said, 'and you've seen quite a few of them since.'

Glasgow University did not see him as 'a schizophrenic'. He was an employee who had schizophrenia. Big difference. His illness did not define him. So often he rose above it. And his work was so important to his well-being. He liked that status. He liked ritual. He liked performing. He liked *being* something. Twenty-seven years in one job. A generation and a half of students.

If he refused to let his illness define his life, the same cannot be said of his piping. Dad taught Donald and me the bagpipes when we were small, first over the kitchen table on the chanter, then down in the cellar on the pipes. Donald loved not just the music but the culture, the camaraderie, the competitions. Mum worried that we loved the drinking side of the culture too much and she had a point. But it was the music that drove Donald.

The last time he played was at the university's memorial for Charles Kennedy, my friend through politics and Donald's from when Charles was rector. The whole political establishment of Scotland seemed to be there. Donald didn't look well. He was struggling for breath even before we started. I said to him, 'Listen, I can do this on my own.' 'No,' he said, 'I'll do it. I liked Charlie.'

We led the procession into the quadrangle. But a third of the way round he had to stop to fight for breath and I finished alone. He never played again. To lose his work and then his piping to *physical* ill health, after doing so well for so long with his *mental* ill health – that was cruel. But he never complained. He just banked the thousands of hours of pleasure gained and given from his playing days; and Donald, I know, would have been so happy that, he having piped the lament at so many funerals himself, today it was Gavin, son of our cousin Susan, and one of his star pupils, who piped him into the crematorium.

So . . . Worker. Teacher. Soldier. Piper. A husband, though not for too long. An insurance salesman too, but money was never really his thing – unless you count giving it away to people you like, and bookmakers.

Of course, even if his illness did not define him, we cannot recall his life without talking of his schizophrenia. But, before I do that, I want to take a break, and ask our nephew Jamie to come and sing one of the remarkable songs he has written about mental illness. This one, inspired by and dedicated to Donald, is called 'My Mind'. The lyrics are on the order of service. So read along as Jamie sings.

I've been in that place
Where the stars are blue
When it rains all day
Though you don't want it to

Nothing bright to see
No horizon to find
All alone in this world
A world that's borne of my mind

MY MIND HAS TAKEN OVER, OVER MY LIFE

The voices are so loud
Drowning out all other sounds
My mind's a beating drum
Tells me evil's ways have won

The crowds, they laugh at me
Codes and words are all I see
Can't share a joke, a laugh, a smile
While the world is in denial

MY MIND HAS TAKEN OVER, OVER MY LIFE

So listen to me now
I'm a person, not a clown
This life is not a game
It's a fight I choose each day

So pick me up when I am down
Dare to turn my world around
Fight the demons here with me
Boy, I could use the company

MY MIND HAS TAKEN OVER
BUT MY LIFE, IT ISN'T OVER

HELLO, WORLD,
GIVE ME A SHOULDER
THAT I CAN CLING TO

That I can cling to
Let me cling to . . .

'My mind has taken over . . . but *my life* it isn't over.' That sums up Donald's attitude to his illness so well.

One of his GPs from fifteen years ago wrote to me after

Donald died and said, 'We were best of pals.' One of his Glasgow psychiatrists said to me, 'Donald is my greatest success story. Holds down his job. Owns his own flat. Drives himself around. Has a passion for his music. Has more friends than any of us. Has a positive attitude almost all the time.'

That last bit was certainly true. 'It is what is it, Ali. I got given a bit of a crap deal, but you've got to make the best of it, know what I mean?'

We were counting up all the different hospitals he had been in the other night. It was like a map of the length of Britain, from the military hospital near Southampton, where it all started, to London, Leicester in the Midlands, Hull in the North, and various wonderful places around Scotland. Donald had fantastic treatment from so many NHS staff right to the end, including near here at Millbrook and then Kingsmill in Mansfield, where he died.

Schizophrenia is a truly horrible illness. You can't see it. No crutches. No sudden baldness. No bandages. No scars. It is all in the mind. People who have it are often pariahs, shunned in the workplace, derided and abused on the streets. And, because of the stigma, it's at the wrong end of the queue for research; the medication takes, on average, twenty years from the lifespan of someone who has it. Dad was eighty-two when he died; Donald, sixty-two.

It is not a 'split personality', that awful cliché, as awful as the way people use the word 'schizophrenic' when they mean there are two views of something, or someone has good moods and bad. Please don't. It minimizes. It misunderstands. It stigmatizes. Schizophrenia is a severe *illness* in which the workings of your mind become separated from the reality around you. And it can be terrifying. Imagine a cacophony of voices in your head, screaming, telling you to do things you *normally* know you shouldn't. Then imagine plugs, sockets and light switches, road signs and shop signs talking to you. Imagine sitting in a place like this with a crowd like this and thinking every single word being said *and thought* by everyone is about *you*. Imagine watching TV and everyone is talking about you. And then imagine snakes coming out of the floor and wild cats charging through the walls and ceilings. Donald had all that and more when he was in crisis. So imagine the strength of character it takes to deal with that in a way that had made so many people love him so much, not out of sympathy – he didn't want sympathy – but out of an appreciation of the real him, unclouded by illness. That is an achievement of epic proportions. Doctors and medication were a big part of his achievement. But he was the biggest part.

Also to have had that and never say 'it's not fair'. I said it, for more than forty years, from the first day Dad and I saw him lying in Netley military psychiatric hospital, terrified, his eyes not the eyes I knew. 'Not fair. Why Donald?' I said it; he didn't. Not then. Not ever. Not once.

Imagine being so keen to be a private in the Guards, making it, doing well but then, with this illness, his career terminated, the prestige of playing in the Scots Guards First Battalion Pipe Band gone. Did he ever say a single word against the army? No. He loved those years. He talked of the Guards with fondness, always, and would be thrilled to know so many former Guardsmen had been in touch. His career in the Guards just ended badly and he got through it, got on with it, adapted, lived the best life that he could. And, if you're wondering why I'm not wearing a black tie, it is because he said to me once, at Gartnavel Hospital in Glasgow: 'If you do my eulogy, make sure I'm in my kilt and my Guards jacket in the coffin – don't forget the glengarry – and you wear my Guards tie.' We thought he was on the way out *then*. He kept going for years.

In the recent days before he was taken ill – one of the pictures is on the back of the order of service – he was looking as healthy and handsome as he has for ages. But sadly towards the end we were seeing and speaking to a Donald most of you never saw. That you didn't is testimony to how brilliantly he and his doctors managed his illness.

He was violent when he was admitted to hospital a few weeks ago, so unusual for him, throwing himself around, refusing medication, tearing out his oxygen tubes, snarling and shouting at everyone. The staff on Orchid Ward – that is the only Donald they ever knew. They were a new addition to his NHS map. But do you know what? When we went from seeing his body at the bereavement centre to collect his belongings from the ward, the nurses sought us out, not just to offer condolences but to tell us how much they liked him. 'Oh, you could tell he was a character,' said one. 'I know I shouldn't laugh but he was funny,' said another. And Donald having listened to his piping CDs in there – loudly – other patients had said they would never hear the bagpipes again without the hair standing on their necks and thinking of Donald. They knew that, beneath the crazy stuff the voices and the visions made him do and say, he was a great guy. The fact *nurses* could see it even as they had to restrain him – three staff members in his room round the clock – underlined that.

The letters and messages have been incredible. Both in volume and content. There is so much grief for Donald because he inspired so much love. When we went to see the body, it was about *saying* goodbye, but I couldn't say anything. I was in bits. Liz [my sister] did say something. She stroked his hair and she said, 'You taught us more than anyone, Don.' He did. Resilience. Fortitude. Courage. Kindness. Not letting even a horrible illness destroy his zest for life and love of people. Thinking of others more than himself, even when life was so tough. And as he lay there, bruised, a bit discoloured, I felt as sad as I have ever felt in my life that his eyes would never open again, we would never again listen to him playing the pipes, never again see our children in hysterics at his observations of other people; sad too that their children as yet unborn would never have the joy of knowing him; that I'd never see 'Donald Mobile' come up on my phone and I answer and say, 'Donald, you phoned me an hour ago. Why are you phoning me again?' and he'd say, 'I just wanted to see how your hour's been. You OK, yeah?'

But I also thought at least he never has to hear those wretched voices in his head again. He really was at peace. Above all – and the next time I went to see him at the chapel of rest I did say this – I said, 'You're the best big brother anyone could ever wish for; and every single person who was ever touched by you had a better life, because Donald Lachlan Cameron Campbell was a part of it.'

My mind has taken over . . . but my life it isn't over. It is now. But Donald can keep on touching us, all of us, every day, until our lives are over too.

" SO PICK ME UP WHEN I AM DOWN

DARE TO TURN MY WORLD AROUND

FIGHT THE DEMONS HERE WITH ME

BOY, I COULD USE THE COMPANY "

70% CRYING, 30% BANTER

BY

Candice Carty-Williams

AUTHOR

As I write this, I'm sitting on a sunlounger in my great-aunt Rose's back yard in Jamaica. The sun is shining, the air means my skin is the best it's been in months, and, even though we're far from civilization, we have WiFi. I should be happy – or content, at least – God knows happiness isn't a real thing. Or maybe it is? I don't know. For me it's not. I am 70% crying and then 30% banter to pull myself through the day. My mum and my sister are here in Jamaica too. They're both loud in their own way. Not performatively or annoyingly loud; just chatty and engaging. Though saying that, mums are generally annoying, aren't they? But my mum and sister are good. They're the funniest people I know, and sometimes I can't believe I'm related to them. While we've been here, they ask a lot of questions and they make the people in the house laugh. I can't do that. I mean, I think I have the ability to do that, but it won't come out. Instead, I open my mouth to talk, and feel a flatness come where words usually would. So I close my mouth, and I go into another room. I've been called 'quiet' a lot on this holiday by my great-aunt and her husband, Uncle Buzz. But my great-aunt is smart, so I think that she understands that my quiet is depression. She tells everyone to let me be alone when she can tell I need it. She keeps saying, 'It's OK that you're quiet – me still love you same way.'

I'd like to be sociable, obviously, and to be able to communicate normally. While I'm not concerned about being the life and soul of any type of party, it would mainly be nice to be able to talk when I want to. I don't know how to describe it, you know. I will try, for the sake of this essay. Maybe it will help me to write it out. Emotionally, I'm pretty all over the place. I cry a lot, though I understand that crying is good for me. If I wake up and know that the day is going to be a bad and very sad one, I'll put a film on that I know will make me cry so that I can attach my sadness to something tangible. When the film ends and I've cried, my brain knows that it's time to close that door and be productive. That happens often, but it's not the crying or the emotion that I'm worried about. It's the . . . you know, I actually can't find the words again, which is weird. Words are literally my job.

OK, maybe if I talk about the *effects* of how I can feel, that will sum it up. It's mainly the way I am with people when I have these 'down bouts' that I have to ride out. That's what I started calling them a few years ago when I clocked that they were here, regularly, to stay. I go into myself. I can't talk. I push people away. I don't care how it makes them feel. Maybe because I assume that me removing myself is best for everyone involved. It's probably quite clear to you, the reader, that I don't like myself very much. But I don't really mind that. I doubt I'm alone in that.

As much as I can be terrible to people, I push that aside to be a good friend. I'm the strong friend. It's exhausting. I'm a rider. If you're my friend, I'm loyal. I want to know how you are, and what I can do for you. I am a good advice-giver. I've been leaned on hundreds, if not thousands of times, by my friends and family. They know that when they come to me, I'll give them judgement-free, practical, positive advice. I gas people up to the hilt. I love people, for all of their isms, because I know that we're all just a big bag of isms trying to get through the day.

I'm not trying to play the blame game here, but we're basically so much of our parents, right? My mum is the most joyful, optimistic-to-the-point-of-dreamy person I've ever met. She has time for everyone, anyone. She loves anyone she comes into contact with. My dad, on the other hand, is a severely quiet man. Anything I know about him I've learned from my older sister, who has spent more time with him than I ever will. I've grown to understand that he's always been depressed, which I just took for quiet, or apathy, and mainly dislike towards me. I don't have the word count to describe the effects this has had on me and my relationships with men, but what I do know is that, despite not growing up with my dad, I'm more like him than my mum. And I truly hate that. But from my mum I get the laughter 30% of the time, so I'm grateful.

I know that therapy will help. I've had it before. But you know the funny thing? I don't hate my down bouts. Because I *know* them. I know how to navigate them. I'm comfortable in them and with them, because there are no surprises and no room to be let down. They feel safe for me. Sadness is safety. But I know this is in no way healthy. This deeply unhealthy way of being is no good way to live. Probably because it's not in my control. One day my luck will almost certainly run out. My friends or family or partners won't have the patience to accept that sometimes I'll just disappear, and that I just lock myself away emotionally for periods of time and then pop back like nothing happened. Until then, if I'm being honest, I'll probably keep trying my luck. I'll probably keep riding the down bouts until the wheels fall off.

"

**I DON'T HATE
MY DOWN BOUTS.**
BECAUSE I *KNOW* THEM.
I KNOW HOW TO
NAVIGATE THEM.
I'M COMFORTABLE IN
THEM AND WITH THEM,
BECAUSE THERE ARE NO
SURPRISES AND NO ROOM
TO BE LET DOWN.
THEY FEEL SAFE FOR ME.

"

OK TO
NOT BE OK

BY

Naomi Campbell

MODEL, ACTOR, ENTREPRENEUR

The maintenance of one's mental health is, to me, just as important as looking after your physical health. In fact, I would suggest a healthy mind is sometimes more important. The two coexist and should not be treated as separate.

It bothers me that in society we still tend to stigmatize those with mental health issues instead of helping them by understanding them and by simply not judging.

I've learned to constantly monitor myself to determine where I am in balancing my own mental health. Like most, I'm a work in progress but I will say this – take time to reset, take each day as it comes, seek help and do not be ashamed of your story; it will inspire others.

YOUR MENTAL HEALTH
DOES NOT DEFINE WHO YOU ARE.

A TALE OF TWO CITIES

BY

BLOGGER, MENTAL HEALTH CAMPAIGNER

Explaining to people what you mean when you say you suffer from mental health problems is a tough gig.

For starters, you never really know who your audience is. You could be talking to the crowd who see you, who understand what living with a maze in your mind is really like. Then there's the crowd who don't understand but who still nod and smile when you tell them about the time that you wrote a to-do list to remind yourself to brush your teeth because you live in fear that you'll forget everything, always. Or you could be talking to the crowd who think they have OCD because they like matching stationery from Paperchase. Or the gang who refer to depression as the feeling they experience when they get to the bottom of their packet of Frazzles.

So you might feel heard and not alone.

Or you might feel like you want to poke a (nicely matching) pencil into your eye.

Mental health issues are also the hardest things to articulate when people only know one version of you.

See, when people meet me (I'm told) it's relatively unfathomable to them that I have this maze going on in my head.

On the surface, I have a good job, friends who aren't arseholes, and I'm able on occasion to make people laugh or feel at ease or less sad. I've campaigned for mental health initiatives and spoken on stages, on the radio, even in

Buckingham Palace. People see someone who's outspoken (read 'gobby'), determined, possibly even confident.

Underneath, however, is another, less fun truth. The other version of me is fuelled by utter panic; there's a pool of self-disbelief and a voice in my head that spends most of its time telling me I'm a complete shitbag. I have panic attacks that have put me in hospital. I experience periods of depression that stop me being able to shower, let alone get to work, let alone be able to speak to a prince.

MENTAL HEALTH IS A COMPLEX THING TO NAVIGATE, AND AN EVEN HARDER ONE TO EXPLAIN, ESPECIALLY BECAUSE YOU NEVER QUITE KNOW HOW IT'LL BE RECEIVED.

So, for the purposes of this, I'm going to try. In perhaps the most convoluted way possible.

Because I figure that if it was easy to explain it would be easy to fix.

A TALE OF TWO CITIES

My mind often feels like it's cut in half. Two different cities, with two very different approaches.

One city is a light, airy space. Full of green parks, balloons and half-cut people, drinking cocktail tinnies with a picnic somewhere fun, looking cool and laid-back in easy summer clothes. Everyone there holds their head high and greets one another with, 'Check you out, stunner.' The people have meaningful jobs and self-belief, and are in relationships that assure them. Everyone gets on; it's easy, it's pleasant, and smells a bit like Cowshed toiletries. It's a safe space, a comfortable one, but it often leaves you feeling like you do when you're on holiday. Enjoy it while it lasts; we'll be back in front of the TV a week on Tuesday.

The other city is grim. A sprawling concrete jungle of misery where people fight. It's cloudy, hard to navigate, and still filled with people drinking tinnies. But, rather than swilling a Pornstar Martini and being pleasant, they're on the lager. Propped up next to a bin, in clothes a size too small for them, screaming 'ugly bitch' at you as you pass. Nobody's got much going for them. If they work, it's in buildings with carpet tiles and plastic plants and no windows. If they don't work, they just shuffle around, sniffing clothes to see if they can make them last another day. It feels unsafe, shady, and it makes you agitated.

THE JOURNEY BETWEEN

During bad periods in my head, each day can come with the constant uncertainty of not knowing in which city you're going to wake up. During really bad periods, you can wake up in one city, get out of the bath in the other, and cry yourself to sleep travelling to somewhere in between.

The pinch point is the journey you take between them. Something takes you from the nice place with the good people to the city that smells like a bin and makes you feel like danger is at every turn. It's like hopping on a bus, and when you're going to Good City you pass through stops like Self-Belief Street and Looking Forward to Tomorrow Park. The bus is well air-conditioned and arrives on time and brakes cautiously. It's filled with people who smell of fresh laundry and who drink super juices to fuel their superpowers.

And when you're going to Shit City you pass through stops like You're a Joke Close and Give Up Already Industrial Park. The bus has piss on the seats and discarded Chicken Cottage boxes on the floor. The windows are misty, so you can't see where you're going, and it's filled with people standing up with their noses in the armpits of another, wishing they could just go home, sit in the dark and cry some more.

THE DRIVER OF THE BUS

I've thought about this and I reckon that your destination depends on who you allow to drive your bus.

Bear with me.

See, you're the boss of the bus. You manage shift patterns, annual leave, performance-related pay (I've gone too far). So you can control who drives on which day, if you feel able.

SEE, YOU'RE THE BOSS OF THE BUS. YOU MANAGE SHIFT PATTERNS, ANNUAL LEAVE, PERFORMANCE-RELATED PAY (I'VE GONE TOO FAR). **SO YOU CAN CONTROL WHO DRIVES ON WHICH DAY, IF YOU FEEL ABLE.**

I arrived at the conclusion that I have at least eleven drivers on my staff. And depending on who I let drive, or who I give a day off, I end up in one place or another.

Here come the girls . . .

SELF-HATE SANDRA

She's a bitch. Her favourite song is a sick little lullaby that's just a never-ending refrain of 'you're shit, and you know you are', and she picks apart everything I do. She questions every email I send, every conversation I have and every calorie I eat. She tells me that I'm not good enough; that I can't win; that I'm worth very little.

She drives the bus a lot, was driving it when I lost the bottle to apply for dream jobs and while I dated some very questionable blokes.

PANICKY PAULA

When P's at the wheel I'm known to walk around with feelings that are a mixture of toilet-chasing nerves and guilt. I always know when she's on shift, because when I wake up I feel instantly sick. Nervous like I've got the biggest job interview of my life, guilty like I committed second-degree murder in my sleep, and panicked that I really have done it. The nerves remain all day and make daily tasks like jumping on a train, making some toast or just popping to the Co-op* feel frightening and impossible. Paula makes the attacks happen.

* When Paula was in charge a few weeks ago, I sat outside the aforementioned Co-op for twenty-five minutes, so convinced that something bad would happen if I went inside that I just drove home again. I ended up not getting the milk I needed for three more days.

DEPRESSED DEBS

I mean, she might as well just drive the bus straight towards a brick wall when she's on duty. She makes me feel like my bones are made of lead when I wake up, and like everything outside the confines of my bedroom walls is only going to make things worse. She ruins my sleep patterns; she makes brushing my teeth feel like an unachievable possibility. She makes me feel two very distinct things: empty and lonely. In the busiest of rooms with people I love, if Debs is at the wheel I feel like the only person on earth.

I hate it when Debs turns up to work, and she's the hardest of all of them to get to take a break once she's there. She's a stubborn cow.

NIGHTMARE NANCY

She does what it says on her tin: makes me have the most horrific, realistic, world-ending dreams that leave me waking up in soaked pyjamas, with the genuine belief that the flat is under terrorist attack.

Nancy clocks off and normally swaps straight away with Paula. They are right clique-y, them two.

WORRIED WILMA

She worries about everything. About that look my mum just gave me, about the use-by date on the yoghurt in the fridge, about my health, the health of others, my relationships, the bloke I don't know but see on the train every morning, my future, my prospects, how my toenails grow.

She's an absolute worry warrior and hasn't been off my bus for nearly twenty-five years. She doesn't always drive but she's always at the back causing havoc.

MUDDLED MABEL

Two words. Hot. Mess. With her, I can't be trusted to remember to pee let alone remember where I parked the car. When she's around I'm all over the place. Confused, disorientated and completely incapable of even picking anything to watch on Netflix.

When Mabel's driving, Wilma can often be heard shouting from the back seat, 'It's probably dementia,' which always makes that shift much more fun.

CRYING CAROL

Carol is overly sensitive and only drives when I am in the darkest alleyways of Shit City. She makes me cry when I see old people on the bus, about whom I make up stories of loneliness, leading to weeks of me worrying about them. She makes me cry when the microwave dings because I'm living on my nerves. She makes me cry in the middle of the Boots

3-for-2 aisle because I'm convinced that everyone will hate what I've bought them for Christmas so much that I'll spend the next one alone.

Carol comes and goes, but she does overtime during the festive period.

KIND KIM

Kim tells me I look nice in the morning. That I did a good job. That I should feel pleased with myself about something or not be surprised when my boyfriend tells me he loves me.

Kim's a lazy cow who shows up for work intermittently at best.

STRONG SUE

God knows where she comes from, but she pops in every now and again, and bosses a meeting or a run or a night out with friends and leaves me feeling epic for days. She takes the rough with the smooth and doesn't flap when things get tough. She's the project manager in me, the good friend, the tenacious one.

I love Sue so much; she's my safe driver, and that's why she's named after my mum.

DETERMINED DEBORAH

She's a force to be reckoned with. She knows my strengths and she rationalizes my lack of self-belief.

She's the one who tells me that 'your boss didn't give you a job as a favour, he must think you're good at some stuff'. She pushes me to do the things I know I'll always be thankful for.

She doesn't drive the bus enough. But she drove it the day I ran the London Marathon, the day I decided to leave an industry that no longer made me happy, the day I said yes to writing this.

LAID-BACK LISA
Being honest, she's literally never been to work.

So there they are. The girls, the drivers of my bus. My workforce. My backbone. My downfall. An erratic, unpredictable and somewhat exhausting bunch of people I've come to know pretty bloody well.

They need controlling, yes. The odd bollocking, absolutely.

But when you know them – how they work, how they tick – it makes it ten times easier to ask them once in a while to get out of the bloody driving seat.

"SO THERE
THEY ARE.
THE GIRLS,
THE DRIVERS
OF MY BUS.
MY WORKFORCE.
MY BACKBONE.
MY DOWNFALL.
"

ANIMAL THINKING

BY

Matt Haig

AUTHOR

Let's start with the blatantly obvious.

You are an animal.

A clever animal, yes. An animal reading a book. But still you are an animal.

Everything you do is an animal doing it.

When you listen to your favourite playlist on Spotify, you are an animal listening to your favourite playlist on Spotify.

When you exfoliate your skin, or meditate, or fill up your petrol tank, or play Monopoly, or sing karaoke, or log on to Twitter, or run for the bus, or beat someone at Mario Kart, or go for a job interview, or shop online, or tie your shoelaces, or run on a treadmill, or ask Alexa something, or read Dostoyevsky, or do ashtanga yoga, or eat some toast, or ignore a text message, or write a birthday card, or select an emoji, or cry at a movie, or book a weekend break in Barcelona, you are an animal doing those things.

Of course, you know this.

Everyone knows that human beings are a type of animal.

Everyone knows that we are mammals.

Everyone knows that – like gorillas, chimpanzees, orangutans and bonobos – we are apes. Great apes.

Everyone knows that, as animals are nature, then *we* are nature. And most of us are aware that – it hardly takes much lateral thinking – if we are part of nature, then we are also dependent on the *rest* of nature.

And, let's be honest, nature is not having a great time right now.

So, maybe the problems we are causing in the natural world – and they are so devastating it can be hard to absorb – are linked to the problems going on inside our heads.

Think about it.

We no longer sleep when we need to, because we stay up later and later watching Netflix.

We no longer eat the kind of stuff humans once foraged.

Our natural instincts to wake up have been taken over by the alarm clock. Our natural instincts to worry about what endangers us have been taken over by breaking news. Our natural instincts to worry about mortality have been exploited by the multi-billion-dollar anti-aging industry.

It is no wonder that, increasingly, nature is seen as a mental health remedy. Eco-therapy is now a thing. And it is increasingly clear from a growing amount of research that what we are doing to mess up the planet is also messing up our health. Studies show that anxiety rates are rising in line with environmental destruction. And this isn't just due to 'eco anxiety' – you know, the understandable existential fear about what our species is doing to the planet. It may be down to the fact that we forget that we *are* the natural world. We can't destabilize the natural order of things without destabilizing ourselves.

And one of the problems for environmentalism and mental

health is that we don't really feel part of the natural environment. For instance, very often when we say the word 'animal', we mean an animal that isn't us. We mean a non-human animal. We don't mean the people we live with or the people we work with. When we talk about the 'animal kingdom', we are not including Sophie in the IT department or Mahmoud in accounts. We are not talking about Elon Musk or Beyoncé or J. K. Rowling. We are not talking about our parents or siblings or children or partners.

No.

In most cases, we are talking about pandas and sea lions and horses and any of the other nine million known species. *Animal* animals.

An individualistic consumer culture that encourages us to always crave something more, something newer, and to dispose of anything old, is reflected in how we treat ourselves. We are encouraged to worry about everything, from our calorie intake to our step count, via our popularity on social media.

The consumer economy depends on our unhappiness.

Every January we hear the cries of 'New Year, New You' as if we are a smartphone ready for an upgrade. We fill our minds with psychological waste, like landfill: all this nonsense about what we are expected to feel and look like and be.

Maybe, as well as trying to rewild the world for biodiversity, we need to rewild ourselves for our sanity. We should see the beauty in the things we have been taught are ugly, just as we should see the value of plants we were trained to see as weeds. There is nothing unnatural or wrong with a line on our face any more than there is with clover or a dandelion in a meadow.

Maybe we need to stop feeling obliged to take part in those toxic elements of modern work, and social interaction, and consumer life, and just to realize that, often, everything we need is right in front of us. It's staring back at us in the mirror. We are as perfect as anything else in nature, because we *are* nature. We came complete. We should take it easier on ourselves. We should learn to breathe again.

It is so much easier to feel at one with the world when we realize the world is us.

" WE ARE AS PERFECT AS ANYTHING ELSE IN NATURE, BECAUSE WE *ARE* NATURE. WE CAME COMPLETE. WE SHOULD TAKE IT EASIER ON OURSELVES. **WE SHOULD LEARN TO BREATHE AGAIN.** "

IT LOVED ME THE MOST BUT HATED ME THE SAME

BY

ACTOR

It loved me the most but hated me the same,

It made me feel safe yet it constantly threatened me.

I tried to keep my distance but it stayed by my side,

It told me to give up and stop trying to hide.

I told it to leave but yet it would stay,

It told me it would never leave even if I packed

    my bags, switched off my phone and ran away.

It told me if I run it will always find me,

It said, 'Go ahead, I'll be right behind, you'll see.'

It made me feel intelligent but told me I was dumb,

It made me feel stressed and took away all the fun.

I can't take it no more, it's too much for my brain,

It made me love and laugh but still caused all the

    destruction and pain.

It loved me the most but hated me the same,

It hurt me constantly, again and again.

It left marks you could see and ones that you couldn't,

I asked it to stop hurting me, it told me it wouldn't.

It made me feel beautiful as if no one could compare,

It also told me I was ugly and that no one would ever care.

It made me feel alone though it was always there.

It told me I have beautiful green eyes

But don't get happy, you still have ugly hair.

It broke me and it tricked me and made me feel wrong,
It fractured my friendships and relationships
But still reminded me I'm strong.
I felt as though we knew each other although we'd never met,
It gave me the confidence to pursue my dreams
And told me, 'You're going to be a star, don't you ever forget.'
Then it told me to die because I'd never really make it,
'Just get it over and done with, tie the rope round your neck
  and break it.'

It made me feel honour, it made me feel shame,
It made me feel I was always to blame.
It loved me the most but it hated me the same.

"

IT BROKE ME AND
IT TRICKED ME AND
MADE ME FEEL WRONG,

IT FRACTURED MY
FRIENDSHIPS AND
RELATIONSHIPS

**BUT STILL REMINDED ME
I'M STRONG**.

"

LIGHT SWITCH

BY

Martha Lane Fox

ENTREPRENEUR

A body covered in scars and a walking stick as an accessory isn't how I imagined myself in my mid forties. An expanding waistline and some wrinkles, sure, but not a complete rebuild of my pelvis, arms and legs. Yet this is the body I inhabit after a monumentally serious car crash in 2004 changed my life forever.

I'm lucky: I can walk, I can stand up, and I can still dance as badly as I ever did, but every day I have to battle an inner voice of insecurity and anxiety about my physical challenges. There are the tiny things, like not being able to wear any kind of shoe with a heel, and bigger things, like battling daily pain and incontinence. These get in my head and wear down my mood, and my temper, and often turn me into someone I don't want to be. And, because I am a lunatic, my working life involves a great deal of public speaking – speeches, panels and debates in the House of Lords. To get through these moments, when I can be feeling so low inside or not in control of my own body, I have a simple trick.

I IMAGINE A LIGHT SWITCH.

A big white old-fashioned one with a huge on/off sign emblazoned on it. I flick that switch from off to ON. I smile, act as though I'm the most confident person I know, and I perform.

TRY IT.

SEASONS

BY

Bryony Gordon

WRITER, JOURNALIST

The first time I got ill, it was Christmas. I was twelve. I hid in my bedroom for almost the entirety of the school holidays, too scared to go outside because of the germs that lurked everywhere, invisible cells determined to kill me. Winter had brought with it a sort of perpetual darkness that seemed tailor-made to suit how I felt – bleak, lifeless, empty. There were many theories put forward by my parents to explain that first breakdown: my hormones; the stress and upheaval of a newborn baby brother; the fact that it was winter. Of them all, the latter was the one that seemed to hold sway, because as winter turned to spring I perked up a bit and stopped hiding my toothbrush under my pillow so I wouldn't infect my family with whatever killer illness it was that I was certain I had. The illness I *actually* had was a serious mental one – obsessive-compulsive disorder – but I was too young to know that. It was 1992. Nobody spoke about the stuff that went on in people's heads, unless it was to describe them as being worthy of being carted off to a loony bin. So I stayed silent.

As I got older, my OCD evolved and grew and told me that I not only had AIDS or Ebola but that I was also probably a serial-killing paedophile who had committed horrific crimes but blanked them out in shock (nobody, and I mean *nobody* ever spoke about this kind of OCD around the dinner table, instead believing it to be an illness associated with cleanliness, so I trudged on believing that . . . well, that I was a fifteen-year-old serial-killing paedophile, despite being nothing of the sort).

I chose to believe the winter theory. I ignored the fact that I had these thoughts all year long, drinking and drugging them away when the sun was out, and when the clocks went back I would be gripped by an icy fear of the total paralysis that would almost surely follow. I had a serious mental illness, and it was caused by the weather. Yes, that was it. A lack of vitamin D. Nothing more than that.

The popular narrative of depression and mental illness backed up my belief in the winter theory. The black dog, dark thoughts, so on and so on. In Britain, everyone got down and low in the winter. They got 'depressed' by the cold. Never mind that in the summer I was also down and low and depressed. I was down and low and depressed but terrified of admitting it to anyone because . . . well, what excuse did I have? My mum would say things like, 'Oh, the weather's so lovely – it's impossible not to feel uplifted!' And inside I would die a little bit. I was a complex fuck-up, a suicidal alcoholic drug addict because I lived in northern Europe. Probably.

It was only at the age of thirty-eight, almost a year out of rehab and newly sober, that I realized my problems had nothing to do with the weather. That it was possible to be mentally ill at any time of the year, in the sun or in the rain or in the snow, on any day as long as it had a Y in it. I was lying on a sun lounger in the south of France, my five-year-old daughter playing in the swimming pool with her dad, the sun blazing, everything perfect, perfect, PERFECT, and I wanted to die. I wanted to die because I was finally having to deal with all the feelings that I had, in part, dismissed as the weather, the feelings I drunk on for so many years. The fact that it was glorious, that everyone seemed to be so happy, only made it worse. What was wrong with me? Why couldn't I just be normal like everyone else? As the heat rose, my mood got ever lower. Drawing the curtains on the sun seemed like a particular admission of defeat, an acknowledgement of the huge amount of work I had to do on the giant great big gaping hole in my soul. At least in the winter I felt some solidarity. At least in the winter I could legitimately hide away, and not have to answer questions about it. At least in the winter I could pretend that everyone else was feeling the same way as me, that everyone else needed a solid course of rehab and four-times-a-week twelve-step meetings, not to mention weekly psychotherapy and medication, even if all they actually needed was two weeks in the Caribbean.

The forecast is not as bleak as I make it sound, however. Because in the acknowledgement that these things can happen at any time of the year, I feel a lot brighter. I know now that my internal weather is always changing, that no single feeling will last forever, that sometimes I will experience four seasons in one day. I am prepared for the rain, the wind, the snow and the blazing sun. I see beauty in them all; I can see light, even in the sometimes seemingly never-ending darkness.

"

I KNOW NOW THAT
MY INTERNAL WEATHER
IS ALWAYS CHANGING,
THAT NO SINGLE FEELING
WILL LAST FOREVER,
**THAT SOMETIMES
I WILL EXPERIENCE
FOUR SEASONS
IN ONE DAY**.

"

IT'S OK
TO SHOUT

THE STORY
I DON'T TELL
BY
Scarlett Curtis
JOURNALIST, ACTIVIST

I called a suicide hotline when I was nineteen years old. While I tend to talk very openly about my mental health 'journey' these days, this is the one story I rarely tell.

There are some stories about my anxiety and depression that are 'fun' to tell and I roll those out freely while the others stay locked away in a box marked DO NOT TOUCH.

TURNING THE WORST MOMENTS OF YOUR LIFE INTO STORIES IS A **POWERFUL WAY TO RECLAIM A MOMENT WHEN YOU FELT COMPLETELY OUT OF CONTROL**.

It turns memory from trauma into folklore and if you tell it enough times you start to feel like you're talking about someone else.

My favourite story about my anxiety is from Halloween in New York. I was dressed as Marie Antoinette (full corset, tutu, slit neck, pink hair, white make-up) and trying to walk across 6th Avenue in the middle of the Halloween parade. The street was impenetrable and I was already an hour into a journey that should have taken me five minutes. The pavement was lined with demons, and police barred every entry into the street to make way for the cavorting, dancing skeletons and mermaids.

After seventy-five minutes of getting nowhere I began to panic. My phone had lost reception, my friends were waiting, so I pushed through hordes of zombies and werewolves to head down into the subway. Hoping to cross through the underpass I was immediately faced by a stern-looking policewoman who said there was no access through the tunnel.

I collapsed. It was the last straw and I was exhausted. Falling to the floor, I sat on the cushiony fluff of my fifty-layer tutu and began to have a panic attack. I couldn't breathe and I couldn't stop crying. The entire world was spinning and my already tight corset felt like a prison. As I sobbed and gasped for air a family of tourists circled round me, quickly joined by others until a crowd of about twenty people surrounded me. They began laughing, pointing and taking pictures, filming me and whispering to each other in a language I didn't understand. I started to shout at them, confused by their laughter, until it hit me: I was a weeping Marie Antoinette sitting on the floor of the subway in the middle of the Halloween parade. I was part of the show. A perfect New York moment in the underpass at 6th Avenue and 14th Street. I picked myself up, did a polite curtsey, pleaded with the officer to let me through the exit and showed up to the party with wet streaks flowing through my white make-up, adding the perfect finishing touch to the best Halloween costume of the year.

I trot my Halloween story out eagerly to divert the inquisition and create the pretence of openness. When you tell people a story about a time that you were vulnerable they tend to think you've shown them the whole picture. I love that story. It's my favourite.

This, however, is the story I never tell.

Three months later, January had hit New York like a kick in the balls. The snow was a suffocating blanket, covering the city in chunks of ice and impenetrable barriers of thick, grey sludge. I was living alone in a country I still didn't know, in an apartment infested with cockroaches that I could never quite bring myself to leave. My family, back in the UK, were sick of me complaining over the phone and 3,459 miles is a long way to come for a night that seemed no worse to them than the hundred before it. Nothing happened that night. Nothing was different from the night before it or the night before that. I just decided I was done. I had been trying for five years to feel some emotion that wasn't misery or fear, and nothing was working.

I walked in my pyjamas through the snow to the pharmacy. I bought the pills and paid for them at the self-service machine so no one would question my intentions. No one had the key to my flat except the superintendent of the building, who hated me and lived ages away, so I knew I'd be safe for a week or so.

This is the bit where I'll skip over the details, partly because I don't remember them, partly because I failed, partly because I don't want anyone reading this to get ideas, partly because I'm still ashamed, partly because it's still too painful a memory to turn into a story.

When I woke up at 5 a.m., I googled a phone number and dialled. A woman picked up the phone and we talked and she saved my life. At 5.45 a.m. I called my best friend and he listened and let me cry and told me I was going to be OK.

I don't really believe in rock bottom but I guess this was mine, although at the time it didn't feel like it. The next day was as hard as the day before but I managed to have a shower. The day after that I managed to eat something. The day after that I managed to go to class. And 1,275 days later things still aren't easy, but they are easier. People describe rock bottom as if it's something magical. They make it sound like you're a diver swimming down to the bottom of the ocean, touching the seabed and shooting back up to the surface. It wasn't like that for me. I lay my body down on the ocean floor and gazed up at the waves that seemed too far away to ever reach. And then I slowly started to swim.

THERE ARE DAYS WHEN
I STILL FEEL UNDERWATER,
LIKE THE WHOLE WORLD
IS SINKING AROUND ME
AND IT HURTS JUST
TO TAKE A BREATH.
**BUT THERE ARE ALSO
DAYS WHEN I FIND
MYSELF POKING MY
HEAD ABOVE THE TIDE.**

And when that happens, and I look down, all I can see is the beauty and magic of the ocean around me, and that cold, hard rock at the bottom of the sea seems really, really far away.

BOYS
DON'T DIE

BY

WRITER, ARTIST

I.

We talked about it casually.
Reserved spaces on my body
For tattooed memory,
And opening lines
Of half-baked eulogies
Filled with pre-emptive remembrance
Noted in real time.

It sat with painful comfort
In the back of my skull,
Its shadow cast, translucent,
Down long tables
Where we talked about living, quietly,
And drank and smoked and laughed,
Knowing some of us wouldn't.

I knew it at fourteen,
In the dimples of schoolboy ties,
And in the twentieth hour of sunrise,
Not from morbid fascination
Or divine inclination,
Just the fact that I was a boy,
And so were they.

For a few years,
I thought it might be me.
We spoke and danced and loved,
Stoned, scared and happy,
Around the subject,
Asking the edge of questions
Lest we fall down the centre.

I knew my friends were going to die,
And after three of them tried,
One of them did.
And I still don't know what to do.

II.

I knew that I would have friends who died because we were boys and there were lots of us and that just felt like part of life. For that and other reasons, I spent a long part of my life believing myself to be an individual, easily detached from the people around me so that anyone could leave and I would be fine. It didn't scare me. We were not the most typically boyish group, avoiding some, but certainly not all, of the pitfalls of toxic masculinity. We grew up together in liberal and privileged households with modern views and morals where, if not always encouraged, we were rarely discouraged from talking about our feelings. Though platonic, our friendships were romantic and our dialogues were open. I never felt embarrassed about talking about my feelings, and was safe in the knowledge that there were people who would listen, and who loved me. We spent more time talking to each other than we did on any other activity. We knew each other's lives so intimately, and we went through our pubescent years with unbridled affection for, and confidence in, each other. I had – and continue to – struggled with mental health, but it was never a secret, though we didn't always have the right words or means of expressing it. We all knew each other's issues, all knew that we supported each other, all believed in each other, and that we'd all be OK together. Yet we also talked about us dying. Exclusively in the abstract, it was nevertheless present in our world. No one was named, no particulars given, but it was there. In this little group that was filled with unconditional love and honesty there existed a morsel of knowledge that some of us would die young. It existed there only because we were boys. It didn't scare us; it was just another seat at the long tables we filled. In my constant overanalysis, for a long time I didn't think about this facet of our lives, so ingrained is it in the life of boys. Soon after we left school, it became something I had to think about constantly, as my seemingly joyous group of friends suffered through increasing mental illness, hidden problems and suicide attempts. When suicide took Kai's life in the winter of

2019, my world broke apart. I used to think I would be OK, and that I was an individual. I am not; I am so much a part of the boys, and girls, I grew up with that I think none of us will ever be an individual, untied to each other; to be OK without each other is impossible. I was not scared of death. Today, I am terrified. Not of my own death so much, but the deaths of those around me, and the knowledge that boys die – this knowledge I once lived with so comfortably – fills me with constant pain.

Every time the phone rings, I am scared. Every time I see a man or boy looking sad, I am scared. Every time I wake up, I am scared. Atop all this fear is something more powerful and more potent. I am so fucking angry. In my little group of boys, liberal, modern, traditionally 'feminine'-leaning boys, where there should never have been an onus of silence, we have suffered loss and pain because embedded in our world is the idea that boys suffer in silence. Even writing this, I feel worried and embarrassed talking about my mental health, not for fear of society but of the voice in my head, stirring, that tells me not to, that my issues are not to be validated, not worthy of conversation. It is so deep in the collective male psyche that happy boys grow up with the thought embedded in their minds that their friends will die. We shouldn't have to grow up with that.

WE SHOULD GROW UP,
INSTEAD, IN THE
KNOWLEDGE THAT OUR
FEELINGS MATTER,
THAT THEY ARE WORTH
TALKING ABOUT,
**VALID ENOUGH TO
DWELL ON AND SCARY
ENOUGH TO TAKE
SERIOUSLY**.

That we all feel sad, and how brilliant a thing that is, not just because it unifies us all in collective solidarity but because to experience emotion of that depth means we can experience emotion at dizzying heights, and how beautiful a possibility that is.

III.

I, and so many of those around me, have in the last year tried to find solutions. Ultimately there are none. So deeply ingrained and systematic is the undermining of male mental health that there isn't an easy one. While we were always an open group, in the last year the necessity for this openness has grown stronger, and we have all learned, and worked on learning, how to talk about feelings. It is not perfect, but we are getting there. It should not have taken a death to reach that point. This is not a problem for boys alone. This is a problem for everyone. I asked the boys I love to give me advice, as I have done so many times through my life, and below is a compilation of what they all said. Crowd-sourced, incomplete and imperfect, their words come from a place of love, truth and fear. All of them, having felt sad, and having suffered through the devastating effects of silence, the loss of friends and the loss of themselves, wrote these words hoping they could help someone, save someone. Some of them might, some of them won't, but if nothing else I hope they serve as a reminder that our friends have good things to say, that boys have feelings and can learn to talk about them, and that they understand us even when we think we are beyond understanding. These are the words of ten boys I love, who have always helped and guided me, and have felt just as sad as I have, reminding me constantly that I am not alone.

- Don't believe the thoughts created in your anxious brain. Talking about them will almost always reveal them as the overwrought fictions they are.

- Watch *Ferris Bueller's Day Off* – I hardly know a more joyous thing.

- It's important to separate yourself from your thoughts sometimes. It's natural to believe that there's truth in all your assumptions and the way you see things, but the truth is we often have things wrong, and it's important to view your thoughts objectively in this way.

- Meditation and mindfulness can help you realize that your thoughts are separate from you, so you don't have to take on the burden of any negative feelings you have.

- It's easy to get fixated and believe that you have it all worked out when it comes to others' opinions of you and your own self-worth, but it's all about perspective. That's why talking to others, be it a therapist, a friend or a parent, is so important. Don't live in the echo chamber of your own brain.

THERE IS NOTHING BETTER THAN A GOOD CRY AND, DESPITE WHAT THE CURE SUGGESTED, BOYS CAN BE VERY GOOD AT IT.

- Know that your mind's capacity for mental gymnastics is extraordinary, and only an outside perspective can free you from the paralysis of anxious conviction.

- Ask the right questions and don't accept the 'right' answers.

- To ourselves and to those around us: dig past pleasantries and etiquette until you reach honesty, because there are fifteen questions worth asking after someone answers 'fine'.

- Be selfish, because it's unlikely that you ever are.

- Do whatever feels right for you, and stop worrying about other things and pressures. Do what makes you happy. I know it sounds clichéd, but I feel that often I don't do what I actually want to or feel under pressure not to, and in the long run this can make me pretty unhappy.

- Feel what you feel; don't try to feel anything that you think you should. This applies to talking to your mates as well: say what you want; don't think there's a right or wrong thing to say or ask, because there never is – it's just about talking more than anything else, whether serious or not.

TALK ABOUT YOURSELF
UNTIL YOU FEEL BETTER.

- Remind each other that we are not alone – and do this lots.

- Acknowledge your instincts, but don't follow them blindly.

- Take a breath.

BOYS MUST BE WARY OF THE TRAITS **THAT WE OFTEN FEEL PRESSURED TO EXIST WITHIN**.

- While one can dip one's toes into any trait, it is important to make sure it does not absorb your true character. The crisis of personality that this may create can make you deeply unhappy. However, if you succeed in owning your traits and not having them own you, your well-being will be much improved and you will feel more content in yourself.

- I never wanted to accept I was depressed, and the only thing that made me realize my emotions, and that I would want to address them, was the process of writing. It was my main help and focus: get it down on paper, almost like a list. Once it is on the page, your mental illness becomes something you can conquer because you can hear your voice, see your words; it becomes a tangible enemy to be defeated rather than abstract voices in your head.

- I was one of those boys who don't speak about their feelings, and let it brew and get worse, which led to wanting to kill myself. Writing, along with reading, helped me accept these emotions as legitimate. One of my professors, knowing my situation, sent me articles to remind me that I was not alone.

TELL YOUR FRIENDS
YOU LOVE THEM.

ASK FOR HELP

BY

Jonny Benjamin

MENTAL HEALTH CAMPAIGNER,
AUTHOR, VLOGGER

I'm currently in a psychiatric hospital. I came in recently after a relapse. This is my **sixth** admission, and my **second** in the last **five** months.

My first admission was **eleven** years ago when, at the age of **twenty**, I was first diagnosed with schizoaffective disorder.

Sorry . . . it's a lot of numbers to take in, isn't it? I've got a big thing about numbers. I don't know why, but I've had it since I was a kid. Growing up, my life revolved around numbers. For instance, if the clock said it was twenty-seven minutes past the hour, I had to say a prayer or else one of my grandmothers would pass away. If the clock struck thirty-four minutes past the hour, I would have to say a different prayer or else my other grandmother would pass away.

Thankfully I no longer have to follow these rituals – though that is partly because both my grandmothers have passed away. But it is also because my mind no longer has the control over me that it used to.

And yet sometimes I find I *am* at the mercy of it, and suddenly everything changes. When I become psychotic, I am a different person altogether. I would like to emphasize at this point that I have NEVER been violent towards another individual.

Hollywood movies might have you believe that anyone who experiences psychosis is dangerous and deadly, but research shows that this is rarely the case.[1]

When I am psychotic, I am more terrified that other people are out to harm me in some way.

My version of reality becomes totally distorted during psychosis. Sometimes I believe I'm in my own version of *The Truman Show*, a phenomenon that has become known as 'the *Truman Show* Delusion', or TSD for short.[2] Everyone around me may argue against my beliefs during this time, but my brain remains stuck firmly in my own version of events.

More terrifying and distorted than this is the point where my thoughts turn to suicide. When I begin to think that I need to take my own life in order to fulfil some sort of purpose that will help the world I'm leaving behind, I seriously need some assistance.

While my mental health is in better shape overall than it was when I was growing up, and I no longer have to perform certain rituals, hear the voice of 'the devil' or mask my severely low moods, it is the acute phases of mental illness that cause me, and others around me, the greatest concern.

1 www.time-to-change.org.uk/about-mental-health/types-problems/schizophrenia

2 www.ncbi.nlm.nih.gov/pubmed/22640240

Tomorrow, on 1 May, I will be discharged from hospital. I feel quite apprehensive about it, but I trust my toolbox of helpful things, from medication to meditation, to maintain my mental health.

MOST IMPORTANTLY OF ALL, I KNOW **I CAN NOW TALK AND ASK FOR HELP** WHEN I NEED IT.

It's taken me most of my adult life to develop the courage I needed to actually do this. I always felt unworthy of it. But now I feel empowered to pick up my phone and dial certain numbers when I really need support, be it my parents, a friend or, more typically, a crisis service like SHOUT. So, I guess numbers are still quite important to me after all . . .

HEY, YOU
AN OPEN LETTER TO MY LATE HUSBAND'S DEPRESSION

BY

Poorna Bell

AUTHOR, SENIOR EDITOR, DIGITAL CONSULTANT

Hey, you. Yes, I'm talking to you.

Come now – don't be shy. Coyness doesn't suit you when I have seen you command the stage in my loved one's brain.

Don't speak in whispers when we both know how deafening your voice was in stapling him to his bed. How your resolve is vast, singular and resolute, though you veil it in the softness of pillows, and the weight of thick curtains pressing the daylight out.

Murderer, is what I wanted to scream at you four years ago, when he took his own life. I believed you had won. And when I experienced depression because he had died, I believed you had come for me too.

But now, I feel like I am looking at you through Plexiglas. You can't touch me, or hurt me.

You might find yourself near my borders, and you might think you can visit. Meander down my path, as if I was an old friend. But don't bother. You aren't welcome. I've seen you off once, and I will do so again.

I WONDERED HOW YOU BECAME SO POWERFUL. BUT THEN I REMEMBERED THAT **THE BIGGEST WEAPON WE EVER HANDED YOU WAS INVISIBILITY**.

When Rob told me you were a part of his life, I didn't know anything about you. It was like someone dropping the name of a pop star I didn't recognize. I nodded along, like I knew what he was talking about, when the reality was that I didn't.

SO YOU SLID UNDER THE RADAR OF STIGMA AND SILENCE, AND YOU DID IT SO QUIETLY I DIDN'T KNOW YOU WERE THERE.

I didn't know it was you saying, 'I'm fine,' as I watched him slowly turn from someone who blasted the Specials and Neil Young and Gil Scott Heron into someone who played no music at all. I didn't know you were the reason why his garden went from being his pride and joy, filled with tulips and alliums and obscure varieties of lily, to an unkempt tangle.

I started to suspect it when I saw his body wasting away, a landscape of flesh that was as familiar to me as my own, from the tattoos down his back to the curve of his bottom. When

I'd come home from work and check the bin, and find nothing there; that he hadn't eaten, because you'd been feasting on him instead.

There is so much I didn't know. I wish I'd known that 'just getting out of bed' wouldn't make him feel better. I wish I'd known that you're written off as a mental illness when you are so physical in your output.

But while I wish there was more I had known to support him better, I do know that the world we are in now is not the same as it was before. More is known about you, and we are better equipped to understand you, to fight you, and to help others when they need it.

Now I know how to recognize you. I know when you have made a home in another person. I can see you with your hands in the fuse box of their mind, flicking the switches off, one by one.

And there is one thing you should know. For all that you did to him, and all that you took from us, I never lost sight of who he was.

On the days when he felt well, my husband returned. He never stopped being loving. He never stopped cuddling our dog. He still made up limericks about his friends to troll them with, performed wizardry in the kitchen, danced to Dolly Parton, and prepared his pots with plants for spring.

I wrongly used to wonder if we would ever have a normal

life, on the days when you visited for weeks and months on end. Now I know that we had a life that wasn't perfect but it was filled with love. And the fact that he was able to do any of the things he did, with you holding him hostage, only makes me love and respect him more.

So remember that I know you. Remember that I have never forgotten or forgiven that you entered my house without permission. And when I see you doing your work in the home of another, don't think for one minute that I will remain silent.

I, like so many others, will come for you.

" MORE IS KNOWN
ABOUT YOU,
**AND WE ARE
BETTER EQUIPPED
TO UNDERSTAND YOU,
TO FIGHT YOU,
AND TO HELP OTHERS
WHEN THEY NEED IT**. "

ON FINDING THE RIGHT MEDICATION FOR YOU

(AND SLEEPING WITH HALF OF LONDON)

BY

WRITER, PRODUCER,
CO-FOUNDER OF THE PINK PROTEST

TRIGGER WARNING: SEXUAL ASSAULT, RAPE

In my mid-teens, I think I felt a smug kind of satisfaction that I wasn't on antidepressants. I've never admitted this before. I guess that's because of the stigma around mental health – but I've never really been bothered by that – I mean, my mental health issues are seemingly a bottomless pit at this point. But I would still spout the rhetoric that 'even though meds were really important and worked for some people, I only needed talk therapy'. This smugness of saying the right thing around the discourse of mental health, while secretly feeling rather pleased with myself that I merely needed therapy once a week to keep the demons at bay . . . Well, now I find it cringe-worthy and nausea-inducing.

Luckily, such is the way with this kind of thing – karma or whatever version of cosmic retribution you subscribe to, I learned my lesson when a family crisis struck and I found myself sitting, suicidal, in a shiny new psychiatrist's office. My very first psychiatrist, a blind date set up by my mother, who watched with growing concern as I became increasingly tear-stained and smelly while my most recent bout of intense depression grew. I was prescribed Escitalopram.

The first day I took the pill I was on a skiing holiday with my family – the perfect destination for a depressed child. I had been warned that the initial side effects might make me hyper-sensitive – which, if you know anything about me as a person, is a terrifying thought. I've been described as 'sensitive' since

I could crawl. But at that time in my life I had felt nothing for months. The thought of maybe squeezing out a tear thrilled me no end. I had forgotten what emotion looked like on me. My mum, who loves activities, had booked snowmobiling in a snowy New England forest. Primed and ready, I had taken my medication, hopped on the snowmobile and immediately burst into tears. The speed and terror of the sheer drops punctuated by trees and large rocks cocktailed with the reuptake of my serotonin being inhibited – hello, feelings, we're back in business.

I look back on my first tryst with antidepressants like a high-school sweetheart – my parents loved you and you always tried to do the right thing by me, but ultimately we weren't meant to be. I plodded along for six months, the human embodiment of Snorlax the Pokémon. I walked around in a state of permanent exhaustion; I was lethargic, sensitive, and had lost that initial warm fuzzy feeling. I slumped back to my incredibly kind psychiatrist feeling like a failure. Maybe smug teen Honey had been right: antidepressants work for some people but not for me, and I just need to double down on talk therapy.

We tried again. My doctor put me on Sertraline with a four-month prescription. I would love to say that this medication solved all my problems and I thrived – but instead I spiralled. I ate compulsively but never felt full. I was angry at myself and constantly exhausted. I'd never felt so volatile and lost in my life. I was more depressed than I had been prior to taking medication. And let me be clear: it wasn't solely the medication making me feel like this – I felt very isolated in my life, and was still tied up in a series of toxic friendships. But still, this doesn't justify the fact that, in secret (and I'm nevertheless very ashamed of this)

I CAME OFF MY MEDICATION WITHOUT TELLING ANYONE. THAT'S LIKE MEDICATION 101. **NEVER DO THIS.** IT WAS DANGEROUS AND STUPID.

And when my mum found out – and she did find out – we had a mini fight on an airport shuttle bus, which resulted in me crying very hard and very publicly.

I had ended my relationship with antidepressants. A horrible break-up that left me and my closest friends and family reeling. But, in private, I felt free.

Two years flew by. I talked fondly of my brief affair with medication. I chipped into conversations saying, 'Oh yeah, I tried that – wasn't for me . . . but super helpful for some people.' Funny how you slip back into stock phrases like that.

Then something awful happened. I was raped. Everything I thought I'd known about my depression before was eclipsed. This was a breed of darkness that I hope I never have to feel again. It wasn't that safe numbness I'd felt before – it was raw and burning emotion, pulsing through my body constantly. I sobbed in child's pose on the floor. My best friend slept in my bed most nights. My dad sent me a childhood photo of myself and said, 'You're still this girl' – a bold choice, but one I have come to appreciate with time and distance. I grieved for a part of myself that I never knew I needed to fear losing. My friends and family gathered around me like an army of soft teddy bears. They protected my heart. I would truly be dead without them – but you know who else came back into my life, gave me a second chance even though we'd ended on such bad terms? Antidepressants. Duloxetine – or Cymbalta – stepped in and gave me the safety net I needed to stay alive.

When I couldn't wake up in the morning, Cymbalta was there. Unlike the usual SSRIs I'd tried, my sweet love Cymbalta was an SNRI. This baby was working overtime to block the reuptake of both my serotonin and norepinephrine, and honestly I've never been so grateful to an inanimate object in my whole life.

On my first day trying the pill, my sister and her girlfriend came and sat with me for the whole day. My psychiatrist had described the adjustment period as feeling like you've been plugged into the electrical grid of the city. He wasn't lying. My sister watched me bounce manically off the walls of the house. She didn't even get angry when I nearly fed her a Thai curry paste containing fish sauce – she's vegetarian and has been since she was three years old. My mind was slightly fried, but at least I had the energy to cook for the first time in a month.

In addition to the initial sugar-rush effect that Cymbalta had on me, my doctor had warned of other side effects. He told me it was likely I'd experience a total nuking of my sex drive. I laughed in his face. In my mind at this point I was never having sex again. Cymbalta had other ideas.

Have you ever looked at a cat on heat and just felt sorry for it? Aimlessly meowing and rubbing itself on surfaces, desperate for any kind of release. Well, that was me for the first six months on Cymbalta. I was the horniest, saddest woman in London. I've always been a sexual person, but this kind of hypersexuality was completely new to me. It was as if I was radiating sexy-lady pheromones: I would walk into a club with my friends, look around, lock eyes with a man and *boom*. I knew we would be hopping in an Uber by the end of the night to bang. It was the weirdest superpower, which I really didn't want – with great pussy power comes great responsibility, and I was in no emotional state to be responsible. Cymbalta and I went on a sexual rampage through London. Like a thicc and thirsty Godzilla. And you know what? It helped me work through something I didn't think I'd face for many years. Intimacy. If it hadn't been for this chaotic sex drive, who knows how long I would have shut down for? After the trauma, when I was getting tested, the doctor asked insensitively if I wanted to go on birth control so if something like this happened again I wouldn't worry about pregnancy scares. I burst into tears and snapped that I'd never let a man touch me again.

CYMBALTA WAS THE ULTIMATE WING WOMAN: **NON-JUDGEMENTAL AND SUPPORTIVE**.

Cymbalta stood at the side of the dance floor and shouted 'Yaas, bitch' as I kissed the second man I'd kissed that night. Cymbalta went above and beyond the call of duty.

I wish I could say this story ties up neatly. I still live with the trauma of what happened to me every day, even though the pain gets less and less. I owe a lot of that to Cymbalta. But can I say with rock-solid confidence that I'll be on it forever? Absolutely not. She might be just a wonderful friend I love dearly through my twenties, and then will tell my children about one day. This magical thing came into my life and helped me get out of bed in the morning.

SO, ALL I CAN SAY IS, IF YOU'RE GOING THROUGH SOMETHING, **KEEP GOING** – AND IF YOU'RE SEARCHING FOR THE RIGHT ANTIDEPRESSANTS FOR YOU, **KEEP SEARCHING**.

And always use protection.

THE THREAD OF SADNESS

BY

Alexis Caught

WRITER, CREATOR & CO-HOST
OF AWARD-WINNING
PODCAST QMMUNITY

I start this essay with a disclaimer – a disclaimer that only minorities need ever say, lest we be held up as a sole spokesperson for our community. I'm a gay man, but there is no way that I could (or should) speak as a representative for the entirety of the glitteringly diverse LGBTQ+[1] spectrum. I'm also very aware that, while my own experiences of navigating a homophobic world have left me with emotional baggage and issues, my race (white) and my modicum of 'straight-passing privilege' have helped to shield me from the worst of what this world can throw at my queer siblings . . . And yet I haven't got by unscathed; few of us have.

So I write this from my perspective as I look at the world around me and wonder why over half (52%) of LGBTQ+ people have suffered from depression within the past year,[2] compared to 20% of the general (heterosexual) population.[3] A wildly troubling comparison that only gets worse: queer people of colour experience depression at rates as high as 62%,[4] while 46% of our trans siblings have considered suicide.[5]

Of course (thankfully) not every LGBTQ+ person experiences mental health issues, but the statistics are scary and give pause for thought. Why does it affect people like me more? The moniker we claimed for ourselves, 'gay', is supposed to mean happy. In 2019, we're told that we have full equal rights and legal equality, that we've never had it so good, that homophobia is a thing of the past (though we know that's not true) . . . But why hasn't our mental health, reflecting our emotional state, caught up?

One contributing factor, I believe, is the thread of sadness.

---

1 LGBTQ+, also referred to as LGBT or LGBT+, is an abbreviation for Lesbian, Gay, Bisexual, Transgender, Queer identities, while the + is used to signify and include the panoply of other sexual and gender experiences such as Asexuality, Pansexuality, and those who are Questioning, Non-Binary and Gender Fluid.

2 The 2018 Stonewall 'LGBT In Britain Health Report' found that 52% of respondents had suffered from depression within the last year.

3 In 2014, 19.7% of people in the UK aged sixteen and over showed symptoms of anxiety or depression – figures from the Mental Health Foundation.

4 Statistic from the 2018 Stonewall 'LGBT In Britain Health Report'.

5 Statistic from the 2018 Stonewall 'LGBT In Britain Health Report'.

THE THREAD OF SADNESS

Innocent playground days: playing with my friends. I can remember being five or six, and everyone was playing the thoroughly problematic game of Kiss Chase (it was the nineties – that's what kids did). Boys chased girls, and girls chased boys in return, all in the hope of getting a kiss when you caught them. But I didn't want to chase the girls – I wanted to chase Zack and yet at the age of five, even without anyone telling me, I knew I wasn't supposed to want to chase Zack, I knew I would be teased if I did, and so I sat it out. I sat alone, watching the others play, questioning why I felt this way – why I wasn't like the others. And I felt sad.

Aged twelve, in Spanish class: we're set an assignment – introduce yourself in Spanish: your name, where you live, your hobby . . . and whether you have a girlfriend or boyfriend. In turn, we have to recite our answers to the class. One boy stands up and says, '*Mi novio . . .*' – the simple accidental use of the incorrect gender prompting a teasing 'You have a boyfriend?' from the teacher and laughter from the class. I turned cold, I felt sick . . . A boy having a boyfriend was something to be laughed at. I felt ashamed. And I felt sad.

Years pass, and despite a virulently homophobic school environment I come out. I feel liberated, although not free (daily slurs and regular acts of violence see to that) but I get through school. (I skip my state school's 'Leavers' Ball' – a watered-down, sickly cousin of the American school prom and public-school formal. There's no way I could have taken a guy as my date . . . Besides, I was the only kid who was out; I was alone.)

I grow up, and I become an adult, I begin to process my gay shame, I become more and more confident in my sexuality. I learn to dance under the rainbow.

Aged twenty, I go on a date: his name is Harry, his brown eyes sparkle and I want to kiss him so badly. It's been a beautiful first date – we laughed, we flirted. My heart is pounding as we eye each other up at the end of the night – are we going to kiss? Our bodies get closer, and we lean in . . . I can smell him . . . Just as our eyes close and our lips begin to cross that electrically charged chasm, a man barges into us on the pavement. '*Faggots*,' he hisses. Our date is ruined. The moment tarnished forever. The spark is extinguished and I go home by myself, feeling ashamed. And I feel sad.

It's 2004: every time I turn on the news I see people like me being debated. Should we be allowed to marry? Are we worthy? A large, and very loud, portion of the media (and the majority of the reigning Conservative Party) believe that my love is less valid – that, if people like me are allowed equality, it will 'undermine the institution of marriage'. Because I am less than. Because I am not equal. And I feel sad.

Years later, my serious boyfriend and I are looking at flats.

It's our first time living together. The excitement bubbles through me – I'm going to be living with the man I love, we're taking this step together. I'm not unlovable; I am loved. The estate agent (*ew*) makes a joke about almost accidentally showing us a one-bed flat . . . And then I remember: two men sharing a bedroom, sharing a bed . . . is something to be laughed at. I am something to be laughed at. My love is something to be laughed at. And I feel sad.

In 2018, a wonderful friend invites a group of people to visit Ghana, the country of her birth, and friends excitedly get in on the plans . . . I can't go. Ghana is one of seventy-two countries where people like me face imprisonment and punishment for our sexuality. I see their holiday pictures, laughing, carefree, exploring, sharing . . . And I feel sad.

I go on my own holiday, with my partner, to a place where our sexuality isn't a crime. As we walk through the hotel, aiming for the beach to catch a romantic sunset, eyes follow us, jaws tighten, unsubtle second and third glances, nudges, nods and smirks follow us. We double back and watch the sun go down from the privacy of our own balcony. I'm on holiday, and I feel sad.

Moments of joy, of pleasure, of goodness are what help heal us from mental health maladies, and the thread of sadness leaches poison into the remedy. It is this that triggers past trauma, PTSD style. It is this that stops many of us from feeling the full effects of joyous moments and occasions. It is this thread of sadness that re-traumatizes, even in seemingly mild ways. It stops us from truly, fully moving forward, from living fully happy lives.

But what causes it? And how do we pull out this thread?

IT IS NOT MY REACTION TO MY SEXUALITY THAT CAUSES ME ISSUES.

IT IS THE WIDER WORLD'S REACTION TO MY SEXUALITY THAT HURTS ME, THAT MAKES ME FEEL SAD.

(It makes me feel angry, indignant, and often pitiful too – pitiful of those who are scared of a changing world. It makes me suspicious – suspicious that they might harbour same-sex desire. But these feelings are a whole other essay.)

And it is this homophobia that we need to challenge, drive out and assign to the past – not just for the sake of the LGBTQ+ community, but for straight people too.

Homophobia is a choking bindweed that steals life, that

flourishes with toxic masculinity and bears no scented flower. It shames straight men for speaking out – lest they appear weak, lest they appear gay. It is fear of homophobia, of being perceived as less of a man, that contributes to a society where men feel the need to display dominance over women (and each other too – a Sisyphean quest for hierarchy) through acts of violence in order to assert their manhood and distance themselves from homosexuality.

WE NEED TO ADDRESS HOMOPHOBIA, CHALLENGE IT, ROOT IT OUT SO THAT **WE CAN ALL LIVE FREE OF THE POISON IT SPREADS**.

So that straight men can live without the fear of it.

So that straight women can live without the aftershocks of it.

So that children can grow up free and unbound by it.

So that queer people can live without the oppression of it.

So that we can enjoy the fullness of our happy moments, and feel the effects of healing moments, without the thread of sadness.

SAYING MY MIND

BY

Kelechi Okafor

ACTOR, DIRECTOR, PODCASTER, WRITER

I don't think I've ever written about the time I took an overdose of paracetamol.

It was at the end of my final year at university. It felt like an answer to the many questions being a young Black woman posed to me in an institutionally racist environment in and outside academia. The compounding factors of a traumatic childhood and a tempestuous family dynamic meant that I was exhausted and wanted some way out. Of course, I made sure to complete my studies first before doing something so devastating. Coming from a Nigerian household, I could feel suicidal, I guess, but still have the self-respect to have good grades.

I remember everything just feeling so bleak. I struggled to live in my own body because so much trauma resided with me there.

What I didn't realize at the time was that the incident served as an awakening of sorts for me. Not in the clichéd sense that suddenly I had a reason to live, but quite anticlimactically that I didn't really have a reason to die.

In hindsight I am very sure that I didn't want to stop existing; I just wanted to stop feeling so lonely and unworthy. There were so many words that I needed to say that were weighing on my mind and that is what depression felt like; I was crumbling under the weight of my unspoken hurts.

One of the girls I hung out with heard of the incident and said to me a couple of weeks later: 'I was so surprised to hear of what you tried to do. You're popular, you can sing, dance and act. Why would you not be happy with your life?'

I felt ashamed. I felt ungrateful. It seemed as if everyone around me was disappointed in me for not living up to the strong Black woman. As far as they could see, I was blessed with many gifts and was audacious enough to still yearn for something more. Something safer.

The day I took the tablets, my boyfriend at the time was at my flat. I'd locked myself in my en-suite bathroom and refused to come out. My housemates spoke in panicked, hushed voices outside the house as they waited for the ambulance to arrive and, even then, what struck me the most was me saying to myself, 'Gosh, you're so dramatic.' Even I couldn't feel sorry for myself as I unravelled.

I was taken to the hospital where my boyfriend called my mum to tell her what had happened. He told me that she had said in her stern Nigerian tone, 'Oh well, if she wants to be irresponsible with her life, that's her problem. All this behaviour is just attention-seeking. When she is ready to behave like an intelligent person, she can give me a call.'

I felt sick.

I felt sick because of what my mum, a mental health nurse,

had said in response to my breakdown, and I felt sick because the smirk on my boyfriend's face as he delivered the news was unmistakable. He followed it up with: 'I guess you only have me now.' He seemed to revel in the isolation I felt, because this strong fortress of a persona I'd built of being a Nigerian warrior princess was falling to pieces and he had a front-row seat.

Based on what those closest to me were saying, to feel so desperately depressed and unhappy was inconvenient and not something that someone so 'gifted' should do. Gifted people can get tired. Not just a physical tiredness but a soul tiredness. To get to twenty-one years old, emotionally limping from the brutalization of sexual abuse as a child, while pushing the boulder of self-esteem up the hill of society's unattainable standards as a Black woman can get tiring.

I would love to write that I immediately started therapy after this experience, but it was another year or so before I worked up the nerve to ask my GP for a referral. What I learned in the year leading up to seeing a counsellor was that nobody could save me because they were barely saving themselves.

When I mentioned to my family that I would be seeking therapy, I was told that it was a futile thing to do because 'Nigerians don't suffer from depression' and if I felt depressed it was because I 'wasn't trusting God enough'. I know that many Black people across cultures hear similar things when they consider seeking support for their mental health. We are made to feel like disrespectful traitors for wanting 'to chat our family's business outside'. Of course, none of this is true.

Nigerians do suffer from depression even if they never call it that. Acknowledging your depression doesn't mean you don't trust God; usually it's a deep distrust of yourself. Going to therapy isn't betraying your family, because the things you might discuss in therapy are classified as confidential and you are usually informed of the specific circumstances where the things you divulge may be shared with a third party.

IT IS FUTILE TO DISCUSS MENTAL HEALTH WITHOUT DISCUSSING **THE GENDERED AND RACIALIZED BARRIERS TO ACCESSING SUITABLE HELP**.

As much as it hurt me that my mum failed to understand my needs in some of my most challenging moments, I no longer hold it against her because, although she worked in the mental health sector, her cultural beliefs took precedence when her own children were involved – in the sense that we all had to be 'strong'. This is one of the reasons that I'm careful about describing other Black women as strong, because it is a racialized trope that has survived centuries. It has been the justification for our enslavement and the violations of our individual and collective bodies. The type of strength that is usually pushed on Black women requires them to be unfeeling and relentlessly productive. It has killed many Black women and I simply refused to let it kill me.

Our families are not irrational for distrusting the healthcare industry, because there have been hundreds of racist acts performed in the name of science. Due to the collective history of colonialism and the transatlantic slave trade, it isn't enough for a therapist to simply talk to us about whatever issues we might bring to sessions if they lack an understanding of intragenerational trauma. I am reminded of Audre Lorde's poem 'A Litany for Survival' in which she wrote: 'We were never meant to survive.'

Audre Lorde's words affect me so deeply because everywhere I look in today's society I am reminded that not only is distraction the true function of racism, as Toni Morrison teaches, but another function of the mechanism of racism is extinction. The intent was that the enslaved and the colonized would build modern society and hopefully die in the process. The fact that Black people are still here is a rebellion in itself. I often wonder if the taking of one's own life is another act of rebellion when we consider blackness, because historically Black people weren't allowed autonomy over their own lives. It is a tumultuous existence to be so tired in a society that refuses to see you because it had hoped you would've stopped existing by now and thus you are rarely represented or reflected accurately within it.

My mum later told me that she cried the day my boyfriend called her from the hospital. She was scared that she was helpless to fix whatever it was that I believed was so deeply broken within me. She was instantly worried that I would be like many of the Black patients she came across in her line of work, who were over-medicated and severely misunderstood. Their cultural nuances were lost on the doctors. Their impassioned responses were misconstrued as anger, and so they became stuck in a cycle where those who were meant to be helping them were essentially causing them more harm.

I didn't let my mum's fears deter me. I didn't let the lack of rapport I had with my first therapist, a white Italian woman, deter me. I was used to my mum's reluctance to hear my truths but it was disheartening to be in therapy sessions and feel like

I was still being gaslighted. I would tell the therapist of incidents that other Black people would understand as a micro or macro aggression, yet she would be adamant that race had nothing to do with it. She told me that things like racism could be tackled by simply choosing to not be affected by it. I ultimately felt unsafe in the presence of my therapist because the most influential factors on my depression couldn't be understood by her, since she maintained a stance that racism was merely a difference in opinion. Even if she understood aspects of the sexual abuse I'd suffered as a child, the institutionalized racism that caused teachers to interpret my detachment as a result of the abuse as 'moodiness' was lost on her.

I knew on a visceral level that I'd had so many things happen to me that would warrant me wanting to give up on existing, but none of them still rang true enough for me to truly give up.

On my second attempt I was assigned a therapist who was Black: a Nigerian woman at that. Even today I am so thankful that I met with her. She was able to give me the vocabulary for so many things that I felt, and I knew I was safe enough to make cultural references, however ludicrous they might have been, and trust that she would understand me on some level. I grew exponentially because of my sessions with her. I then went on to have two other Black female therapists and found these sessions to be literally life-changing because my self-awareness was commended while I was invited to challenge myself in rediscovering vulnerability.

To some people it might not matter what race or ethnicity their therapist is, but for me, and other Black women I've come across, it has played a major role in unpacking the 'dirty laundry' our culture frowns upon us sharing because we know we are in a safe space.

I started my podcast, *Say Your Mind*, because I know first-hand the power of speaking your truth. The letters that I receive from men, women and non-binary people telling me that they've sought out therapy because my podcast inspired them to do so, will always be one of my main reasons for continuing to make episodes. There's nothing glamorous about what I say on my podcast. I simply insist on sharing my views and my vulnerabilities and quirks.

I use tarot as a way of sharing general life lessons that I garner from deconstructing the images on the cards. This resonates deeply with listeners across different cultural beliefs. I sometimes share things I've recently discovered in therapy. I also dissect and comment on current affairs based on my perspective as a Black woman, which listeners greatly enjoy as sometimes I might posit an idea they hadn't otherwise considered. The favourite part of the podcast seems to be the last segment where I express my anger at whatever might be happening in the news or world at large that week. My therapy sessions showed me that anger isn't necessarily a bad thing; it's what we do with it that matters. Many Black women are subjected to emotional trauma because they suppress their anger about the ways they've been violated, for fear of being labelled an Angry Black Woman.

MY PODCAST HAS BEEN PART OF MY HEALING AND A WAY OF ENCOURAGING OTHER PEOPLE, ESPECIALLY BLACK WOMXN, **TO FEEL WHAT THEY FEEL AND NOT RUN FROM IT**.

The only way out is usually through. Many listeners write in asking me for advice on how to become confident and to speak out in the way that I do. The only consistent advice I give is to never give up on yourself, even if at times you disappoint yourself, and to seek a safe space to talk through whatever you might be dealing with. Saying my mind saved me and I know it can help other people.

When I think of depression, I think of a deep blue sea with waves that can sometimes overwhelm me. There are only a few times when the waves subside and you can look for something safe to grab on to so you don't drown. It is important that families, friends and mental health practitioners learn to be conversant in the nuances of mental health and marginalized cultures and identities, so that in those moments when the waves ease off they too can be the safe thing we hold on to.

"

THE ONLY CONSISTENT
ADVICE I GIVE IS
**TO NEVER GIVE UP
ON YOURSELF**,
EVEN IF AT TIMES
YOU DISAPPOINT
YOURSELF, AND TO
SEEK A SAFE SPACE
TO TALK THROUGH
WHATEVER YOU MIGHT
BE DEALING WITH.

"

THE SUMMER YOU CAME OUT WAS LIKE A LONELY ISLAND

I LOST A £25 SAINSBURY'S VOUCHER AND COULD TASTE MY PULSE IN MY THROAT

BY

Kai-Isaiah Jamal

SPOKEN WORD POET/PERFORMER, WRITER

You take a train to the other side of London, where nobody says your right name. You painfully wake at a time so early that not even the sun has entered the dance floor of a hallow sky. You have probably cried yourself to sleep and smoked so much green that your lungs have moss in the bottom of them. But you take a train to the other side of London in the dark early hours, in a suit that clings to every part of you that you are trying to slice, so much so that the man on the bus tells you that 'God will not save you'. In a city you don't even know. To do a job that doesn't pay your bills or even to sleep in your friend's spare room. You keep telling her that it is just until you find your feet; every night you sleep, you dream that they are cut off. You don't have enough of a tongue left to tell yourself that you dream in metaphors. But of course you will search for deeper meaning. You will overthink and read into your 3 a.m. insomniac paralysis; dreaming about losing your feet is a sign to stand by your principles. As if that is not what made you homeless. As if standing in your truth and setting your boundaries didn't mean you lost your mother and your lover all in the same summer. Didn't mean you lost hope in deep, in unconditional, all the traditional ways of prayer. You search for a deeper meaning in everything, try to sing some devil out of your stomach because this man is telling you, 'God will not save you,' and you know you cannot save yourself either. And you drop to your knees on a summer's evening and scream into the same hallow sky, 'Just take me now.' Howl and hurtle every limb you have into one another with enough force that they could all shatter into a million pieces of porcelain and take you back to where it all began. You take a train to the other side of London, to ask people if they will sign up for a scheme that means they will receive fresh food to their door. The irony being most days you eat a bowl of cereal because you are still spending your food vouchers on cigarettes. Can't stomach anything to make you feel heavier than you do. Can't swallow anything whole, anything that don't be smoke. The irony is, you are asking everyone on the high street if they have a moment, or for some time, asking if they are fine with their finances. Asking all the questions you have nothing but a shaking head to respond to. Mouth shaping, 'Excuse me can I talk to you for a second'; eyes saying, 'I haven't spoken to anyone for seventy-two hours and I think I'm dying.' Everyone replies:

'I'm busy.'

'I'm not interested.'

'I just don't care.'

And all the men at work still call you beautiful and tell you that you haven't been with the right man yet and, instead of packing your paperwork and leaving, you laugh, with no joy in the pit of your stomach. You change the subject, talk about the weather or weekend plans, as if you have any. As if your last penny wasn't spent getting to this job on the other side of London. As if you haven't listened to Biggie Smalls and tried to text your father that you are Ready To Die.

You take a train home to this side of London, with eyelids of lead and eyelashes crossing like praying hands, exhaustion sitting under your tongue like a silent prayer. You find a way to pick your feet up and convince your shadow that you are something worth being tied to. Tethered by ankles. Mine too. You fumble in your pocket and pull out your headphones. Bump into seven different shoulders, say sorry each time until you turn into a whisper. You press your cracked screen that is about to die, like everything around you. You tell the girl who is breaking your heart that you love her, knowing you will never hear from her again. Unless she wants to fuck a boy with enough on his chest for her to feel like she's rebelling against her family expectations. You want to call your friends, or your mother. You want to call anyone with an ear and enough time to listen to you do nothing but cry. But you don't. You go on a dating app and allow all the girls to misgender you, apologize if you correct them because you have been saying sorry all day and it is all you know right now. Now your face is lowered into your screen, just so that man on the corner doesn't spit on your shoulder again because you can no longer pretend that everything doesn't hurt. Thirst and the need for therapy are keeping your mouth shut. But you are bumping into aggressively impatient shoulders in Victoria Station, walking back to your friend's house and all you have to your name is your mother's disappointment, addiction and a £25 Sainsbury's food voucher to buy at least one meal that will make you smile this week. But you reach into your pocket and your voucher is gone and all you can feel is a finger-width hole and an incoming tide approaching your bottom lashes. You pace back and forth on this one piece of road asking anyone if they've seen a card on the floor and everyone replies:

'I'm busy.'

'I'm not interested.'

'I just don't care.'

Despair and desperation dance on your vocal cords until you sob into your palms knowing that you haven't got the heart for one more thing to just walk away from you. There is a woman with a child crossing the road towards you; everything pours from you. Wanting nothing more than a hand in yours, you text your ex and tell her that you want to see her, even if it's a lie. You just want to see somebody who has never really seen you. She tells you:

She's busy.

She's not interested.

She just doesn't care.

So you write her a poem, send it as a voice note just so she can hear how tired you are. With a whisper, just so she can see how small you are from the other side of London. You will write a poem asking her if the wind is hurting her too today, if the sun is nothing but a forceful hand touching a body that you do not want to be touched; ask her if she loves you any more even with all these broken porcelain pieces that she might be able to hold together.

So instead you ask if she ever knew that masculinity is the loneliest island you knew. Why? Because men don't hold other men, only in the gay porn you watch and wash yourself after. Only the man in the gay club who told you that you could carry a baby for him. Only when we are dying. Never when we are crying. Only when we are drunk or limping, only in the rugby games or the football cheers. Only in the irony. Only behind ears or curtains that know not of what we do behind them. Only when we are babies or children. Only sometimes, never always, never when we need. Maybe when we bleed, but not like I bleed. Never when you're trans. Never when you're trans. Never when you're trans and depressed. Never when you're trans and oppressed. Never when you're trans and undressed or when your head makes more sound than your mouth. Never when you are silent. Violently silent. When you are dying. When you are ready to die. Never when you are on the other side of London. Never.

Only when you survive. We only hold one another when you survive the worst summer on the other side of London and have lost everything including a Sainsbury's food voucher, a mother, a lover, most of your friends, a voice, your smile and your sanity. Only when you are writing a poem about the worst summer you ever lived through and because you lived through. Who knew that maybe, just maybe, if one of the boys told me they also wanted to die, we would have found a way to live, together? Through the sticky weather and the heartbreak. The fast-paced hungry days and slow aching nights. Maybe we would have found a way to fight. Maybe:

NOBODY WAS BUSY. SOMEBODY WAS INTERESTED.
EVERYONE CARED.

'The Summer You Came Out Was like a Lonely Island – I Lost a £25 Sainsbury's Voucher and Could Taste My Pulse in My Throat' is a poem/stream of consciousness that reflects on the summer when I came out as a trans man and stepped into the painful silence of male depression, the inaccessibility to resources and dealt with the violence attached to presenting outside a binary.

I very rarely write about this period of my life, for fear of having to relive it in some way.

THIS PROVES WE CAN CONTINUE TO MOVE EVEN WHEN WE FEEL NOTHING BUT STUCK.

THE PREGNANT MAN

BY

Hussain Manawer

POET, WRITER, ACTOR

You can't have expected me to tell you
When I didn't understand myself
But when you begin to fight the feelings
You start to fight yourself

I rally the troops
As this war it sends no warning
And as I begin to face this battle
There is no one I could be calling

As time presses on this tumour begins to grow
Transfixed to my inner body
It's not long at all now
Until it's time for your show

I knew it from the start
You were there inside of me
As much as I would try to hide
Your darkness would brighten me

Compressed against our thoughts
This battle is underway
Going against everything I was taught
I will live to fight another day

BECAUSE YOU CAN'T HAVE EXPECTED ME TO TELL YOU

WHEN I DIDN'T UNDERSTAND MYSELF

BUT WHEN YOU BEGIN TO FIGHT THE FEELINGS

YOU START TO FIGHT YOURSELF

Then you kick in the night
And wake me up during my sleep
How can you be so impactful?
For someone who can't be seen

I hide you so well in front of others
Nobody has got any clue
But behind closed eyelids you come to life
And my heart you go straight through

You latch on to my feelings

Trap my inner health

Destroy any form of emotion

So you can have me to yourself

At first I didn't understand

And some days I still feel like I don't

But I've learned if I don't speak on this matter it won't help

But the question is, do I want this problem to be solved?

You've come to show me you're all I have

So I only walk alone

You see that doesn't make sense

Because you are STUCK with me in my zone

And yes I can't change my words

But I can raise my tone

And yes I can't change my skin

But I can strengthen my bones

And yes I can no longer fly

But I can say that I have flown

And I will live to fight another day

Because I refuse to have you on my throne

So raise your body armour

As you walk through that door

Adopt the traits of your father

Pick yourself up from the floor

Prepare for war my little soldier
For you will take no more
As you learn the journey of a martyr
After all, it's true what they say: all is fair in love and war

So, you can't have expected me to tell you
When I didn't understand myself
But when you begin to fight the feelings
You start to fight yourself

"AND I WILL LIVE TO FIGHT ANOTHER DAY

BECAUSE I REFUSE TO HAVE YOU ON MY THRONE.**"**

SYMPTOMS

BY

POET, PRODUCER, AUTHOR

It's the little things
Like the pain in my hands
Like the blocking of my ear
Like the spewing on my shoes

It's the little things
Like no one who understands
Like the overwhelming fear
Like I've got it all to lose

It's the little things
Like keeping in touch
Like getting on a train
Like remembering to eat

It's the little things
Like communicating the density of 'rough'
Like it being too big to explain
Like admitting complete defeat

It's the little things
Like washing up a plate
Like having a shower
Like yawning in conversation

It's the little things
That make the big things hard to handle
That make the little things feel like
They're strangling you
Before you can face the big things
And see the little things
As a symptom of
The big things
That seem so big that they're improbable
That maybe you're just being impossible
That perhaps it's all just *you*

But it's the little things
That need some time
That need some patience
That need acceptance
That need forgiveness
That are there to protect us
Despite the pain

They're a shout and a scream
To remind us
That the big thing is a lot
To remind us
Our brain is all we've got

THE LITTLE THINGS ARE
SENT BY THE BIG THING
TO SAY TAKE A STEP BACK
AND LOOK AFTER YOU.

TO ALL MY FRIENDS
I DON'T HAVE TOO MANY

BY

Rosa Mercuriadis

HEAD OF CREATIVE AT
HIPGNOSIS SONGS FUND LTD/
THE FAMILY (MUSIC) LTD,
FOUNDER OF SICK SAD GIRLZ

All my friends are dead. Well, that's not entirely true, but a good amount of the friends I made between the ages of twelve and eighteen are now dead. For clarity I am twenty-eight years old this year. All my friends should not be dead. But nonetheless a lot of people I love are dead, and for the most part they were not physically ill.

I also happened to be on drugs between the ages of twelve and eighteen. My life has always felt like it was being lived in the extreme: super, soaring, beautiful highs and crashing, heartbreaking lows, with not much in between. The way I used drugs was no different.

I am/was/have always been sad, anxious, powerless, depressed and unmanageable. I have always felt my feelings in a big way, overwhelmed by life on life's terms. As my mother would put it, I have a sensitive constitution. When I moved from London to New York at nine years old, an educational evaluation told my parents they thought I was depressed. I cried and screamed about going to school every day for no discernible reason; I was just fucking sad. A sadness that never really left me. Later I would realize that these were my earliest panic attacks. At the time they were viewed as another attempt at being overdramatic by my family, who crowned me the Queen of Sheba for all my particular demands and dislikes. From there I grew up a little and found boys and drugs and things that distracted the still-sad committee of voices in my head.

"I HAVE ALWAYS FELT MY FEELINGS IN A BIG WAY, **OVERWHELMED BY LIFE ON LIFE'S TERMS**."

Drugs often work for sad girls and I have a penchant for downers, which numb the pain. I ran from the sadness until running stopped working for me. The high doesn't keep you high enough; your body starts to give up the fight. The drugs catch up with you, and by eighteen I had been to rehab a few times and spent most waking hours praying that maybe I would just cease to exist. I wanted an easier and softer way out of this life. Which I can probably imagine is how these people I love ended up dead. I can think of at least fifteen overdoses, a handful of drink-driving crashes, and a few suicides of people I love. And it's fucking heartbreaking. It's hard to bury a friend and keep going; it's hard to be the survivor of what feels like some sort of nuclear fallout because I made it to shelter first.

By the grace of some power bigger than me, I have been ten years sober this year. At eighteen I went to rehab for the last time, and for the first time in my life felt the calm of surrendering to the powerlessness I had (can still have) in my life. I am powerless when faced with drugs, alcohol, sadness, fear, depression, work, shopping, men – the list goes on ad infinitum. But I have found a solution and ways of coping: an incredible community of other alcoholics who are sick and sad and just like me and who have afforded me the ability to live this life. My sobriety has built this life for me, has given me the ability to withstand the sadness and sickness I feel. Given me the opportunity to create spaces, as we do with @SickSadGirlz. It is cathartic and brilliant and complex. It is beyond-my-wildest-dreams incredible. I have almost everything I've ever wanted from life and I think I've worked really hard for it. From a job I love to being able to walk freely through the world without fear of people, places and things I used to be terrified of – my teenage self wouldn't believe this is real.

The harder part is watching the people you thought would also grow up, get sober and share funny stories about the bad, hard, sad days not make it. There are very few of those people left for me. My shared experience is a dying breed. And I want them back.

I want to stop making comments to deflect the hurt, like, 'It's OK! All my friends are dead!' when another one of us dies. I want to work harder to find an even-keeled life I never thought was possible. I want to say I'm OK and mean it. And I want to tell you I fucking love you. I love you. I love you. I love you. And I know it won't save you, but at least I won't regret not telling you if I have to bury you too.

"

I AM POWERLESS
WHEN FACED WITH
DRUGS, ALCOHOL,
SADNESS, FEAR,
DEPRESSION, WORK,
SHOPPING, MEN –
THE LIST GOES ON
AD INFINITUM.
**BUT I HAVE FOUND
A SOLUTION AND
WAYS OF COPING . . .**

"

In my own life I find music to be really helpful with my woes. Here are some suggestions.

'Still Ill' – The Smiths

'Someone Great' – LCD Soundsystem

'Hope There's Someone' – Antony and the Johnsons

'All the Umbrellas in London' – The Magnetic Fields

'On the Low' – Hope Sandoval

'But Not For Me' – Billie Holiday

'I Guess That's Why They Call It the Blues' – Elton John

'In My Life' – The Beatles (Johnny Cash's cover is also great)

'My Body Is a Cage' – Arcade Fire

'Steal My Sunshine' – Len

'These Days' – Nico

'Wuthering Heights' – Kate Bush

'Good Feeling' – Violent Femmes

'Combat Baby' – Metric

'Why Don't You Find Out For Yourself' – Morrissey

'Love Makes You Feel' – Lou Reed

'Fast Slow Disco' – St Vincent

'Nina' – Anaïs

'Expectations' – Belle and Sebastian

'Torn' – Natalie Imbruglia

'Teenage Kicks' – The Undertones

'(No One Knows Me) Like the Piano' – Sampha

'Parting Gift' – Fiona Apple

'Mama Said' – The Shirelles

'Stay Schemin'' – Rick Ross, featuring Drake and
    French Montana

'Straight To Hell' – The Clash

'My Problem Is You' – Jackson Browne

'911' – Tyler, the Creator

'Brand New Key' – Melanie

'I'm So Tired' – Fugazi

'idontwannabeyouanymore' – Billie Eilish

'After Hours' – The Velvet Underground

THE C-WORD

BY

ARTIST, WRITER, BROADCASTER

My grandad called it his nerves.

My mum calls it her mood.

I call it a lot of things.

We are the mental ones in our family, and it should come as no surprise that my mum and my grandad are the ones I have the closest bond with – we understand each other better than most.

There are many ways in which we communicate with each other, and with the outside world, that we are not well, that our brains are fragile or we need some space. These ways are varied but often similar – anything from being short-tempered to having to navigate self-doubt, wallowing in deep sadness or long bouts of low mood and low energy. These all contribute to unhelpful thoughts and feelings that persuade you to think *you* are the problem, *you* are at fault, *you* are the worst – that the world is against you.

A ritual for the three of us is to take to bed, to remove ourselves for a while, and distance ourselves from the world outside. Some people find this approach unhealthy. They see it as a failure; to them, we're 'common'. They find it 'slobbish' and link our fat bodies to our supposed inability to care for ourselves. Staying still, pushing away the world for a bit and taking time to breathe isn't necessarily a bad thing – sometimes taking to bed is what we need . . . and sometimes it isn't, but we still do it anyway, and that should be OK.

Sometimes I take to the internet in the hope of normalizing depression and reaching out to others, but then I begin to worry about the overshare, and think maybe some things don't have to be, or shouldn't have to be, on the internet.

IF THERE'S SOMETHING REALLY ANNOYING ABOUT THE WAY POOR MENTAL HEALTH MANIFESTS ITSELF, **IT'S THE CONSTANT INNER MONOLOGUE ATTEMPTING TO BOTH DERAIL YOU AND LOOK AFTER YOU AT THE SAME TIME**.

Another trait that isn't very productive is self-medicating – finding small bits of happiness, solidarity and consistency in booze, food or other props. In recent years I've found that happiness in yoga, running and history books, which is sort of embarrassing for a council-estate kid from north London.

Even with all the self-care regimes, therapy and systems of care I have in place, I seem to spend a lot of time thinking about depression – why it is so present in every generation of my family and why it bonds us together. Each of us has lived a life that is full of trauma – trauma that has had a lasting effect, trauma inflicted upon us as a result of growing up in poverty, with parents who are processing their own trauma. We were raised in sub-standard social housing, surrounded by really complex social issues – depravity, violence – all while attempting to survive, to get on, to keep going.

Something that I feel is missing from our discussions on mental health is the C-word: class. Mental health discourse often likes to present a world of brain parity, a culture in which we all experience the same sort of mental health stuff; therefore we can be 'fixed' or 'cured' with one remedy. If you look at the voices that take up public space during Mental Health Awareness Month, you'd think depression and its cousins only affected the white middle classes, most of whom have letters after their name.

At a time when we're all attempting to acknowledge privilege I think it's more vital than ever to acknowledge class in conversations on mental health. Being 'common' and poor has informed so much of my family's relationship with our brains – from the speed with which we are able to address problems to the help that is available to us. The lack of support in navigating complex healthcare systems, understanding the languages and terminology of mental health and, most importantly, the slow and painful acknowledgement of how our social standing has contributed to the way our brains work . . . and don't work.

When I bring class into conversations like this, folks often respond with an eye-roll – the experience of the working classes, particularly in relation to mental health, is often belittled as a chip on the shoulder. So, here's my part of that chip in black and white – and a provocative one it is too.

IF YOU'VE GOT MONEY, SOCIAL AND CULTURAL CAPITAL, HOUSING STABILITY, AND COME FROM A HOUSEHOLD WHERE TALKING ABOUT YOUR WELL-BEING IS A THING, **THEN CHANCES ARE YOU ARE GONNA BE MORE LIKELY TO FIND YOUR WAY THROUGH THE MENTAL HEALTH BULLSHIT**.

Chances are you'll also have immediate access to the finances needed to support you during the bullshit, and so access to the systems and services that can support you at your time of need. Plainly speaking, if you've got £75 a week to spare, you can talk to someone and access care – some of which you might need almost straight away. If you can pay for your well-being, then you will get it faster. If you can take time off, have private healthcare, can understand the lingo being thrown at you, then our current healthcare systems are all so much easier to navigate.

Can you see why that chip on the shoulder feels completely unfair? Simply because I was born in a different bed to other sufferers, my ability to access the care I need is restricted.

Now, for the record, I'm not saying that those of you reading who are more privileged don't suffer. I'm not saying it's an easy ride, or that you don't have your own barricades to climb; what I'm saying is, your experience is different, and that needs to be on the table in conversations like this.

With every hashtag set up to help us talk more, with every campaign to get people sharing, with the phrase 'mental health' now so commonly used it just sounds like you're asking for soy milk in your coffee, you would have thought we were moving towards a better place – a place where the boundaries of class are no longer restricting our access to support. Unfortunately I feel that this promised utopia is not a reality.

The waiting lists for services have got much longer, the system is under pressure to do more with less, and many simply can't wait for help. This results in preventable deaths. We're forced into group therapy and assessed in a ten-minute phone call. We're taught what language to use to describe where our heads are at, so we can get signed off work for rest and care, but we have to make sure we don't use language that is too graphic, for fear of being sectioned.

All this stuff is political; like it or not, we can no longer claim ignorance, ambivalence or, worse, denial. As we slowly edge towards the deconsecrating of British socialism and find ourselves heading for an aggressively capitalist state in which our wealth determines our wellness, ask yourself: who is going to be disproportionately affected, and who is already disproportionately affected, by the decisions of our elected leaders to cut services, restrict spending and privatize healthcare? Who wins in a society that favours the rich, and what happens to those of us whose fragility is shaped by our class?

"WHO WINS IN A SOCIETY THAT FAVOURS THE RICH, AND WHAT HAPPENS TO THOSE OF US WHOSE FRAGILITY IS SHAPED BY OUR CLASS?**"**

DID YOU HAVE A DANCE?

BY

COMEDIAN, WRITER

Throughout my teens (and sometimes still now), whenever I got home from a party my mum would say, 'Did you have a dance?' She said this because she knew I loved to dance (not with any sort of skill), but she also meant it as a kind of code. It meant: 'I'm slightly annoyed that you've woken me up because you forgot your key, but if you danced then it was probably worth it.' She understood that if I had danced at a party I'd had a good time, that I'd maybe snogged a boy, possibly taken my shoes off somewhere inappropriate and stepped on a bit of glass, and probably spent an hour laughing on the top deck of a night bus (N65).

For me, the difference between happiness and sadness is the difference between movement and stasis. The happiest times of my life have all involved moving: dancing, running into the freezing cold sea screaming, cycling down a hill to the pub, spinning round in circles for no reason except it feels *so good*, or sprinting through an airport to tell the man I love that I love him. (Really, this should read as 'getting an Uber Pool across London to tell a boy I've fancied for four years that I like his trainers'.) I loved the aimless locomotion of being fifteen; the pointless lingering with friends on street corners, waiting for someone to be brave enough to try their fake ID in a newsagent, followed by a mass movement to Enfield because a friend's friend's brother had a 'free house'.

I think I appreciate that feeling even more now because I

know what it's like to feel paralysed by fear, depression, anxiety and chronic illness. I know what it's like when you have to spend months in bed replaying memories over and over in your head in a hypnotic rhythm that ultimately leaves you believing that not only will you never have fun again, but you've never really had any joy before. I've had an illness – known as migraine-associated vertigo – that means constant vertigo, flashing lights that blind my eyes, the floor rocking uncontrollably, numb limbs and brain fog among other things. When I've been at my worst, I've had dreams about running for a bus, only to be met by the crippling sadness of not being able to walk to the bathroom when I wake up.

And I've found mental illness to be just as paralysing: living in fear – or worse, the fear of fear – can mean that putting one foot in front of the other and choosing to leave your house feels impossible. There's a lot of talk about the 'fight or flight' mechanism that kicks in with anxiety, but I'd like to see the animal version of me fight a lion in the wild with shaky hands and overwhelming nausea. For me, the fear has much more stillness. When I'm ill, I can't move. And what feels even worse is the inability to even make plans that involve moving, because the horrible voices in your head tell you, 'You won't be able to do that. You won't *ever* be able to do that again.'

And so you wait. Any ill person will know the pain of waiting, without any movement in the right direction. Waiting for a doctor's appointment, waiting to feel better, waiting for the night-time so you can go to sleep, waiting for Christmas because everyone loves stuffing. I've been to ten doctors (mostly men) and tried nine different medications, which have all made me sad, sick and finally heartbroken every time they don't work.

In Victorian times this illness was known as 'floating woman's disease' (something to do with 'vapours' and 'hysteria') and would mean institutionalization. As with so many illnesses that mainly affect women, I don't feel like much has changed since then, due to a lack of research and an inability to take women seriously. Today, male doctors are less likely to prescribe appropriate medication for women than men; they're more likely to presume women's illnesses are 'just psychological', and medication still isn't being tested on women. I've been made to feel totally responsible for my own pain, which then makes me unbearably sad when I don't get better.

A whole community of mentally and physically ill women is waiting – waiting to be seen by a doctor, waiting to be well enough to go back to work, waiting to hear about whether they will be deemed 'disabled enough' to be eligible for disability allowance. And I'm lucky – I'm white, I'm middle class, I have the NHS, often I can walk. So many people don't have these privileges.

Women are not being taken seriously by medical professionals, partly because pain is seen as our destiny. ('Women are born with pain built in. It's our physical destiny,' as Phoebe Waller-Bridge reminded us in her show *Fleabag*.) But imagine how successful, how powerful, how happy we'd be if we didn't have period pains, fibromyalgia, premenstrual dysphoric disorder, multiple sclerosis, endometriosis, migrane-associated vertigo . . . The list goes on and on. It's not fair that the thing that joins us is suffering, and yet we still feel so isolated.

WE NEED TO DEMAND MORE FOR OURSELVES AND OTHER WOMEN. **WE NEED TO MOVE AND DANCE BEYOND THE PATRIARCHAL MEDICAL SYSTEM THAT KEEPS US TRAPPED, A STRUCTURE THAT CONSPIRES TO KEEP US STILL.**

It makes sense that with movement comes happiness. Free movement is an extreme privilege: it means you're not stuck behind a till waiting for your shift to finish; it means you can live somewhere safe, where your free movement isn't under threat; it might mean you're on a train to see your mum, or on a cheap EasyJet flight to a hen-do; it means you're not in prison or under a curfew – and it means you're able-bodied enough to leave your house. But the movement itself can contribute happiness. As we've all been told by our GPs, a little bit of exercise a day can BOOST your endolphins (?). (What are they? How can I get them? Why do I feel so angry when I do yoga?)

The act of movement itself can also signal to your body that change has come. The part of your brain that sends messages like 'You shouldn't do that!', 'You can't do that!', 'Last time you did that you got anxious!' is in fact without language. Telling yourself 'It's going to be OK' won't necessarily retrain your brain. It's the act of *doing* that reassures your anxious mind that you are in fact fine, that you're not running from a lion – you're just getting on the tube/walking around the block/making a phone call. And then you've done it. Through your action you've told your body that it's OK; it doesn't need that fear any more. Through movement comes change. 'Movement': the word itself evokes thoughts of political change. Indeed, people often embark on pilgrimages with the hope of personal transformation. Anthropologist Victor Turner suggests that the act of moving – going on a pilgrimage – allows us to perform and explore new identities. He noted that it is the liminality of a pilgrim's space – between or outside societal constraints – that allows for freedom, exploration and, for me, happiness. Sometimes we enter a liminal space (full of 'potential and potency', as Turner suggested) by choice: a trip to the seaside to clear our heads and break our routines.

But, as ill people, we can find ourselves pushed out of society against our will. And particularly as ill women – according Hélène Cixous in 'The Laugh of Medusa' – 'we've lived in flight, stealing away, finding, when desired, narrow passageways, hidden crossovers.' But there on the borders, on the thresholds and crossovers, we will flourish. I think I do this through making comedy and through writing. As Cixous says so beautifully, 'Flying is woman's gesture – flying in language and making it fly.' Through writing, song, laughter and dance, we can fly, not just float. 'Flying women', not 'floating women'.

And so anyone who identifies as a woman (and, indeed, any minoritized group) – and particularly as a woman with mental and physical illness – has to move out of normative spaces, which are spaces with learned fear. Patriarchal spaces where doctors make you feel like it should be OK to be in pain.

AND WITH THE ACT OF MOVING, SHIFTING LITERALLY OR MENTALLY, COMES A SHIFT IN IDENTITY. **HOPEFULLY, TOWARDS HAPPINESS AND PEACE.**

In other words, 'it's the cliiiimb' (Miley Cyrus). And so now I walk with a walking stick when I have to (something I was too embarrassed to do for a long time) and, when I'm feeling up to it, I go to a party and have a little dance. I try to make the choice to move beyond constraints put on me. I make comedy because 'boys don't like girls for funniness' (*Angus, Thongs and Perfect Snogging*); I make collages and paintings even though I didn't get into art school. But often I'm too sick and sad to get out of bed. I think that's OK too.

IT'S OK TO BE VULNERABLE

TWO SIDES TO EVERY STORY

BY

JOURNALIST, ACTIVIST

I am a burden. I am a liability. I am a worthless human being who does not deserve help. I am ashamed of this deep, dark hole inside me and I will not show it to anyone. I am boring. I am a drain. I am invited to parties out of pity and everyone is disappointed when I show up. I am so ugly that my face offends those who look at me, so disgusting that to be in a room with me is unbearable. I am unworthy of help, unworthy of love, unworthy of friendship. One day they will all get sick of me. They will get sick of my moods and my tears and my constant needs and they will all disappear. I am a bad person. I am a burden.

You are my best friend/my child/the love of my life. You are hurting and in pain. You are a victim of a force bigger than you, and none of this, none of this, is your fault. You are the light of my life and that doesn't change when your life is dark. I do not love you because you're in a good mood. I do not love you because you are funny, clever, busy, hard-working, able to get out of bed in the morning. I love you because you bring joy to my life. I still love you when you feel anxious and sad, because I love you and not who your brain is telling you that you are. I can see the person underneath the fog and that is the person I love. I cannot fix this but I can be there for you. Let me be there for you. I have made some toast and Marmite and a warm cup of tea.

PLEASE LET ME IN.

ANXIETY

BY

Ben Platt

ACTOR, SINGER, SONGWRITER

There's a worry I feel every day
It distracts from my work and it ruins my play
It can pop in and out
It can whisper or shout
And it certainly won't go away

It's a worry I've learned how to bait
There are places I know that it's bound to await
Like a long airplane flight
Or a space that's too tight
They have all become places I hate

But this worry is oft unannounced
I can rarely predict when it's going to pounce
When it happens I'm stuck
I'm a ripe sitting duck
As it hits in alarming amounts

There's a worry that won't let me speak
And it's got me believing my body is weak
With just one simple trick
It can tell me I'm sick
And turn everything needlessly bleak

It's a worry that makes me feel shame
It says, 'Look at the comforts you've got to your name!
If you can't just calm down
With this privilege around
Then your cowardice must be to blame'

But this worry is no one's but mine
Maybe yours is much worse or perhaps you feel fine
I can only connect
And give equal respect
To find hope that our worries align

There's a worry that loves to surprise
And the truth disappears when it looks in my eyes
I can know what is real
And then suddenly feel
That my logic and reason are lies

It's a worry that I have to serve
I could wonder 'Why me?' but I don't have the nerve
When so much of my life
Is unclouded by strife
I think worry's the least I deserve

BUT MY WORRY
IS ONLY ONE VOICE

I'VE DECIDED THAT'S
REASON ENOUGH
TO REJOICE

WHEN THE
PEOPLE AROUND

MAKE MORE
VALUABLE SOUND

**THEN TO WORRY CAN
FEEL LIKE A CHOICE**

SEEN AND HEARD

(CAN YOU SEE THE
HOLE IN MY HEAD AND
OTHER RAMBLINGS)

BY

Emilia Clarke

ACTOR

When the essence of your job is to be looked at, it brings into sharp focus a whole host of musings that can make you feel pretty bad if you're not careful. When your job also entails being a young woman and being looked at? Well, this is a path that womankind has been treading for centuries. When you're being looked at for your living and you have suffered a brain injury or two, that calls into account the very nature of how you trust your mind . . . Here we land ourselves in some very murky waters.

I was just getting hold of what it felt like to be a young woman when good fortune landed me the job of a lifetime.

The Mother of Dragons didn't start out as a dragon-riding warrior queen with little thought to how quickly she could burn someone alive. She began scared, alone and abused, sold to the highest and biggest bidder. She – I – we walked that line together. My own insecurities, fears and femininity out there for all to see, naked in every sense. I was starting to understand how it felt to be a woman who was being looked at, while people around the world tuned in to begin their *Game of Thrones* addiction.

This turned out to be the less tricky part. I was a newbie in my profession, a young sapling sprouting growth in the industry of my dreams. So much to learn, so much energy to give to this learning, so many opportunities to show this male-dominated world what a young woman was capable of. So far, so dragon-riding good. Then my brain exploded.

That really is how it feels, by the way: a mini explosion in your head, as if you can physically feel the blood being set free and wreaking havoc. Clinically a brain haemorrhage, simplistically a stroke. My ball-busting plan to take on the world, one slave owner at a time, was scuppered. If only I could keep my cool. This only proved halfway possible if I kept my head injuries a secret from the world that was now looking.

How the world sees brain injuries, I've found, is with the face of someone trying to work out a very complicated maths equation: largely confusion muddled with concern and a total lack of understanding with regard to the science behind it all. And I don't blame them for a second: before my injuries that was me too! But this realization is a relatively new experience for me because, for nine long years, I kept them a secret. I did everything in my power to make sure no one found out that I had survived two brain haemorrhages. Why? Because I was finding it hard enough having people look at me for a living, dissecting my face and body to the point where my image was quickly becoming all I could think about when I stepped outside. Throw in a brain injury or two, and here we have a problem.

I was convinced that everyone could see the holes in my

head; that they could actually *see* the holes in my armour, my confidence, my self-belief. Where they saw a young woman trying on the film industry for size, I saw in myself a total imposter, too sick to be taken seriously and too weak to play *any* mother, let alone a mother of dragons.

Now, I had no idea about mental health. Naive as that sounds, I had heard of depression, PTSD, and people who had tried to take their own life, but never in a million years did I think that it was something I might be struggling with. But here I was. In the thick of it. How I saw myself was no longer for me only: I took on the belief that everyone I encountered could see it too, my failings. If only I had a cast on my leg or a patch over my eye, a sign that said CAREFUL, WARNING: THIS GIRL IS UNWELL, I might have seen the ways in which people are capable of showing compassion, but for me and for many this is not an option. Hiding is; and I gladly threw on my acting camouflage.

I am one of the lucky few, the lucky few who have been raised by good people, surrounded by good friends and with enough of an understanding of humanity that I could apply it to myself. I decided to care about my brain, which had been through hell and back and managed to survive it, so that I could look around and recognize that the life I was living was actually full to bursting with love, kindness and laughter.

It was a long road to get there, don't get me wrong, and

there are still plenty of rooms and days when I feel like I'm the sham who's about to be caught out, whose broken brain is out there for all to see, as I'm quietly escorted to the nearest exit.

Now how much of this is being a woman? How much of this is being an actor? How much of this is the way my mind works, or how much of this is due to me still trying to comprehend which part of my brain has left me for good, I just can't say. But the good news is that I know I'm not alone – not just because I'm a recognizable face, or because I'm privileged enough to have a support system that will give me hugs on demand, but because I am one of the 50 million people around the world today living with a brain injury. And if *they* can do it, well then I guess the Mother of Dragons better get on and do it too.

"

I DECIDED TO CARE
ABOUT MY BRAIN . . .
SO THAT I COULD
LOOK AROUND AND
RECOGNIZE THAT
THE LIFE I WAS LIVING
WAS ACTUALLY
**FULL TO BURSTING
WITH LOVE, KINDNESS
AND LAUGHTER**.

"

DAY 16

BY

Hannah Witton

VLOGGER, BROADCASTER, AUTHOR

Day Nine in my hospital room, I'm weak and tired. My permanent state of being is lying down with my eyes closed, but I never sleep except with the help of a very strong pill at night. My voice is a quiet whisper; it takes energy to talk, but I don't have anything to say anyway. As it has done multiple times a day for the last several weeks, a pain surges through my abdomen and I have to force myself to open my eyes, roll out of the bed, put my slippers on and slowly shuffle to the toilet. When I sit down I realize I've forgotten my water bottle, but Mum is there in the doorway with a sad look on her face handing it to me. I'm going to be here a while; best to stay hydrated.

All in all, I probably spent hours, maybe even days, on that toilet during my hospital admission due to a flare-up of my ulcerative colitis. That's a lot of time all alone, ill and in pain to sit and think. About health, about life, about my life. I went through phases in what occupied my brain during that time. Each individual session on the toilet could last up to an hour but I was never bored. I was too ill to be bored. At the beginning I would stare at the speckled hospital floor and make out shapes and stories like you do with clouds. I hadn't seen a cloud since being here. There was a window in my room but I couldn't see the sky from where I lay in my bed, and on Saturdays and Sundays really loud construction took place; the noises shattered through my body. Everything hurt.

My body could felt the slightest disturbance. The nurse's trolley wheeling outside my room – I could feel it when it went over a bump; if someone grazed my hospital bed, I could feel it; if my hospital-room door slammed shut instead of being gently closed, oh boy could I feel that.

In the floor speckles I saw faces and animals; I'm pretty sure I even saw a dragon once. Each visit brought new discoveries but I could never find the same thing twice. My nails and my nose were another fascination. I picked and I picked until there was nothing left of my nails and the skin around them and there was nothing left to dig out of my nose. My fingers went where no fingers had gone before. Then there was the song, just one part of one song that was stuck in my head for days and days on end. It would go round and round, and it scares me to acknowledge exactly why this particular part of this particular song dominated my brain. I've never had mental health issues; physical health issues, sure – I was diagnosed with ulcerative colitis when I was seven years old. Hospitals, needles, drugs – I got this. But I've always been a happy person, despite everything. The song was in fact a comedy song by Bo Burnham; I've been a fan of his for many years. It's called '#Deep' and, yes, you're supposed to say the hashtag because that's #comedy. The lyrics in my head go:

If life makes you wish you were dead
Just put on a good movie then promptly put a bullet in
  your head
Spend forever asleep
'Cause life pales in comparison to living the dream
Hashtag deep

I DON'T KNOW IF I WAS SUICIDAL. THE PASSIVE THOUGHT ABOUT STOCKPILING PARACETAMOL CROSSED MY MIND BUT I COULDN'T IMAGINE ACTUALLY TAKING THEM ALL. **I JUST WANTED THE PAIN TO BE OVER.**

I wanted this life I was living in that hospital room to be over. I thought about my life a lot, everything I'd done. My achievements, things I'd experienced, places I'd been, friends I'd made, the kind of person I was, and I came to the conclusion that if I didn't wake up I'd be content with the life I'd lived.

But on Day Seventeen of being in hospital I had emergency life-changing surgery. I woke up in a lot of pain but a different kind of pain, and I no longer wanted to die.

Having a stoma has been a lot to adjust to, and I've never so clearly understood the connection between my physical and mental health. As my body recovered from the trauma and became stronger, so did my mind, but it took months, a year. To be honest, I don't know when I'll ever be 'fully recovered' from what happened, but I'm not there yet. My brain, however, feels good; I've talked about what happened with friends, family, online and with other people who've gone through similar things, which has really helped. And my body feels good too. I set myself the challenge of running five kilometres before the end of 2018 after literally having to learn to walk again after my surgery. And I did it! And I'm still working out, which is helping my body and helping my brain. Having a stoma and a massive scar has forced me to care less about what my body looks like but care more about how it feels. I work out to build and maintain my body's fitness, and I'm building and maintaining my brain's fitness by talking and sharing, not trying to bury what happened but acknowledge it.

YES, I WANTED
TO DIE. IT'S A
HARD THING FOR ME
(A HAPPY PERSON)
TO FACE THE FACT
THAT I HAD
THOSE THOUGHTS.
**BUT NOW,
I WANT TO LIVE.**

INTO LIGHT

BY

Elizabeth Day

JOURNALIST

We dug a hole in the ground
in which to bury our shame.
We stopped our hearts and stilled our blood
in order to avoid detection.
And somewhere in that dark, deep soil
we shielded ourselves from a flood
that never came.

We forgot that vulnerability is connection,
that solidarity is forged around
things going wrong,
not right.
That sometimes the only fight
worth having
is the one against the judgement we imagine
thrown like orange peel from the cheap seats.
And that the greatest feats
are ones budding from the truth of who we are.
Not the hall of circus mirrors
in which we reflect the meanest distortions,
trying to live our lives
in a box of the smallest proportions;
our limbs in perpetual commotion,
our thoughts cut to fit,
a pattern that is not of our making.

I want to know
before I resign myself
to a half-life of half-buried intent,
before I redesign myself
to a plan that claims to be heaven-sent,
who was it who asked us to feel repentance
for sins uncommitted?
And why did we give our consent?
Who was it who pitted
us against our truest selves?
Who catcalled and made us confess
to guilt even though we were guilt*less*?
These ill-formed voices
who have no skin in the game,
who clothe us in their worn-out shame.
I am tired of their jeering
of their peering into the ugly corners.
I am tired of their eclipses
that force my belief into ellipses.
Because maybe – what if – here's a thought –
the dark is only dark when buried?

So.

I CHOOSE INSTEAD
TO BURROW UP
THROUGH THE SOIL,

UP THROUGH THE DARK,
HEAVY SOIL OF
MY HUMILIATION.

AND I WILL EMBRACE
THE NIGHT

**WHILE HOLDING
MY SOUL UP
TO THE LIGHT**.

FAILURE

BY

WRITER, DIRECTOR, BROADCASTER

For some it's an experience, an essential rite of passage en route to manhood. For me, failure was an intimidating skyscraper that dwarfed anyone in its shadow. There's something so vicious about the word that it's almost as storied as the worst kind of heavyweight champ. So here's to the unbeaten, calloused and bloated belt-holder. Failure. Fuck you.

Growing into these ears and awkwardly long arms were two of the many worries I had as a teenager. Puberty for me was mainly avoiding anything that resembled breasts due to their ability to turn me an Arsenal shade of red. I'm a black man. My people don't blush, but boobs had the power to betray my melanin.

Outside my unavoidable genetics, a silently building ideal began to grow. I was learning the code of manhood. Not deliberately, but socially and culturally. The man-shaped armour I'd started to wear taught me to never reveal the chink I knew existed. That vulnerability was failure.

London in the eighties was the backdrop to my formative years, while my parents' uprooted African culture took centre stage. The ability to be both working-class London and unashamedly African caused a constant friction within me.

The distance between the two worlds was vast, yet some beliefs were shared. In both cultures being a man did not include weakness or failure, and being a good man was all I wanted.

" FEAR AND FAILURE MADE MENTAL STRENGTH A DISTANT MEMORY. **BUT NO ONE IS TRULY FEARLESS AND FAILURE IS INEVITABLE.** "

My first run-in with failure played a part in finding myself on a therapist's couch. Session one was a masterclass in what I knew to be true bumping into its harder, scarier self. Of course I wasn't going to cry and of course the therapist agreed. A statement contradicted by him nudging the tissue box closer. He knew exactly what sat on that ugly floral couch and he knew it was about to blow.

The first time I really cried as a man was when I believed I'd let everybody down. Feeling that, when it counted, I didn't do what I said I would; I wasn't good enough. Failure was an admission of weakness, an inability to deal. More so, because of the way I'd culturally been directed, a convincing male performance was one that NEVER buckled.

My failures professionally, romantically and everything in between saw me at my most frail mentally. Believing I'd fallen in the opinion of those I love most made me not want to go outside. Believing I'd never again reach the best that I'd achieved and lost by failing made me not want to try. Fear and failure made mental strength a distant memory. But no one is truly fearless and failure is inevitable.

At my worst, I was forced to accept my shadow and be comfortable with him. Being me in the light was easy; my best self I knew well. But that shadow has become a far more important acquaintance. It's that relationship that has taught me my triggers.

It's that relationship that has helped me understand that the opinion of those I love will never shift because they love me back. The highs I'd found and lost professionally or romantically were never really the highs; they were an experience I'd only surpass at a later date. They'd become nothing more than a measuring stick for the middle, NOT the top.

My mate, the geezer who likes to lurk in the shadows, told me that when my integrity is challenged, the trigger I didn't know existed gets a solid push. Reluctantly, he also shared the fact that having a trigger isn't failure; knowing that it exists in itself is success.

The 'man armour' I wear today is full of cracks, dents and openings, but I know every mark and scuff intimately. I still have fears, but they will never again define me, because no one is truly fearless and failure is inevitable. So here's to the unbeaten, calloused and bloated belt-holder. Failure. Fuck you.

"

HAVING A TRIGGER
ISN'T FAILURE;
**KNOWING THAT
IT EXISTS IN ITSELF
IS SUCCESS**.

"

A SECRET

BY

Jamie Flook

WRITER, JOURNALIST

Under the night sky I am gazing upon ancient stars, a cacophony of screeches rasping inside my mind, fighting each other for space. The stars are both mortal and endless.

When Scarlett invited me to contribute to this book, I didn't even need to think about it. The opportunity to write something that might help alleviate the isolation that many feel during times of mental distress was too great to turn down. This is the book I wish was around years ago. Having agreed to contribute, I then brainstormed about twenty ideas and realized that approximately nineteen of them were absurd. I was left with one idea on the page. I would need to talk about my own mental health.

Holy guacamolc.

Some people think I'm a bit crazy, but that's just people who know me. What people don't know about me is that upstairs there is a war going on. Well, I'm a guy – I'm supposed to be mentally invincible, aren't I? If I get injured, I think it's supposed to be straining one of the ol' biceps in a tug-of-war or slicing open an artery while engaging in jungle warfare. I'm supposed to be icily untouchable. I'm supposed to be Arnie. Or James Bond. Or Han Solo. But I'm not.

I'm me.

That's not a diss on movie icons by the way – I love those guys. Looking back, I think my mental health afflictions started very young and I am sure the same can be said for many people. I know a guy with mental health issues who once told me that around the age of five or six he dreamed of becoming an astronaut and then when he was a little older he wanted to become a hammerhead shark. He's now got qualifications coming out of his ears and is as bright as they come. When I was a child one of my afflictions was OCD, which meant even numbers began to play a hugely uneven role in everyday tasks. Certain things had to be done two, four or even eight or more times. I had it for quite a while until I realized that zipping open my pencil case twenty-two times every time I needed to write something was incompatible with actually getting anything done with my pen.

The common magical idea when you are young is that the world is your oyster. Quite why the dreams of youth are tied up with the existence of a saltwater clam is a mystery to me. Perhaps it has something to do with oysters' status in some lands as a delicacy. It can't be anything to do with their adventurous spirit, as to the best of my knowledge they spend most of their time 'asleep'. The thing is, though, society doesn't tell you that as you get older you're going to get absolutely battered again and again and again. And again. We accumulate damage.

I have duelled with depression on and off for a long time. There, I said it. I never thought I'd write that for people to read, but sometimes you have to stick your neck out to help things change. He who dares wins, hopefully. Less frequently I have also experienced anxiety and panic attacks. I have had anxiety all my life. The National Curriculum practically enforces it in state schools in the UK, just in case wider society doesn't already do a grand enough job of gutting your psyche on a daily basis. I remember that at school I thought I was the only person in the world who felt that way.

The panic attacks started later but have, thankfully, only appeared on a small handful of occasions, and for me they come completely out of nowhere. The first time was when I was working as a sales assistant in a high-end shop where customers could be savagely rude and abusive. I didn't feel in any way threatened or scared but it still happened. I remember I was operating the till and my hands started shaking violently. How I didn't scatter the customers' change all over the shop, I don't know. Jack Douglas would have been proud.

Depression is the most prolific of the three amigos. At its worst it strips you of all hope. Without hope you feel . . .

Empty.

I liken depression to a painting entitled 'The Torment of Saint Anthony' by Michelangelo. In the artwork the saint is standing on a cliff edge while being lynched by a mob of terrifying demons. When you have depression the demons dig their claws in to you and nobody hears you scream.

Nobody hears *them* scream.

OF COURSE SOME PEEPS DON'T UNDERSTAND DEPRESSION AND MISTAKE IT FOR MERE SADNESS, **BUT THAT'S LIKE MISTAKING AN ATOMIC BOMB FOR A BUNSEN BURNER**.

I remember years ago when I first realized that I had depression. It was like I had plunged to a whole new secret depth of an intense, all-consuming feeling of hopelessness within my soul that I never knew existed. Everything suddenly became pointless and even the most trivial tasks became a massive effort.

However, having now admitted the above, I feel compelled to prepare for some of the comments that I know will come my way. I know guys don't like to admit this stuff for fear of being judged. I get it. I really do. Phrases such as 'man up' and 'grow a pair' spring to mind. The controversial psychologist Dr Jordan Peterson says that we should teach people to be more resilient, but I'd say, how about we teach people not to be so judgemental? I think the shame surrounding depression is at least partly caused by people who express lofty disdain on a subject they know nothing about. 'Oh, we didn't have all these mental health issues in my day.' No? I don't think Hemingway was just polishing his shotgun with the safety catch off. This code of silence is killing people. We need to try another way.

I'd also like to add that I don't think there's a right or wrong way to survive with depression. Everyone is different. Some folk find it difficult to get out of bed, and in my book that's

OK. Some don't want to go to work and when it becomes long-term I think we sometimes call them benefits cheats. In such situations I'd ask, what is wrong with our workplaces that they are often so dread-inducing to people with mental health issues?

If you don't feel comfortable talking about depression yet or whatever issue affects you, maybe write about it instead. Find your rhythm, write down what you are feeling, and then when you are ready, show it to someone.

This might sound deluded right now, but it really does get better. You can get through the hellfire. Nowadays, each of my writing accomplishments feels like a small victory over depression, but before that just getting out of bed was really a victory in itself. I don't want to come over all preachy, though; I know how hard it is. The empathy I extend to others I do not always apply to myself, and I guess the same might be true for you.

If you have depression or any other mental health issue, talking about it can help humanity learn. We are all destined to reach life's end the way things were before our lives began, as stardust storming through the galaxies. Life is short; the journey is long.

"

IF YOU HAVE
DEPRESSION OR
ANY OTHER MENTAL
HEALTH ISSUE,
**TALKING ABOUT IT
CAN HELP
HUMANITY LEARN**.

"

THE LONG GOODBYE AND MANY SWEET HELLOS

BY

JOURNALIST, AUTHOR

Dementia snatched the freshness of September in 2009.

In all the years before, I had enjoyed the return of crisp morning breezes. Even though I was bullied so relentlessly, I always loved the return to school. Mummy would be the one to give me the money for stationery, to announce my entrance in classrooms. As always, I chose colour. I longed for the pink stuff with sassy quotes and a pen with a fluffy cap to top things off. But no! That was too dangerous at my secondary school in Palmers Green. I settled for the space-themed purple, blue, green galactic stationery. It still conveyed a strong message to my classmates. I was set to explore worlds that they knew nothing about. Way back then, my gender nonconformity was loud, with a promise to get louder. Having been blessed with queerness, violent gusts of conflict engulfed Mummy and me in the summer between Year Twelve and Year Thirteen in 2003. She begged me to get back into a box of masculine safety I had never actually lived in. I refused. I had tasted the freedom feminism promised me. My body, my gender and my future were mine for the taking. The beginnings of a rather radical self-acceptance had been set in motion when I chose to go to sixth form at a girls' school started by a suffragette. I was ravenous for the freedom to be as feminine as my spirit needed to be. Willing to fight for it. Willing to die for it. So we fought. She had burned all my magazines and cosmetics while I partied like a debutante unleashed in Tufnell Park. Returning to the

"
I WAS RAVENOUS
FOR THE FREEDOM
TO BE AS FEMININE
AS MY SPIRIT
NEEDED TO BE.
**WILLING TO
FIGHT FOR IT.
WILLING TO
DIE FOR IT.**
"

battlefield, I called home in Bush Hill Park. The finality of this betrayal made me scream at her:

'*YOU'RE NOT MY MOTHER!*'

Just like Zoe from *EastEnders* did.

She didn't respond with Kat Slater's killer line:

'*YES I AAAAAAM!*'

Her name, Castella, means castle in Spanish. I once believed myself to be the blood in her stone. I never had to call her name when I was sick in the night as a child. Our bond was intrinsic, intuitive and spiritual. Our separation was a violent one. I needed to escape.

I ran off into a life of friends' spare bedrooms, hostels, bedsits, and sitting in offices begging for income support. Estranged from the only family I had known, I metamorphosed into a forthright, mouthy bird, utterly unaware of my own fragility. I flew off to Paris, Martinique and back; battered by people and incidents no one ever deserves. I suffered too many crash-landings for anyone to ever consider themselves well and fully operational. Yet I kept going. The drugs didn't work. They definitely made things worse. But they helped the complex PTSD from numerous assaults and the sensation that I was drowning as my gender dysphoria filled my lungs with dirty water. I could not speak or share what was still pure and innocent about me. So I kept chugging along and crashing. I crashed out of university without the decent qualifications my peers gained, but not quite with nothing. I had some knowledge of why life was so hard and why it was set to get even harder. My prodigal return was complex and quite queer. But I wasn't quite ready for the news that my mummy had started the peculiar and sad process of forgetting things.

In a mental health assessment centre in Edmonton my father, my aunt, my sister and I sat by the window. My mummy sat facing the doctor at his desk. The sun poured in behind us, and I hoped it made our faces dark enough for her not to make out our strained facial expressions. I had chosen to have a Grace Jones hi-top fade. I wished to appear as strong and striking as her. I did not feel strong or striking that day. I was helpless. We all were. The doctor asked my mum basic questions. What did she do for work, etc. He asked her to count. She struggled to get past ten. He asked her to count backwards. She couldn't. He asked her when her birthday was. She had no idea. He asked her when my sister's birthday was. She had no idea. That morning, knowing that she was going to have her memory tested, she had written our birthdays down in her small notebook. I had seen her do it. She looked so put together. Regal in rich aubergine, her skin plump, her body still buxom. She had seemed worried, anxious to get things right, but in a nervous, giggly way. Nevertheless her natural disposition was cheerful. A healthy middle-aged black lady with gorgeously cared for shoulder-length sisterlocks. She looked young for her age, in the way we so often do. She still knew what it was to look 'put together'. In the face of a barrage of questions from an expressionless doctor whose middle name was Objectivity, my mummy revealed herself to be the child.

I sat there and said to myself:

'*Oh my god. She's going . . .*'

My mummy was an ocean liner who had cared for me with grit and glamour. *Castella the Unsinkable*. I stood on the dock waving goodbye to the most rounded and intelligent woman I had known. She was my Windrush. Birthed in an era of warm waters where all seemed filled with promise. A lifetime of impeccable service, brief bouts of seasickness and 'good-god-how-are-we-gonna-make-it-through's on the choppy seas. This doctor, who couldn't possibly know the scope of this loss, commanded that we now thank her for her service.

'*For an educated woman who went to LSE and has had such an illustrious career, the fact that you weren't able to answer these questions adequately is worrying.*'

The confusion of the past nine months suddenly painfully clear. Her kindly colleagues at her local government job who had done their best to do the right thing by her. The forgotten appointments with the occupational therapist. Her futile attempts to keep her computer skills up to date with evening classes at the local women's college. It all made sense now.

This wasn't mere menopausal forgetfulness. It wasn't occasional. It wasn't even chronic. This was degenerative. This was permanent. This was a spiral. This was the beginning of her end.

My sister beside me was tearful but stoic and respectful. I was a wreck. A deplorable wreck with soaked cheeks and juddering breath. I couldn't wipe my face because then everyone would have seen my smooth chocolate ganache foundation smear. So I just sat there, dejected, with the heavy awareness that this would be the longest goodbye I would ever know.

The previous Christmas, 2008, my mummy had sat my sister and me down at our dining table covered with a tablecloth of spices and elephants. The home smelled of a hybridized wholesomeness: basmati rice, gravy, turkey, parsnips, sweet potatoes and puddings. She gifted us the sentence we would need to survive without her:

'*I love you both, unconditionally . . .*'

There was something covenly about our triangular seating arrangement. She bound us with the preciousness of her sincerity. She had lived for us. All resentments had dissipated. My presence there, back at home, was a ceasefire. She'd given us books, a solid domestic training, and the black goldmine of confidence necessary to love ourselves in a country we were learning did not love us back.

The Christmas of 2009 was quieter. From festive to furtive. My sister and I sat upstairs in our burnt orange bedroom, consoling ourselves with red wine, weed and reality TV. Mummy had now forgotten how to cook. My sister picked up the slack. I'd done the required running around. We had made our bodies busy. It helped. Just before he went to bed our father stood in the doorway of our bedroom:

'*Your mother's diagnosis has come through in a letter. Dementia, early onset Alzheimer's.*'

He said it with solemn gravitas, like he was reading a telegram. The silence that followed was cloyingly thick. We chose to chuckle at how emotionless he was. The parent who cared for our emotional well-being was gone. We laughed from a deep, bitter well, knowing we now only had each other.

Mummy became our child. We took care of her in shifts. Eventually the car was sold because, even though she could still drive as if on autopilot, the day would come when she couldn't, and no accident was worth waiting for. She wouldn't go out alone any more. At first giving her direction reminders was enough, and then it wasn't. Then came the tantrums. She became convinced that home was elsewhere. If the door wasn't locked, she would bolt.

We were gasping for technology that would help us deal with our new reality: the family with 'the runaway mother'. We would roam the streets asking:

'*Have you seen a black lady?? She comes up to my shoulder??? She has shoulder-length hair in sisterlo– like, really thin locks?*'

I resented the gormless faces of nothingness that softened once people realized we weren't trying to sell them anything, and now they had nothing of value to offer us either. I would be crying in the back roads of Enfield Town hoping that the local radio announcements would see her home before lunch. Howling my mum's name into the breeze of Jubilee Park as a sunset's once-neutral beauty held a nefarious promise of the worry that night-time would bring.

'*Please come home, Mummy. Please come home.*'

To be in my twenties worrying about my mum on the mean streets of north London was a superbly cruel reversal of the natural order of things. She was most often brought back by the police. Discovered some place random and shepherded home by sweetly serious butch women and broad-shouldered gents with light jokes and booming, sonorous voices. They arrived looking amused but never with the exasperation I would have expected. My mummy's biggest adventure took her from Bush Hill Park to Liverpool Street. She had been found at evening rush hour standing near Broadgate Tower with her pillowcase stuffed with her nightclothes. The officers who brought her back were as pleasant and reassuring as always. Mummy walked in like Olive from *On the Buses* waxing rhapsodical about how great they were:

'Honestly! They were ever so lovely. They got me a lovely cup of tea and they were ever so kind.'

We chortled awkwardly as they explained that she must have got on the Overground train and bustled her way through the ticket barriers with no ticket – of which she had no recollection. The brief relief was transferred into anxiety and fastidiously double-locking the front door after every departure.

It was fortunate that my sister was wise enough to source the most progressive literature to guide us in caring for her. *Contented Dementia: 24-hour Wraparound Care for Lifelong Well-being* by Oliver James. It was good to read about the pointlessness of asking her questions she could not answer, and how validating her perceptions of the world was always the best course of action. We found this most helpful when she raised people from the dead. The one time I let slip that my maternal grandmother had died, her grief knocked us all for six. She spiralled down as if her mother had not been gone for almost a decade.

So, instead, Grandma became a being who was very much alive and doing what she had always been doing. Like the wife of Detective Columbo, she was just never on camera. Hence, Grandma was pioneering with Jehovah's Witnesses in the early evening, buying chocho, yam and dasheen for soup at the market in the morning, getting her hair done for a christening; often she was at church and coming home shortly. I took it upon myself to bring her favourite aunts, Miss Lou and Miss Lize, for her. Just like her accents and the sea moss on the wide Sargasso Sea, we drifted poetically on the Atlantic between the Caribbean and the British Isles. She had regressed to childhood, so it made sense to tell the stories of her childhood in Jamaica. She'd spoken so lovingly and frequently of these industrious women who lived happily man-free in their own homes with their own money and knew nature so well. It was delightful to give their spirits back to her.

What was most comical was her reaction to any black person who happened to be walking by. She just assumed that she knew everybody black. She would greet them heartily:

'*Oh, 'ello!!! GOOD MORNING! Y'all right, love?!*'

Then, after they'd smiled broadly, shocked into friendliness, and had walked past and were out of earshot:

'*Ah forget mi forget her nyame.*'

Or, if they were too sullen to break out of our collective urban training of enforced silence, she would say:

'*Awww, she couldn't hear me . . . She was probably busy.*'

Day to day, for the most part she was just quite unfazed, happy and easily pleased. A polite and good-natured citizen.

I came to miss my mother's admonishments, but I was elated that her queerphobia ceased to exist. I had begun my transition before her eyes. In teenage years, allowing my gender nonconformity the air it needed resulted in homelessness. Coming home as her prodigal daughter was nowhere near as radical as one might have imagined. She would find my knickers in the dryer and put them on my pillow. After all, they were easily identifiable: loud and tacky; a Brazilian-cut cyan lacy number or a fuchsia thong with a tiny yellow bow on the front. She'd watch me make my eyelids tropical and line my waterline with white eyeliner with indifference. If the make-up look was too editorial, she wouldn't hesitate to say:

'*Dat nuh look good.*'

However, a cute black girl nude palette with gentle orangey coral blush and subtle lip gloss, wearing the floral blouses that got me the good tips at my waitressing jobs would elicit:

'*You look very pretty.*'

On those days I felt like I was wearing a priceless antique tiara.

I still assuaged my grief destructively. Daily texts to dealers who made me feel like a very valued customer. Daily visits to the off-licence where I could depend on being called 'darling'. Daily visits to men I never knew and will never know the names of. Fired from job after job because of my addictions, I resigned myself to brokenness, until one day . . . I didn't.

I went to rehab and finally got the healing first wistfully

detailed to me in the black women's literature on my mother's bookshelves. She had gifted me *Rock My Soul: Black People and Self-Esteem* by bell hooks when I moved into my first bedsit in Muswell Hill. I read her copy of *The Color Purple* by Alice Walker in one midsummer night. Also *I Know Why the Caged Bird Sings* by Maya Angelou. She had taught me that we had a canon of our own, and all these books prepared me to recognize and truly see how precious a work was created by Janet Mock in her memoir *Redefining Realness*. This was the book I took with me into rehab that revealed myself to myself. As a result my mummy got to see me get sober and ensure my transition was a gloriously miraculous one.

In recovery I took my mummy to Wales. She would get up to go to the loo at least once an hour it felt like. The stress of it was only manageable because my sister and I alternated the nights we shared her bed. She had always loved Wales. The green rolling hills a more placid version of the Jamaican landscape she grew up in. She adored Welsh male choirs with their softly booming voices. She spoke lovingly of Paul Robeson, and she had read of his time here being embraced by marginalized working-class communities. I am so thankful I got to refresh her with the quiet and the green air of the place, but also to be around such friendly white people who didn't mind greeting us first when we went out to get our bits and bobs from the shops. Here she lost the jitters that London instilled in her. Her London of the sixties, seventies and eighties with Enoch Powell, SUS laws and the National Front had inflicted its wounds. I'm not sure if she had forgotten those memories yet. Her random flinches and wide-eyed anxieties made me wonder. I got to take her to one of the places in Britain she liked best. That was our last holiday.

I continued to visit her regularly in the months that followed. When we went to the supermarket I would try to capture the eye of the cashier and communicate her dementia to them by mouthing the word or by telling our storied situation through my facial expressions. It always worked. I discovered that people were sensitive, vigilant and, for the most part, quite nice. By now, I was so used to the violence meted out to me for being visibly trans in early transition that I was stunned to be looked at with any sort of fondness. With her, I was just a child looking after their mother. Our relationship had been purified. As I purged my pain in therapy and recovery groups, I could return to my mummy in tears. She would ask:

'*What's wrong?*'

I would distil my complicated emotions for her.

'*I fell in love with a man and he hurt me.*'

She would respond:

'*What a silly bastard! You're better off without him.*'

Another day I would say:

'*I'm just upset and lonely.*'

She would say:

'*Aw, babes, I'm sorry. I understand. You're so lovely. You'll be OK.*'

She spoke prophetically and I believed her.

My father took her back to Zimbabwe, his mother country. The weather is nice. She has a live-in carer. I chose not to say goodbye. He didn't tell me the precise date they were leaving and . . . I imagined I would go and see her there one day when I felt brave enough. I thought that maybe I could just wear baggy shorts and baggy T-shirts, not paint my nails and attempt some semblance of gender neutrality because de-transitioning for me, no matter how temporary, is more of a short-story concept than a realistic option. Alas, I am and have always been too buxom, curvaceous and boisterously feminine for someone mistakenly assigned the wrong gender at birth the way I was.

I won't ever get to 'say goodbye' as most people do when loved ones pass on. It's not safe enough to do so.

Nevertheless, in the years I joined in looking after her I got to reintroduce myself as her daughter who shares her hair texture, body shape and looks so much like her own mummy.

In the notes section on my phone I have saved something I wrote that I will never be able to bring myself to delete.

09/04/2013

On hearing the news of Maggie Thatcher's death:

'Oh that's a shame! Cos I knew her and she was a lovely lady!'

Find it so funny that a lifelong Labour voter with Alzheimer's can feel a warmth and familiarity when seeing her image.

Just so uncanny that she's completely forgotten her own mates but now has warm feelings for her political nemesis.

In spite of its Orwellian whiff from a similarity to the final scene of *1984*, it is a funny gem of a moment summing up something I learned from her.

LIFE MAY COMPEL YOU TO HAVE EMPATHY AND COMPASSION FOR SOMEONE YOU MAY HAVE ONCE WRITTEN OFF COMPLETELY.

It's not outlandish to posit that no Jamaican mother born in 1953 ever imagined giving birth to someone who would grow up to be an out and proud black transsexual woman. Yet she did. And she loved me. As I was and as I am, unconditionally . . .

BLACK BALLOONS OVER MY HEAD

BY

Robert Kazandjian

WRITER, TEACHER

I keep it quiet as kept
Yeah, I think I spent most of my life depressed
Only thing on my mind was death
– Earl Sweatshirt, 'Nowhere2go'

I was seven years old when my little brother and I graduated from disturbing our dad's sleep in a cramped double bed, while Mum slept peacefully across the hall, to having our own room and, more importantly, our own bunk beds.

Obviously, big bro privilege meant I had the top bunk. For a moment, I basked in this new-found independence. But coupled with the freedom of my own bed came a sudden loneliness. I was alone with my thoughts and my thoughts revolved around dying.

Death wasn't abstract for me: Dad's family were genocide survivors; my grandad had passed away in Cairo; a brain tumour had cut my auntie's life short; my uncle died when the Airbus he was travelling in crashed into mountains in France; racist murderers poured lighter fluid on a man and set him alight outside our local park.

I was fixated on the inevitability of my own death, the death of my family, friends, the teachers who spent their days telling me off, complete strangers, Gladiators, Power Rangers. I felt an intense pressure in my chest and the urge to burst out of my skin, desperate to take my essence elsewhere.

So I did what boys are supposed to do when faced with something that terrifies them: I shut up about it.

I carried this backpack full of nightmares into adolescence. Waves of fear would overwhelm me, often while I was doing mundane things we take for granted: eating my elite breakfast mix of Coco Pops and Frosties; standing beneath the warm stream of our shower; turning the page of an X-Men comic. Night terrors wrecked my sleep, so I stayed downstairs with the television, hoping I'd pass out on the sofa to the sound of canned laughter.

This preoccupation with death contributed to the depression and anxiety that I suffer from. Of course, when I was a teenager, nobody attached those words to me. Instead, I was angry. I was disruptive. I was lazy and unmotivated. I was on report. I was excluded. I was stoned. I was on the roads. I was antisocial. What was the point in all the learning I was expected to do? What was the point in loving? In living? Everything felt so cruelly meaningless.

The idea of suicide always lurked in the dark walkways of my mind like some goon, waiting to jump me when I had my guard down. I didn't feel attached to my existence on this hurtling space rock. But at the same time my fear of death meant I was too shook to take my own life. The fear was keeping me safe. The Grim Reaper was my guardian angel.

I stumbled into adulthood doing way too many of the things people do to feel good, to numb the fact that I often felt awful. That could mean pushing my body to its absolute limits in the boxing gym, or when I got on it with the boys.

Rather than speaking to my coach, a tough man with a quiet, gentle heart, about my problems, I chose more hooks and uppercuts. Instead of being open with my mates about my feelings, I hoovered up powders and necked pills until the sun came up. I sought out extremes, because, in the midst of the chaos, I felt in control.

Soon black balloons pop
Let it be the day the pain stop
– Denzel Curry, 'Black Balloons'

Then in the space of a few days last summer everything unravelled. My depression and anxiety were pummelling me. Everything hurt. A lump of lead sat in my chest, weighing me down, poisoning me. The weekend descended into a massive bender. I could've reached out to the friends I was with, my best friends. Instead I opened another can and snorted another coke-white slug.

By late Monday morning I was on an island full of flags and narrow minds. It's a place famous for its prison. I felt trapped. I was the little boy on the top bunk again, desperate to burst out of my skin. It was seriously hot. But I felt cold. My fear evaporated. I was ready to die. I didn't want to be there. I didn't want to be. The passive suicidal ideation I'd silently, stoically lived with for years mutated into something monstrous and unavoidable.

So when I opened my eyes on Wednesday morning, still trapped on this island, I put in earphones full of Kendrick Lamar to block out the sounds of the living, creating the illusion I wasn't about to die alone. I hurried to the beach. I was going to walk into the sea and disappear forever.

I lingered at the water's edge. The morning tide, chilled by a night beneath the cold moon, lapped against my feet and numbed my toes. This was the beginning of nothingness, I thought.

And then I felt a hand on my shoulder. I'd been followed. I turned round. In that person's eyes I saw fear and panic and sadness at the idea of a world without me in it. I hesitated. I wavered. I changed my mind.

In the weeks and months that followed I resolved to speak about how I felt with the people closest to me, those who had been there all along. Then I wrote an essay about my experience. Finally, some fifteen years after I clocked I was struggling with my mental health, I sought professional help.

Now I feel I should weave a message into this piece, or it

might read like a Dear Diary of Doom entry. The message is this: we suffer individually, fighting silent battles, wrestling with our own private demons. This pain launched me into a darkness that I've long been running away from. I don't want to be alone in this. In fact, I know I'm not alone in this. And that means you are not alone either. This is me reaching out.

WE CAN FIND OUR WAY BACK **TOGETHER**.

REMEMBER

BY

Jamie Windust

WRITER, EDITOR, PUBLIC SPEAKER, MODEL

Right. Mental health. Truth be told I have been sat here for quite a while thinking of what to say. It's been about three weeks that I've had this tab open on my laptop, just with the title, sitting there, ready to go. I've written from my heart and things I've never told anyone publicly, and deleted them, and then regretted it, and then deleted them again. Not really wanting to dive in, but knowing that I should. Being preoccupied or making myself busy so that I didn't have to delve into my mind-bank and talk about things that I haven't spoken about before. And what played out before me is a parallel of what happens to so many of us when it comes to discussing our mental health. We know that it's something we should be addressing, but doing so is a whole other situation. It's scary, but important. One of the best things about sharing our stories is showing other people who may feel like they're alone that they're not. Although that doesn't necessarily alleviate their problems, it can allow us to find clarity in our mindset: acknowledging how we are feeling is a big first step.

I'm sure we've all heard the common quotes about mental health. Like, if we had a broken leg, we'd go and get it fixed, so why don't we allow ourselves to try to fix our mental health problems? I've always found that analogy reductive. Yes, we should ensure that our mental health is as secure as our physical health, but the major difference between a broken leg and mental health problems is that admitting that you have a broken leg won't cost you your job. It won't cost you your relationship, or your friends. It won't be as hard to discuss; it won't be as hard to gain allyship or empathy. It's not likely that, when you go to a doctor with a broken leg, they will say that they don't quite understand, and that you should just start thinking differently. I'm not saying that these results should stop you from talking about your mental health; I just think that the analogy is a little too black and white.

As a non-binary femme-presenting person, I often feel I don't have autonomy over my mental health. The only thing that I do have autonomy over is ensuring that I try to make it manageable. When it comes to trans and non-binary representation and visibility, we are living through changing times. A heightened visibility may seem on the surface like a good thing, but it can lead to increased vulnerability and lack of safety in public spaces. When my words and body are profiled and shared to thousands of people worldwide, many brands and organizations think that their job is done. They think they've ticked the box, and that all is now well with the world. But what it actually means is that people like me, in privileged spaces where we are profiled by these organizations, are left in a vulnerable situation: we are suddenly shared to thousands of people who may have offensive opinions about our very existence.

But what about the impact on everyday trans people who

are suddenly under society's microscope. The people who just want to live and thrive in their respective fields are suddenly asked to speak for all trans people. And this takes a huge toll on our mental health.

Imagine this for a second, if you're not trans, (cisgender/ cis): you're constantly asked to explain yourself and your gender to people you don't even know. You have to exist in a world that won't allow you to navigate it until you've told them 'who' and 'what' you are. Have to repeat yourself tens of times a day before you can even begin what you actually want to talk about.

Transphobic hate crime in England and Wales has trebled since 2014. Trebled. Of these crimes, 46% involved an act of violence.[1] But what about the transphobic hate crimes that aren't reported due to a lack of support or care from our forces? The shattering statistics on the trans community feel like weights on our chests – though the sad truth is that we already knew that this was our reality. We know that all-too-familiar weight on our chests. Trans women of colour have a life expectancy of thirty-five years, yet we are still not reporting and screaming about the murders of these women across our cities and in the US. The impact on our mental health is hard to even comprehend, let alone take action on, because we know that it's a mammoth hill to climb. We know that a lot of the injustices we face aren't under our control. We know that

1 https://www.theguardian.com/world/2019/jun/14/homophobic-and-transphobic-hate-crimes-surge-in-england-and-wales

applying for that job, or looking for a new home, can come with so many barriers that cis people just don't face, but we don't have the support or allyship from our peers to be able to handle these 'everyday scenarios'.

Taking self-care seriously and ensuring that I try to maintain a good mental health space is something like that final trial they do on *I'm a Celebrity* . . . You think you're making progress, holding your star firmly in your hand, and then suddenly it's wiped out by a huge inflatable ball. I often feel like I have a hold on my mental health, and a grasp on how to navigate my way within a cis-centric world, and then suddenly I'm reminded with a hit of 'tranny' or a gust of 'what the fuck is that' that throws me back into the reality of the outside. I think something that also unites many people, gender aside, is the realization that mental health problems need to be dealt with.

OFTEN WE FALL INTO COPING MECHANISMS THAT BECOME SO COMMONPLACE, WE DON'T EVEN REALIZE THAT THEY ARE IN FACT **RED FLAGS WE ARE WAVING AT OURSELVES**.

They become so ingrained in our routines that we just continue with our day, and don't notice the obvious hurdles that we need to be addressing. For me, alcohol was a space where I could forget. It was a place that wasn't necessarily a dependency situation, but a coping mechanism to forget or to numb the trauma. It was a space that allowed me to forget things, and to blur the instances of prejudice that loomed round every corner. Sex too. Sex addiction, or a compulsion to have sex for reasons that feel beyond my control, or that I know are toxic, was something that I never even knew I was capable of.

It became so ingrained and commonplace that I didn't even realize that these were problems I was forming with intimacy as a result of transphobia, and poor mental health. I thought I was just being a twenty-one-year-old in London. The constant hook-ups, allowing myself to feel fetishized and used as a means to share some form of love and intimacy with someone, became nearly a daily occurrence, and this in turn meant that the cycle of mental health problems that I was facing really gained momentum. The wheel began to spin.

Having mental health problems because of transphobic prejudice, leading to an outpouring of alcohol- and sex-induced activities, then led to even poorer mental health because of the impact these actions had on me: I was in a bizarre and dark place that I wasn't really aware of. If I'm totally honest, I'm still in that space now. There have been times this year when things have just become too much for me to understand or deal with. For example, Pride Month this year was one of the most rewarding yet most difficult times for me. As someone who is still navigating the media world and the work that comes with it, I found myself with opportunities and experiences that I'd never had before, and fell off track with the message that I should've been portraying and sharing.

Activism and influencers are now becoming merged and intertwined and, for me, that felt conflicting. Yes, I enjoy the influencer work as, truth be told, it pays the bills and allows me to continue the work I'm doing elsewhere for the community, such as my award-winning magazine *FRUITCAKE* (love a plug, don't we). But it also felt like I'd fallen into a vacuous world that didn't have a strong resonance for me. Although being in those spaces as a visibly queer, non-binary person was an act of defiance, this visibility isn't going to change the world. It's not the grass-roots fight that so many of us carry on day in, day out. I felt like I'd let myself down, and let my community down, and truly tumbled into a spiral of negativity, comparison and self-doubt. I fell back on to my coping crutches, turning to alcohol and sex, and also turning into a reclusive person. I was shutting out people who wanted to help, and not allowing myself to breathe.

I am one of the world's leading people when it comes to self-detriment, I truly am, and I hate it about myself. I used to disguise it as 'perfectionism', but in actual fact it's a voice that is not positive in any way. It stops me seeing the good in what I'm doing, but magnifies my mistakes and failures so greatly that they overshadow any positive work I do. Even as I sit here, just one year into my post-university life, having worked and achieved things that I would never have imagined possible, I could still give you a long list of the things I've done wrong. The mistakes that I made this year truly left me feeling like I'd just ruined it all. Ruined the message I am so passionate about, and ruined the hopes and expectations of the trans and non-binary people who look up to me as a voice.

BUT I NOW REALIZE THAT WE ARE ALLOWED TO FAIL AND MAKE MISTAKES.
WE ARE, AT THE END OF THE DAY, ONLY HUMAN.

And, more importantly, we are the only people who are living the lives we lead. I am the only person who has lived and worked at the things I have achieved, with my brain and my thoughts. And sometimes I get it wrong. And what I've learned from analysing my mental health and speaking to other trans and non-binary people about it is that we can always, always learn. We can ensure that if we do trip up, we get back on the trans-rights horse (yes, there is one – it's beautiful, don't you know), and continue the work with the same burning ethos we had at the beginning.

But what I have also learned is that we can do other work that makes us happy and allows us to survive and be financially stable, as long as it correlates with our beliefs. For me, a lot of the work I do is solely focused on my identity, my trauma and my lived experience, so it's really rewarding and nourishing to do separate work that's for fun and not emotionally laborious. We are allowed to do things that don't cost us our mental health, all the time, when it comes to activism and fighting for what we believe in.

And to everyone out there who is a fighter, and an activist and a pioneer, know that you're allowed to do that. Know you're allowed to do things for fun sometimes, because the fight inside of you will still burn as bright, especially when you give yourself a break.

Sitting back and analysing what you have done wrong is fine, as long as you don't allow it to consume you, but allow it its time and its place, and then use it to propel you forward in a direction that is even better. A direction that encompasses more people, and allows them to be involved in the fight that you started, because we are all in this together.

One experience that really showed me the progress mental health can make when you reach out for help was at university. During my final year I encountered a lot of stress due to my studies, but also a new stress that I hadn't really expected. I'd started speaking to this wonderfully intricate and wonderfully northern guy on Twitter on 31 December 2017, and you know when you start speaking to someone and there's none of that awful baseline conversation that's like:

Him: Hi
Me: Oh Hi!
Him: How are you?
Me: Oh yeah I'm good thanks, you?
Him: Yeah just chilling, wuu2?

It's just straight into the hilariously embarrassing and borderline cringe deep end of conversation like:

Him: Do you think you could wear flipflops inside a boot and it still feel comfortable?
Me: Oh absolutely, or why don't you just build the

boot around the flipflop and then create some form of boot/flipflop hybrid called a bootflop or a flipboot?

Or just without any warning it would be:

Me: God isn't hummus great

Him: I could literally bathe in hummus and instead of letting the plug out, I would just eat my way out. Enjoy your lunch.

We were virtually inseparable from the get-go. Constant messaging on Twitter turned to phone calls at midnight, turned to voice notes all day, turned to Skype calls, turned to watching films at the exact same time, and then pausing them at the exact same moment so that we could ring each other halfway through and discuss them. (Can I also just say, as a side note, that the only two people I've ever been in what could be described as a borderline relationship with have been in love with Hannibal Lecter . . . I've literally just realized that as I'm writing now . . . interesting.)

But as with all internet relationships and musings that happen over the airwaves, it came to the conversation of meeting. I was obviously keen, and he was also keen. We planned for him to come down over Valentine's Day (I know – intense, right, but also pretty cute). I booked a window seat in a restaurant in town that I'd always thought would be fun to go on a date in because it looked romantic and there was ivy everywhere. He told me that he was excited, and raring to come down. We made plans, and due to the fact that this was one of the few times I'd ever really been interested in someone and had that same level of attention back, my brain didn't really know what to do. It went into overdrive. My final year of university was no longer a top priority, and meeting this elusive man from the north (don't worry, it wasn't as scary as that sounds) became all-consuming. Every waking moment I was concerned with whether or not he still liked me. Whether or not he was still planning on coming down for our Valentine's rendezvous.

A few weeks later, and a week before our planned first physical date, things changed. He started sharing things about himself that were incredibly personal: it was his right to share these parts of his life with me, but they were a lot to listen to. I would describe myself as an emotional sponge – taking on people's emotions and feelings as if they were my own – which led me to feel all kinds of things during those weeks when he was incredibly low. His tone and demeanour changed, and subsequently so did the conversation. No longer were we having off-the-cuff chats about hummus and obscurity; we entered a darker and more sinister avenue of chat. Let's just say, he was not in a good place mentally, and was essentially sharing these parts with me.

On one hand I was grateful and honoured that he could share these things with me, and on the other I was concerned and worried about how this would play out in the long term. Like a lot of people who have friends or partners with mental health issues, many of the problems and discussions we were having were uncharted territory. It was real and honest. And I didn't know what to say.

Whenever I would ask if he was still coming to see me, he would share how that was never part of the plan. That this wasn't something that was going to be real, and that this was just a nice, budding online friendship. As someone who hadn't been in this situation before, and had pinned all of my hopes and dreams on this one guy, I felt devastated. I didn't really know what to do any more.

Our mutual film-watching became frustrated as he would fly off the handle if I wasn't free, or if I'd clicked PLAY at the wrong minute. This is when I sought help. My mental health was failing me, and I knew that I needed to remain focused if I was to finish my final year with the grades I wanted. I spoke to the free therapists at my university about the situation, with the amazing Dawn, and we started a relationship that helped me get out of the bizarre, love-induced hole that I had fallen down.

Speaking to someone about the ways in which I was

navigating this faux relationship felt foolish at first. I think we all get that. When we first speak to someone in a therapy-style scenario, we feel like we are the only ones ever to have these problems. Me more so in this instance as I was aware that Dawn had never encountered someone who was also non-binary. Another layer to the trifle of the mental health pudding. But she really helped me. Through all of our chats and discussions, she got me to a point where she knew I'd be able to handle myself with the dialogue that was happening between me and my northern mystery man.

One night I decided to ring him. It was a few days before he was supposed to be coming down, and after chatting with Dawn I knew that I needed truth and clarity with what was going on here: I couldn't be wasting more of my time trying to figure out what was happening if it took such a toll on my mental health. I went outside with my packet of cigarettes as I knew it was going to be a chain-style situation, lit the cigarette and sat with his number on my phone for the duration of the first B&H Superking Blue. You know when you ring someone and every fibre of your being is telling you to just hang up and run away? You know that what's about to ensue is going to be gross and icky, and you would rather, in the short term, not have to put yourself through that? But in the long term, older Jamie would thank that Jamie for going through the phone call.

He answered, and we had a fairly normal chat for the first few minutes. I was on my 398th cigarette mouthing silently a combination of 'oh my god oh my god oh my god' and 'this is the worst thing that's ever happened' – because, you know, I like to keep things dramatic and hilarious. Finally I spoke what I needed to say:

'Can we just talk about this? Your mental health. My mental health. What's happening here. I've discussed with you at length how I've not dated before and am invested in you and think you're wonderful, but I feel like you're not there at the moment, and that's fine, but I just need to know so I can then move forward. Call me selfish, call me this and that. But I need to preserve my sense of self here, because I really like you, but I can't continue if this isn't something you also have on your radar.'

I vomited that out and quickly moved the phone away from my ear to yell a few more 'OH MY GODS', and awaited his response. We spoke it out. He confirmed what I'd thought, that this wasn't really anything for him, just a distraction from his own mental health problems. He told me he'd never actually had plans to come and see me, and that he was sorry for that, but that's how he felt. Although this was all blisteringly honest, and I felt like my whole body was momentarily shutting down, I then experienced a *Doctor Who* style regeneration (the Christopher Eccleston to David

Tennant kind). I felt relieved. I felt proud that I'd been able to actually vocalize this to someone, and moved on. I was thankful for the therapy from Dawn that had led me to this point, and was thankful also that I was able to navigate a new situation to do with mental health in a way that preserved mine, and allowed him to share and talk about his.

I hung up and obviously had a massive cry, and the following day deleted his number, removed him from my social media, and four days later proudly walked into that adorable restaurant, changed the reservation to a table for one, and enjoyed a celebratory dinner on my own, resilient and stronger (also poorer – Christ, that restaurant was expensive).

I was happy that I was able to treat my mental health in a way that felt proactive, and also realistic. For so long I had thought that prioritizing my mental health above that of others was selfish and narcissistic, but what I learned is that by ensuring that my mental health was in a better state, it wasn't a case of prioritization. It was a case of mutual respect. It allowed me to actually bring my self-respect up to a level that was healthy (not above someone else's).

I still hold that time with Dawn near and dear to me, as it was the first time that I had dealt with a situation in a manner that allowed me to learn more about myself, and how to navigate these situations in the future. I still use her advice, and still adapt the message to fit new and equally complex scenarios in my life. So, if you're out there and are trans and feel like therapy is too cis-centric, I hear you and I feel you. However, the problems that we think are going to occur often never materialize, and the help and support we receive surpasses gender, and works for us as people. As human beings.

*

If we look specifically at the moment, our young trans people are suffering the most. Services for young trans and gender non-conforming people are being halted and postponed due to the scaremongering from right-wing transphobic people of all genders. Predominantly, services like Mermaids, which help young trans and gender non-conforming people and their families in the UK, are under attack from a lobby of TERFS (Trans Exclusionary Radical Feminists). This movement of so-called 'child protection' has meant that funding for these groups has been put at risk, with the most recent being the near pull-out of the Lottery funding for Mermaids after the Lottery were met with a barrage of transphobic 'concern' when their donation was announced.

This new generation of trans people, is entering an environment that is toxic and disruptive. They just want to be able to begin their journey to their truest selves, without all of the rigmarole that comes with that. Hopefully within the next two years in the UK we will have a more streamlined and less mentally invasive Gender Recognition Act that will allow people to self-identify without having to undergo intrusive and unnecessary medical and mental assessments that take years upon years to carry out. We need to be able to show our young pioneers that the world is changing for the better, so that their mental and physical well-being is prioritized as they continue their journey through the world, as gender diverse people. But, for that to happen, we as older trans people (I'm only twenty-two but I feel about fifty lol) need to be able to fully tackle and get to grips with our own mental health, so that we can support people who are more vulnerable than us. Internal allyship is so integral and vital right now. We need to be holding the hands of the trans people of colour in our lives. The trans disabled people, the trans working-class people, the trans migrants and asylum seekers and trans prisoners who are not given the same freedoms that many trans people like myself are afforded. We can't wait for cis people to rally together for us, because that's unfortunately not always realistic. We instead need to ensure that we truly have each other's backs, as the violence that our community is facing is truly a pandemic.

What baffles me about the state of trans mental health, and mine also, is the fact that people are surprised when we explain how we are feeling. They're shocked at the ways in which we are seen, in the words of Munroe Bergdorf, as 'second-class citizens'. When people actually listen to us and hear about the ways in which we are systematically undermined and abused, especially our trans siblings of colour and working-class trans people, they can't quite believe their ears. But what pushes my level of baffled to new heights is that they're asking us how it can change. Asking the oppressed how to stop the oppression. And that's what impacts my mental health the most: the fact that, despite the onslaught of transphobia from all angles, we are so often perceived as being the people who also have to end it. We are seen as the group that has to not only constantly fight, but prevent the need to fight. Transphobia isn't something for trans people to constantly explain, and then subsequently crack open and turn on its head. It's our job to live freely, openly and happily, and for other people to learn how to support us while we do that. It's pretty simple when you think about it. We are having to tell people to think about how to treat us like human beings – that is sadly where we are at in 2019.

I want this to be a lesson to other people, and ultimately to myself, that no matter what trauma and violence we face, we should be able to find spaces to talk about it. Whether that's in a diary, or with a therapist, or just out loud in the middle of a field, know that keeping it in isn't going to fulfil the needs you think it will. I know it's clichéd to say 'We need to talk more', but when you are on the fringes, and part of a marginalized community, having a voice is one of your most political and powerful tools.

Our words have meaning – it's something that trans people often forget. We feel like our words and our experiences fall into nothingness, as we are so often ignored and shunned. We sit here and pour our hearts out, only to be gaslighted or told that we aren't even valid in the first place. But know that there is power in what you say, and power in the words you speak.

I think, ultimately, the worst thing about the prejudice we encounter is that none of it is our fault, yet it's one of the biggest issues we face as a community, day in, day out. The trebling of hate crimes against trans people in the UK is a sure sign that the abuse we suffer is getting worse.

And if you're reading this, and this is all new information to you, then take this opportunity to continue your education and pursue allyship with your heart and your mind. Know that your allyship to us is something that we shouldn't have to ask for or cherish. It should just be commonplace. You shouldn't deserve a medal for it. Acknowledge your privilege and use it to support those who need help.

To everyone, and specifically the members of the LGBTQ+ community who don't know their history, support trans women of colour with every fibre of your being, as they're the reason why we are able to celebrate pride. This collective conscience of allyship, love, empathy and warmth will make a huge difference to the mental health of so many trans people around the world.

And to all my trans siblings out there, wherever you are, however far you've come, know that you are loved. It's going to be dark, and it's going to be terrifying, but it's also going to be so warm and bright. Finding your feet in the community is one of the most precious things. Being surrounded by fellow trans and non-binary people for the first time and being able to unclench your jaw, relax your shoulders and just breathe is something you'll never forget. There are going to be such moments of love. Moments of community and moments of true, unfiltered emotion. Remember that. You are so loved.

"

WHEN YOU ARE
ON THE FRINGES,
AND PART OF
A MARGINALIZED
COMMUNITY,
**HAVING A VOICE IS
ONE OF YOUR MOST
POLITICAL AND
POWERFUL TOOLS**.

"

THE TIME FOR TRAUMA

BY

Lauren Mahon

RADIO PRESENTER,
CO-HOST OF YOU, ME & THE BIG C PODCAST

It's 6.30 a.m. on Tuesday 8 January 2019. And I am sat watching the crystal-clear waters tickle the talcum sand on a remote Thai beach. The rising sun soothes my aching bones and the only sound is that of the breeze whistling in my ears. It's paradise. It's serene. And I'm on the verge of a panic attack.

Not for the first time.

Since my cancer diagnosis in 2016, keeping my mind occupied has been my *numero uno* coping mechanism – whether that be getting myself good and lost in a box set, or the company of my crewdem, or incessantly scrolling my fave social media accounts (hello, @raven__smith), or throwing myself feet first into all things GIRLvsCANCER (I've long said my business was built on the world's most elaborate distraction technique). But, yeah, essentially I cope by being a busy bitch.

Answering emails means I can silence the consistent thoughts that my cancer will come back and kill me.

Back-to-back meetings mean I can ignore the anxiety that this new ache or pain is indeed a tumour.

Scheduling social media content means I might just be able to *shhhhh* the notion that something really bad is right around the corner.

And creating spreadsheets for the latest Tit-Tee shoot means I am able to ignore the crippling grief I feel almost every single day for my body BC (before cancer).

It's not just the cancer that causes my mind to whirr into oblivion. The usual thirty-something stresses feature heavily too. We're talking our old pals imposter syndrome, body image issues and lamenting over a distinct lack of love life. So is it any wonder that, more often than I'd like to admit, I spin into a deep state of overwhelm? Overstimulation of synapses buggers my cognitive function and fucks with my emotional state. Much like a glass full to the brim, add the slightest drop and *boom*, my mental cup runneth over.

Thing is, it's hard to see the wood for the mental health issues when you're in it, isn't it, lads?

It all accumulated for me one morning when I awoke to a brain that felt as though it was crawling. White noise so loud I wanted to scream over it. I couldn't settle. So I did what any millennial worth their weight in avos would do – I attempted to meditate. But in the stillness it wasn't calm I found. Oh no, friends. Instead, the deeper the meditative state, the deeper the nausea and dismay I felt. My body became restless, like I wanted to rip out my own bones, as panic began to rise in my throat and burn my eyes. I sat up gasping for breath between heavy sobs.

You see, in silence there is nowhere to hide from trauma. The stitches in the wound of my cancer experience were still intact and in order to heal I needed to unpick those bad boys.

But, rather than deal with the situation at hand, before you could say 'cognitive behavioural therapy', there I was frantically shoving on my running clobber and legging it towards the canal. Your girl was *literally* attempting to run away from her problems. As fast as her little legs could carry her.

Less than ten minutes passed before my sprint slowed to a stroll. And, like something out of a shitty rom-com, there I stood, in the pissing rain, crying at the side of a canal. I was broken. I was lost. All I wanted to do was rip open my skull, grab my grey matter and rinse it in the murky water by Hackney Marshes. But, as human anatomy does not allow for such things, I opted to take myself home in the hope it would pass.

Spoiler. It didn't.

Back at home I sat in my wet clothes, letting whatever this was wash over me. No stifling the streams of tears. No trying to quiet the thoughts I've spent every waking moment suppressing. Then, as life tends to do in moments of crisis, it threw me a lifeline. I unlocked my phone to call my sister for some words of support, and the screen lit up with my last opened app: Instagram. OBVS.

What greeted me were the following words from author Iain S. Thomas, which had been reposted by a pal. They hit me like a tsunami of simplicity.

It was as if they'd been written just for me. In that moment. To bring me back to myself.

And now I'm leaving them here for you. Just in case you might need them too.

THE NEED TO DO NOTHING

If you do not make time for yourself every single day, literally give yourself time to do nothing, your body will take all the time you owe it, all at once.

And you will sit there, on the side of your bed, and you will cry and say under your breath between sobs,

'What is wrong with me?'

But you are not weak and there is nothing wrong with you.

You have just forgotten to give yourself time.

I still have a hell of a long way to go in the process of my healing, that's for sure. But in those moments, when panic and its pal trauma pop over uninvited, I no longer lock myself in the next room with the TV turned up loud. I simply pull up a chair, pop the kettle on and wait while it boils.

BECAUSE, IN GIVING
MYSELF THE TIME
TO DO NOTHING,
I'VE GIVEN MYSELF
SOMETHING.
**PERMISSION TO
FEEL IT ALL.**

STIFF
UPPER LIP

BY

WRITER, FORMER DOCTOR

It suits us very nicely not to think of doctors as humans. It's nothing malicious; it's not that we don't care. It would just be too much to deal with knowing that we're entrusting our survival to someone who has the occasional 'off day'; an extra worry to add to the already insurmountable pile of concerns facing every hospital inpatient.

But the truth is, of course, that every healthcare professional has a life of their own. Clanking boilers, toddlers who haven't slept in five months, raging psoriasis, credit-card debt, a cat who insists on shitting in the hallway. And, even though the mask rarely slips, the job is often brutal. The endless hours, the missed birthdays and Christmases, and the awful days when things don't go to plan and you lose a patient. We learn in GCSE physics that every action has an equal and opposite reaction, and as a doctor you'll never feel pain *equal* to what a family member suffers but there's always an opposite reaction, and it really does take its toll. Not that you'd ever know, of course – the stiff upper lip is as much a part of a doctor's uniform as the stethoscope.

Changing this baked-in 'get on with it' mentality among medics is difficult, but there's a hardcore kernel of us attempting to do something. For my part, I tried to get it across in my books *This is Going to Hurt* and *Twas the Nightshift Before Christmas*. Just because you wear scrubs you're still allowed to cry. It's OK to not be OK. It's not a sign of weakness to feel overwhelmed or underappreciated.

I'm starting to think our message might be filtering through, and that this ocean liner might be slightly adjusting its route. Twitter may be a pernicious skip fire for the most part, but it does mean I'm easy to contact, and I receive a lot of private messages from doctors. They've told me in their droves that they used to think they were the only ones who weren't coping, the only ones who felt trapped by the pressure. Every time I receive a message like this, it's a vindication and an honour, and it makes every second of the last few years absolutely worth it.

And yet the feedback that has had the most impact on me has come from the seven doctors telling me that I'm 'histrionic', or that I need to 'grow a pair'. These are people so lost, so deep in a distorted mythology about what it means to be a doctor, that they've utterly galvanized my resolve. My DMs are open. Tell me to 'man up' any time you like – as long as there's a culture of denial within the profession I'll never stop. Or tell me that you agree and you're doing something to look after yourself or effect change within your hospital. Or better still, tell me how to fix the clanking sound in my boiler.

" JUST BECAUSE YOU WEAR SCRUBS YOU'RE STILL ALLOWED TO CRY. IT'S OK TO NOT BE OK. **IT'S NOT A SIGN OF WEAKNESS TO FEEL OVERWHELMED OR UNDERAPPRECIATED.** "

HOW CAN
I COMPLAIN?
BY

James Blake

SINGER, SONGWRITER, MUSICIAN,
RECORD PRODUCER

It's especially easy to poke fun at the idea that a white man could be depressed. I have done it myself, as a straight white man who was depressed. In fact, I still carry the shame of having been a straight white man who's depressed and has experienced suicidal thoughts. And still, when discussing it with most people, I will play down or skirt around how desperately sad I have been; instead I emphasize how much happier I am now. I emphasize the work I had to do to get to a better place, and how it was hard work and fruitful work, and how I empowered myself by doing it. I usually focus on how I regained control and an enthusiasm for living ('*Nice one, mate!*'), not on how I lost it. That is the last of my defensiveness.

I remember doing an interview with the *New York Times* where the interviewer asked me why my childhood was painful, and how I got to such a dark place in my late twenties. I told him, 'You know, other kids, bullying, etc.' – and instantly regretted my brevity. He said something like, 'Right, so a pretty standard childhood then.'

Fuck. After all this public talk of depression and anxiety, and many albums of expressed pain, I felt exposed as a fraud, but I was relieved not to have shown my cards and revealed how pathetic and weak I must have been when I was younger. Maybe he was right. He'd probably been through worse and wasn't complaining about it.

I picked up a resentment towards other people from school. My parents were very loving and supportive and, unusually for my generation, still together. I went to school completely unequipped to deal with certain kids who were taking their fractured and in some cases abusive home lives out on me. I know that now. I was 'too sensitive', and I never learned how to act. I was a baby who'd been kept away from germs, and now I was getting ill from anything and everything.

(I should say now that I have many happy memories of childhood, especially of my parents and of certain friends who I could count on, and that my inability to focus on those positives probably didn't help.)

During my school years I spent thousands of hours walking on my own with headphones on or playing piano in the practice rooms, often going there first to cry in private and then occasionally with a mind to play. I was addicted to video games from the age of twelve, rarely going out to socialize. I had a few 'best' friends over the years who, looking back, I didn't know well. But I'm grateful for having had them.

I put girls on pedestals and worshipped them, but only ever remained their friend. I fell in love many times and it was never reciprocated. I had no automatic right to them of course, but they kept me around for years and allowed me to be bullied and humiliated by their friends, accidentally betraying me out of awkwardness. I resented their understandable, youthful inability to know what to do with a sensitive boy who made them laugh and feel good about themselves, but whose body they did not want.

Boys would see my sensitivity as weakness and, while I was sharp and quick-witted, I wasn't sporty, which was my first mistake with them, I think. Again, I didn't know how to act. I wondered for years whether I had some behaviour disorder. I still wonder. In any case, year upon year of capricious bullying and humiliation followed.

These feelings of betrayal, persecution and rejection I kept to myself. In the crude gender stereotypes I was aware of at that age, I thought I had the sensitivity of a female but in a male's body. I joked my way through it and made sure nobody ever saw me cry. I remained a virgin until the age of twenty-two, because I was awkward and unable to be natural around women. I was afraid of the vulnerability of sex after so many embarrassing attempts at it. (The song 'Assume Form' is, in part, about finding the ability to feel safe during intimacy.) It seemed to me that it had taken my success as a DJ for women to pursue me, and then I distrusted them for their sudden, transparent interest, so I pushed them all away. Slowly the face of every woman morphed into the faces of the girls who I felt had betrayed and humiliated me. And the face of every man became a bully who would underestimate me and try to kill my spirit.

Becoming relatively famous, my persecution complex turned

into a self-serving narcissism, and my obsession with proving my worth to people who'd underestimated me was now being rewarded financially. To those ends, my first emotional language – music – had been the vehicle. I wanted to show everyone what they'd missed out on for all those years.

To some extent I succeeded in that, but I became so self-obsessed and isolated that I wasn't the success I seemed to be on paper. And so the chasm grew between my alias – the guy with the 'Pitchfork best new music 8.0+', with the uncompromising and flourishing career, who seemed in control of everything – and the man-child who for many years was hurting, spiralling, never leaving the house, wasting away in an ego prison, refusing to collaborate, allowing himself to be bled financially and taken advantage of by his friends and their extended family, playing video games and smoking weed fourteen hours a day and not taking any care of himself whatsoever until he was in a black depression, experiencing daily panic attacks, hallucinations and an existential crisis. I was asking questions like 'What is the point of me?' and saying I didn't want to live. I became afraid of the growing fog of war outside my house because of what I knew people expected of me if I entered it: a normal interaction and, even more impossible, a new album.

I wanted people to know how I felt, but I didn't have the vocabulary to tell them.

I have gone into a bit of detail here not to make anyone feel sorry for me, but to show how a privileged, relatively rich-and-famous-enough-for-zero-pity white man could become depressed, against all societal expectations and allowances.

IF I CAN BE WRITING THIS, CLEARLY IT ISN'T ONLY OPPRESSION THAT CAUSES DEPRESSION; **FOR ME IT WAS LARGELY REPRESSION**.

I'm still not sure I fully believe I am entitled to be depressed or sad at all, because I'm white and cisgender and male, and life for people like me is undoubtedly the easiest of any group. But my privilege didn't make me want to stick around, and it makes me feel even more embarrassed for having let myself go.

When the delusional mental force field of whiteness finally popped (the 'psychosis' of whiteness, as Kehinde Andrews puts it, which most white people are still experiencing – I was still able to reap the now obvious benefits of being white, straight and male but without the subconscious ability to ignore my responsibility to the marginalized), I started having the uncomfortable but rational thought that my struggle was actually comparatively tiny, and that any person of colour or member of the LGBTQ+ community could feasibly have been through exactly the same thing and then much, much more on top of that. A plate stacked until it was almost unmanageable. For me it became embarrassing to mention my child's portion of trauma and sadness.

Combining that thought with the normalized stigmatization of male musicians' emotional expression in the media, I felt like I must be the 'Sadboy Prince and the Pea'.

But my girlfriend verbally slapped some sense into me, saying it does not help anybody, least of all oneself, to compare pain. And that was good advice to hear from someone who'd been through what she has. I can only imagine how frustrating it was for this Pakistani woman to watch me – with all my advantages in life – self-sabotage and complain like I have. Fuck.

And then you look at the statistics: according to the *Yale Global Health Review*, 'in 2015, the crude suicide rate [in the USA] for white non-Hispanic males aged 40 to 65 was 36.84 per 100,000 people – more than twice the rate in the general American population'.[1] If it wasn't already clear that we have more than enough representation, we're huge in suicide too.

1 'White Male Suicide: The Exception to Privelege' – yaleglobalhealthreview. com/2017/05/14/white-male-suicide-the-exception-to-privelege (14 May, 2017)

Given this, I think it's worth examining why many privileged white men can end up feeling they have no legitimate claim to pain, and then never deal with what they can't lay claim to.

Even while writing this I'm visited by the thought 'Who even cares? There are much bigger problems in the world than white men who feel sad.' (*This is a bloody laughable thing to write your first piece on – get some perspective, arsehole, and put away your tiny violin.*) But you know what? I'll continue because I think we need to advance the conversation around mental health for everyone, and it's the only experience I feel qualified to talk about.

From systemic toxic masculinity ('Boys don't cry', basically) and an ostensibly homophobic fear of sensitivity being beer-bonged into us by our friends, family and the media from as early as we can remember ('Chug, chug, chug!') to the slow realization as we get older that the world is actually stacked towards our success, we end up thinking that our individual psychological decline is shameful.

I believe it is psychologically dangerous for our egos to be built up as much as they are; for the importance of success to be so great; for the world to open its doors more to us than to others (most of us wilfully ignore that those advantages exist, though we feel them deep down, and subconsciously know that it is unfair and that we must capitalize on them). It is dangerous for us to be made to feel we can do anything and be anything, to gain an understanding of women as a resource rather than a lesson in empathy and love – and then find in all our capitalistic and egoistic fervour that we have neglected to take care of that other muscle that enables our survival: the mind.

I for one felt like Donald Trump, starting with $413 million and ending up broke and lying about my tax records. Maybe then it's no surprise that so many disaffected white men identify so deeply with him. (It should be noted that I *absolutely* don't.) That and our shared love of doing anything we want and saying whatever we like without consequence to ourselves.

That shared love has rightly led to a debate about what white males are entitled to say and do. I believe we're entitled to no more than anybody else, which at this point requires a lot of listening and rebalancing. I also believe everybody is entitled to pain, no matter how perceptibly or relatively small that pain is. I don't want the shame around depression and anxiety in privileged people to become worse any more than I want it for the marginalized. Because without addressing that pain we end up with more cisgendered white male egomaniacs who bleed their shit on to everybody (and some of them will write albums about it).

"

IN ALL OUR
CAPITALISTIC AND
EGOTISTIC FERVOUR...
WE HAVE NEGLECTED
TO TAKE CARE OF
THAT OTHER MUSCLE
THAT ENABLES
OUR SURVIVAL:
THE MIND.

"

THINGS WE DON'T SAY

BY

Yusuf Al Majarhi

WRITER, ARTIST

I was told not to talk. Everything is secret in Syria.

'You are not a man if you don't have a secret.'

I was told never to tell anyone that I was ill, that I was bullied, that I was hungry.

I was told not to talk about my mental health. If you have a mental illness in Syria they will call you 'crazy'. It is easier not to say anything.

And then it got too dangerous. And then I left . . .

Aleppo to Turkey to Greece to Macedonia to Serbia to Croatia to Slovakia to Austria to Germany and France.

So many countries, I don't remember them all.

By bus, by boat, we walked, we walked, we crossed borders, we walked, we did not cry.

Three hours in the water off the border of Greece: *Do not cry, do not complain, do not think.*

No one will save you, no one will feel how you feel.

In Slovakia there was an eleven-year-old child with us and two fifteen-year-olds. The eleven-year-old was really cold; we were all cold. I collected crisp packets and I made a fire to keep us warm.

Do not talk about being cold because everyone is cold.

Do not talk about being angry because everyone is angry.

Do not talk about missing home because everyone misses home.

Do not talk about being scared because everyone is scared. Everyone is scared.

Four years of moving and then a moment of kindness: a woman, a kind woman who asked for nothing in return.

I have the right to feel human.

I have the right to feel human like anyone else. I'm a refugee and people look at me like I'm not a human.

People talk about refugees like we're not humans.

We are all the same.

We want to be loved, to eat food, to have an education, to have a home, to have a purpose.

I miss my family, I miss my country, but today I can talk.

We all have a tough life. Mine is not that different from yours. We could have shared that. We could have talked about it.

If we had all talked about it then, it would have been better.

To be human is to talk.

I have the right to feel human.

" TO BE HUMAN
IS TO TALK.
**I HAVE THE RIGHT
TO FEEL HUMAN.** "

IT'S OK TO ASK FOR HELP

HOW CAN I HELP?

BY

Scarlett Curtis

JOURNALIST, ACTIVIST

Helping someone who is going through a mental health crisis is one of the hardest things in the world. It's a little like showing up to a gun fight with a hairbrush as a weapon. When your brain is imploding and the sky has turned dark, it's very hard for anyone to say the right thing. If you've ever found yourself trying to help someone in your life and having no words to soothe them, the first thing I want to say is: you are not alone.

As human beings, when faced with a crisis, our first instincts are usually to try to help, fix or provide context. These are all harmless ways to react but sometimes, when the problem doesn't make sense, the solution doesn't make sense either. Sometimes you just can't help. Sometimes trying to fix someone's brain can make it worse. Sometimes providing context makes the person you're talking to feel even more alone and even more crazy. It's hard to say the right thing. Often there actually just isn't a right thing to say.

You might never be able to say the right thing to help someone through a bad moment, but here are some ideas of things you might not want to say, and things you might want to say instead.

WHAT PEOPLE SAY: Honestly, babe, some people, like, don't even have a house or enough food to eat. Some people have cancer. Some people don't even have legs because they got chopped off by a tractor in a freak farming accident! Some people have *real* things to be depressed about. I seriously think you need to get a bit of perspective. Your life is great!

WHAT I WISH I'D SAID: Do you think I don't know that? Do you think I don't lie awake at night HATING myself for being this unhappy when my life is this great? Do you think I don't feel guilty every single day for feeling this way when I'm so lucky, so privileged, have everything I need and yet still feel like the bottom has fallen out of my world and I'm being sucked through into the Upside Down? By saying this you are confirming my darkest thoughts: that I'm a spoilt idiot who can't seem to appreciate the beautiful things in my life, who only sees the dark side of everything. I know you're trying to help, but pain is not relative. Pain is pain, and as long as a human being is in pain nothing else matters. I need you to tell me that you see how bad my situation is. Even if you don't really understand it. I need you to be there for me. Instead, now I'm just worried about that person who's had their legs chopped off by a tractor. Thanks for that.

WHAT PEOPLE SAY: You just need to come out with me tonight! Let's get drunk. Let's go dancing. It will take your mind off things!

WHAT I WISH I'D SAID: I understand that you care about me and want to help me feel better, but right now going out to a club, drinking alcohol and dancing sounds like my own personal, sweaty version of hell . . . with EDM. It also sounds like a recipe for a panic attack. Sometimes the things that help people without anxiety to feel better are the things that make people with anxiety feel like they are walking naked into a room full of strangers and being forced to do the cha-cha. Right now, what I need is to stay home, watch a film, play a game on my phone, cry and get an early night. I really hope you have fun at 'da club'.

WHAT PEOPLE SAY: It honestly doesn't sound that bad . . .
WHAT I WISH I'D SAID: WELL, YOU KNOW WHAT? IT IS THAT BAD. PLEASE GO AWAY.

WHAT PEOPLE SAY: You're probably not depressed. You're probably just tired and hungry. Have something to eat and go to sleep, and I promise you will feel better.
WHAT I WISH I'D SAID: You're right. I probably am tired and I probably am hungry. Depression makes me not want to look after myself, because I don't feel that I am a person worthy of self-care. Thank you for your suggestion; however, your suggestion also made me feel like you just punched me in the face while wearing a knuckle ring. It was terrifying for me to open up to you and tell you how I feel

and, while I know you're just trying to be kind, now I feel like you think I'm making up my problems and I'm making a big deal out of nothing. I want you to listen and to tell me that my pain is real. I also would like a snack. Please can you make me some toast with Marmite?

WHAT PEOPLE SAY: My cousin had anxiety and she went to see this woman who gave her this magical potion and every single one of her problems went away.

WHAT I WISH I'D SAID: I'm really glad that a magical potion worked to heal your cousin's anxiety, but it's actually rather unhealthy and dangerous to recommend alternative treatments to someone with a serious mental health condition. I'm a huge fan of alternative treatments and I think they can really help some people, but I don't want to get myself fixated on the idea that something is going to SAVE ME, and ignore traditional treatments like therapy or medication. Thank you so much for the tip, though!

WHAT PEOPLE SAY: You're being dramatic and crazy right now . . .

WHAT I WISH I'D SAID: AM I? AM I REALLY? (OK, breathe.) Anyone who has been through a mental health issue will have been told many times that they are dramatic and probably that they are crazy. They may have been told it so many times that they've started to believe it. Just like you probably wouldn't tell someone who's just been stabbed in the arm that they're being dramatic for crying, when I'm having a panic attack or uncontrollably crying please just let me feel my feelings.

WHAT PEOPLE SAY: But what are you actually anxious/sad about?
WHAT I WISH I'D SAID: Nothing. And that's the problem. Nothing has happened and yet I feel like the world is ending. I feel terrified every second of every day. I feel grief like nothing I've ever experienced before and there's nothing in my life to be sad about. Sometimes people feel sad about nothing. Sometimes people feel scared about nothing. That is mental illness. I hope you can understand that.

WHAT PEOPLE SAY: I love you and I can fix all your problems.
WHAT I WISH I'D SAID: Unfortunately, you can't. You are one person and you cannot fix me or save me. You also shouldn't have to. You can support me and be there for me, but this is my battle and no one person is going to be able to pull me out of this. When you're going through a period of bad mental health it's incredibly tempting to believe that a partner or a friend or a parent can save you, but the reality is

that only I can save myself. I need to take some time to do the things that will make me feel better. You are a lovely person, but my brain and my life are not your responsibility. When you tell me you can fix me, you make me believe it's true. You're creating a co-dependent relationship and that's the last thing I need right now. Make me toast, hold my hand, but please don't tell me that you are the answer to my problems. You're not.

THINGS YOU COULD TRY TO SAY INSTEAD:

- I'm so sorry, my love, that sounds awful.
- I can come over. I'll be there in ten.
- You are going through a really hard time. You need to stop being so hard on yourself and look after yourself.
- Cry on my shoulder. (I never liked this top anyway.)
- Yes, your make-up has run down your face and to your neck but you still look beautiful!
- You're allowed to cancel things right now. If you had a broken leg no one would expect you to go to work/a party/a meeting, so you need to think of it like that. You have a broken leg in your mind and you need to let it heal.
- All your feelings are valid.
- This is real. You are not making it up.

- You are in pain and you can't get better on your own. This is just like any other kind of illness. You need help and you will get better.
- We can be quiet for a minute.
- Do you want to watch a TV show?
- Hold my hand and take a deep breath. We can get through this together.
- I know you feel weak but you are so bloody strong. You are fighting a battle that nobody can see and just the fact you are still sitting here today is one of the biggest achievements anyone has ever made.

I AM HERE FOR YOU.
I LOVE YOU.
THIS IS NOT YOUR FAULT.
THIS WAS NEVER
YOUR FAULT.
IT WILL TAKE TIME, BUT
THIS WILL GET EASIER.

A YEAR OF EAT, PRAY, LOVE IN BEDLAM

BY

Nadia Craddock

BODY IMAGE RESEARCHER,
PODCAST CO-HOST & PRODUCER

TRIGGER WARNING: FOOD, EATING DISORDERS

Ten years ago, I spent a year in Bedlam, Europe's oldest psychiatric institution, known today as the Bethlem Royal Hospital in south London. I like to call it my Eat, Pray, Love year. I ate (reluctantly), my mother prayed (voraciously), and without a doubt it was the copious servings of love that got me through. Hardly Elizabeth Gilbert's version of *Eat, Pray, Love*, but it was undeniably a year of growth and discovery. Mine was just more literal. Growth: around fifteen kilograms. Discovery: I had to change.

It's surreal thinking back to that time. My world had become so small and insular, and I only half cared. What's less surreal is how long and difficult the 'journey to recovery' was in the years that followed. I was back on the hospital waiting list within ten months of being discharged, and then again a year later. I did the rounds of being a day patient, outpatient and having private therapy. I tried various twelve-step programmes for a time and, in moments of desperation, some alternative therapies. It all felt a little disheartening. I thought recovery would be straightforward once I had *decided* to get well. It's all in the mind, right? The trouble was that, like all abusive relationships, it was difficult to step away. Anorexia was very alluring, and it was all that I knew.

*

I sometimes think about what I could have done in my Eat, Pray, Love year, confined to about one thousand square feet. What would *you* do? Read? Write? Learn a new skill? Revive an old one? Watch *Game of Thrones* on loop? Work your way through every film on Netflix? I could have read *War and Peace* and the entire works of Shakespeare with time to spare. I could have learned the lyrics to *Les Mis* and been able to quote from every episode of *Friends*. I could been fluent in Spanish. I could have done so many things. I did nothing. It's so easy to forget that I was unwell.

*

That year was consumed by routine. Each day began with a military-style early-morning wake-up call and weigh-in. We were herded, one by one, into the clinic room to be weighed by zealous (but kind) night staff, probably eager to finish up and get home. After confronting one fear (weight gain), the rest of the day revolved around another (eating). There were six visits to the dining room (three forty-five-minute meals, three fifteen-minute snacks), which were accompanied by 'rest periods', where we all sat together full with post-meal anxiety and/or rage.* I then spent most of the rest of the day sleeping

---

* Rage could be directed at staff for doing something egregious (e.g. not weighing out the cereal properly) or, more often than not, at a fellow patient for being annoying. Obviously everyone was unwell, but jeez Louise people could be jarring. I'm amazed I never slapped anyone that year. I'm STUNNED no one slapped me.

or pacing the corridors, like a caged animal.

Sometimes there were visitors. My little sister was in Year Eleven at the time and I remember my parents sending her in, so I could 'help' her prep for her GCSEs. I think she hated coming, but it gave me a sense of purpose and identity outside anorexia and the ward. I was a big sister. I was very good at exams. There was a world out there waiting for me.

Sometimes we had therapeutic groups. These typically descended into a space for us to air our grievances about milk or yoghurt or (more often than not) each other. Reflexology and meditation were popular though; you couldn't talk in those. Sometimes we went for escorted walks in the hospital grounds, which incidentally are beautiful. Sometimes we could do arts and crafts off the ward. I did pottery. I still have some of the bowls I made. Sometimes we watched horror films late at night. Sometimes the emergency alarm would go off and we would be reminded that scary things were happening all around us. We would stop watching horror films for a time. Sometimes patients would escape. It would be funny at first to hear that someone has jumped the fence (freedom!), but then you would end up wondering where they were running to and you would be relieved to see them back at the dinner table.

*

I didn't recover that year, but I did learn a lot about mental health. I witnessed others' emotional turmoil that I have never known and hope to never experience. I saw that, like all mental illnesses, eating disorders do not discriminate by gender, age, sexual orientation, race or class. Some patients had children. Some were children. The youngest patient when I was on the ward was thirteen, the eldest was over sixty. There were always a few men. I was not the only brown person. Some patients were fancy. Some weren't. I remember one patient going on leave to go to Ladies' Day at Ascot. Another patient three rooms down had been living in a hostel prior to being admitted and never went on leave. They were the same age. I don't think either are still alive.

It's hard to pinpoint how things turned around for me. My life today is unrecognizable from ten years ago. I wouldn't have dared to even dream it. Don't get me wrong – I don't have everything figured out. I'm not married. I don't have kids. I am not happy ALL THE TIME. I don't have hundreds of friends. I am not verified on Instagram. I am not excelling at work, earning six figures, or changing the world. I can't hold a three-minute plank. I'm awkward and clumsy and say the wrong thing. I get very anxious. At thirty-three, I still spend too much energy caring about what other people think and wondering if I belong. I wish I was tidier, more confident and funny. I am working on being kinder to myself. I am trying to practise self-compassion. I am coming to realise that we can all have years of stillness, whether it's due to a break-up, grief, illness or just needing to be still. I am coming to know that being still can help us grow. Being still can help us discover. It's OK to be still.

IN THE END, LOVE AND COURAGE SAVED ME, DESPITE THE HEARTACHE AND THE FEAR. **THERE WILL ALWAYS BE HEARTACHE AND FEAR, BUT THERE IS ALWAYS LOVE AND COURAGE.**

I don't know what I weigh today, but I do know I'm still growing and discovering, and that is a true gift.

HOW TO BE AN LGBT ALLY

BY

Mitch Price

STONEWALL YOUTH CAMPAIGNER
OF THE YEAR 2016

As long as homophobia continues to exist in society, young LGBT people will still be a disproportionately large statistic among those facing mental health problems.[1] Young people identifying as lesbian, gay, bi and trans have a significantly higher chance of experiencing bullying at school, of accessing mental health services and even being driven to self-harm or suicide. Things are improving and these numbers are decreasing. However, some young LGBT students are still in dire need of positive voices to affirm and validate their identities, rather than having them mocked, misunderstood or questioned. Unfortunately, this is not just an issue in schools. Thousands of LGBT people of all ages in the United Kingdom remain unable to be open about their identity, while those who are out may face public harassment or even rejection by friends and family.

MORE THAN TWO THIRDS OF LGBT PEOPLE **AVOID HOLDING THEIR PARTNER'S HAND IN PUBLIC**.

[1] The following statistics have been taken from the National LGBT Survey, published July 2018, updated February 2019.

The successes of the past decade have improved the lives of LGBT people. Equal marriage allows couples to marry regardless of gender and sexuality. Protection acts, such as the Equality Act 2010 in the UK, make it illegal for gender identity and sexual orientation to be grounds for discrimination in the workplace. These are great accomplishments, and many LGBT people's lives reflect the equality they now lawfully receive. Nevertheless, there is so much more to be done so that every LGBT person no longer has to face abuse on a daily basis, or – for that matter – on any kind of basis. It should not take LGBT people self-harming for people to finally acknowledge the inherent and persisting problem of homophobia and transphobia in Britain.

A TOTAL OF 24% OF LGBT PEOPLE **HAVE ACCESSED MENTAL HEALTH SERVICES IN THE PAST TWELVE MONTHS**.

It is likely that everyone knows someone close to them who is LGBT (whether you know about it or not). You might be asking, 'How can I help to make things better for them?'

Everyone has the ability to do so much to show their acceptance and support for their LGBT family members, friends, peers and work colleagues. From my experience, consider these following points on how you can become an LGBT ally (trophy not included).

Express your support and acceptance of LGBT people. When LGBT people face abuse, the negative and prejudiced voices often override the murmurs of acceptance and the silent thoughts of support. So verbalize your support to show LGBT people your view.

Don't make lesbian, gay, bisexual and trans people the punchline of your jokes. While mostly said with innocence and without the intent of harming anyone, negative comments like 'that's so gay' (to give one example) can make people equate homosexuality with something bad or something that can't be taken seriously, and encourages prejudice.

Call out abuse, challenge abuse, stand against abuse. If you feel unable to do this, stand with the person facing the abuse so they know you're with them.

Educate yourself to educate others. Most homophobic and transphobic prejudice stems from ignorance. Educate yourself so you can teach others. For instance, people don't often realize that you can be both bisexual and transgender. By talking to people about these topics, you can change minds and stamp out all forms of prejudice.

Don't assume heterosexuality. Don't assume anyone's sexuality or their partner's gender until they tell you. I've had experiences where I've been made to feel uncomfortable when asked, 'Do you have a girlfriend?'

It's OK to feel blue. Encourage your friends and family to speak openly about their mental health so that you can help them help themselves. LGBT people are even more likely to face these problems. Take proactive steps to show your care and appreciation for everyone surrounding you.

The world will be a much happier, safer and improved place for all if these forms of discrimination are stamped out. It's going to take a while to do that . . . but following these steps will help you make your contribution.

IN THE PAST TWELVE MONTHS,
A FIFTH OF LGBT PEOPLE
HAVE EXPERIENCED
A HATE CRIME, AND
90% OF THE MOST
SERIOUS OF THESE
WENT UNREPORTED
**BECAUSE VICTIMS
THOUGHT 'IT HAPPENS
ALL THE TIME'.**

The benefits of full social equality and acceptance are not limited to LGBT people: everyone, regardless of sexuality or gender, will live happier, safer and more reassured lives by knowing that their LGBT friends and family members aren't at higher risk. Change your life slightly to massively change the lives of LGBT people. Come out for LGBT equality by showing your support.

HIS
BEST MAN

BY

COMEDIAN, CAMPAIGNER,
WRITER AND ARTIST

Firstly I'm sorry but I'm starting this story in London. I know it's boring but sadly it has to be London because, much to the disapproval of the GP assessing me for asthma, that's where this bish lives.

By 'this bish' I mean me, and by me I mean a twenty-five-year-old Jack on 27 December at 4.45 p.m. who is walking into the Tottenham Court Road branch of Paperchase after having just been asked to be . . . *drumroll* . . . a Best Man!

A best man. BEST MAN!!!! I've often pondered throughout my life whether I'd ever be given the job of best man. For an eighteen-stone gay comedian who's never quite held down a relationship of his own, this may well be the closest I get to being a bride.

Rochelle (the real bride) has already asked me not to wear anything that upstages her but I'm not sure if that was an ambiguous competitive signal that in fact means 'COME TRY UPSTAGE ME, YOU BIG FAT POOF! THAT'S WHY WE'VE ASKED YOU TO BE BEST MAN!'

On this day, Rochelle is my now future sister-in-law and she is going to marry my thirty-eight-year-old brother Sean. I'm happy for them.

Sean and I haven't always got on that well. The age gap, sibling differences (he's more of a lad's lad) and the fact that I'm about as straight as the sound waves of a Kylie Minogue megamix crafted specifically for a Pride parade on a Balearic island – well, these have meant there's a slight chasm between us.

Sean had actually asked me once before to be his best man for his previous engagement. His ex-fiancée was called 'Anonymous Name To Conceal Identity' and in my mind she had all the charm of a banana skin left out on a windowsill in Spain. I did NOT want her to be my sister-in-law. I did NOT want to be his best man. I did not really care about them.

Rochelle, in contrast, is someone who I very much want to be my sister-in-law. She's forty-one. Fun. Chatty. Filthy sense of humour. She makes me genuinely laugh. My brother moved in with her not long after his previous engagement ended and they fell in love quickly, much to mine and my mum's delight. Now they want to get married as soon as possible.

Anyway, cut back to before I walk into Paperchase . . . It's 27 December at 2.30 p.m. and Sean, Rochelle and I have just had an almightily bowel-destructive trio of pizzas in Franco Manca. My brother hasn't as yet strictly proposed to Rochelle – they just verbally agreed it last night, so over lunch we're planning how he can propose. They decide they want to buy a ring so they can propose at 6 p.m. in front of the giant clock and statue of two lovers kissing that dominate the front entrance of St Pancras International Station. I think it's very #straightpeople and then I remember that is exactly what they are.

Very sweetly, they ask me to meet them later and take the proposal photo and, as the newly asked best man, naturally I help to facilitate this plan.

It's 27 December at 3.45 p.m. and I'm now putting them in an Uber to Hatton Garden. All I know is that this is where lots of jewellers are because of the many, many shit British independent films about diamond heists.

Sean and Rochelle don't have much money to buy the ring but they don't care. This is spontaneity at its best. He is proposing at 6 p.m. whatever happens, even if they have to procure a salt-and-vinegar Hula Hoop like in *The Vicar of Dibley*.

My brother has never been in an Uber before, mainly because they live forty miles out of London and because our dad was a black-cab driver, so Uber is a huge point of contention in our family. Sean feels slightly uneasy about having to get in but, as we're against the clock, I tell him that his moral compass can fly the fuck out of the Prius that Dimitri (4.97 stars) will shortly be arriving in. I also tell him how lucky he is to have such an esteemed driver.

They go off to diamond-shop and I casually stroll down Tottenham Court Road for an hour, popping into what I call 'shit shops' to look at ornamental items in Boxing Day sales that I almost certainly don't need but will buy as 'presents' for other people, and which by April I will claim ownership of.

Then I see the giant two-storey Paperchase. Now if

you know the geo-politics of Tottenham Court Road, you will know that the Paperchase is a dangerous place that catches you off guard if you identify as 'a stationery perv'. I am a stationery perv. I love the stuff. I can't get enough. The key to my heart is a pastel-coloured Moleskine notebook (lined) with accompanying pen. I've got a semi just writing about it.

Now, as I enter Paperchase at 4.45 p.m. on Tottenham Court Road, I have to remember that I am here as part of my new job as Best Man and wedding planner to get them a fuck-off huge engagement card that they can open at St Pancras. And I really want to find a special one.

I stand in front of the congratulatory engagement card selection and with each glance at each row of cards this cloud of sadness washes over me.

Every card says 'Happily ever after' or 'Wishing you many loving years to come 'or 'May you grow old together'. Every card is about longevity and sadly that is something we don't have.

Rochelle was told this morning that her cancer is terminal. That it's incurable and it's spread.

I'd picked them up from the specialist cancer unit at the top of Tottenham Court Road and taken them to the nearest pizza place, because what else do you do?

I put them in the cab to a street of jewellers to find that ring, because what else do you do?

I am buying them a card that I want to be perfect, because what else can I do?

Some bastard swiftly picks up the last 'Feyoncé' engagement card, which has a doodle of Beyoncé on the front and a joke about putting a ring on it. I perhaps wouldn't have got it anyway cos Rochelle would want something classy and, while Beyoncé is a class act, I don't think she's appropriate right now.

I scour through every row to find something suitable. Look in the sale section, trawl the lenticular postcard rack, see if I can maybe even turn a 'Well done on your new job!' card into something funny about how being married to my brother will be like hard labour. But it won't.

All of a sudden I start snapping at a sales assistant who's volunteered to help me. Well, actually, I guess they're paid to help, but I am being truly manic right now so this is definitely volunteered assistance.

'WHY DON'T YOU HAVE ANY BLOODY CARDS THAT AREN'T ABOUT BEING TOGETHER FOREVER! HUH!!!?! **WHY IS IT ALL SO LAME AND DREAMY!**'

The sales assistant blames Christmas on their lack of stock and I roll my eyes.

Now it's 5.45 p.m.; an hour has passed. I am going to be late if I don't leave soon and then I see it.

A perfectly square, large gold card that says 'Congratulations! With All My Love'.

I buy it and write inside on the 73 bus, trying not to be jolted or knocked. I say how much I really love them both. How much I am here for them both and how I can't wait to be their best man.

It's 6 p.m. and Rochelle gives me her crutches and props herself up by the statue. My brother and I stand ten feet away, he gives me his camera and he takes a deep breath. Walks up to her. Sean gets down on one knee and proposes, and the two of them kiss underneath a huge Tracey Emin neon sign that says, 'I want my time with you.'

It says it all.

We go to the St Pancras Renaissance Hotel and drink a fuckload of gin, see where the Spice Girls shot the 'Wannabe' video and we 'cheers' to the bride and groom.

It is 16 March and they're getting married. Sean and I are in matching burgundy suits. I am so proud to be their best man and the ceremony is gorgeous. Rochelle manages to walk down the registry-office aisle completely unassisted and she looks insanely hot. Sexy as fuck. I have sadly not upstaged her at all but I'm not even livid about it.

At the reception I do my (what I'm calling) infamous Best Man speech about how we are here today to celebrate the now. How this wedding is probably the truest celebration of a wedding because it is purely about love and love alone. How, unlike my parents' wedding, it's not about the financial benefits of marriage (less tax) or about money because neither of them have any.

We laugh. We eat. We drink. We dance and it is truly a happy day.

Someone takes a bite out of the wedding cake before it's cut and the mystery is never solved. (It was not me.) A DJ called Clive keeps speaking intermittently between nineties and noughties floor-fillers and all of us kindly mock his accent as he starts singing 'I'm just a luuurrrve machine, faaaading me fan-tasy, gimme a kiss or three – and I'm fine!' It is a beautiful night.

Today it is 4 May. It's the day I am writing this essay/story/ random jumble of words.

I am days past the deadline to hand this in to top gal Scarlett and the big guns at Penguin. And there's nothing else I can write in the world right now but this. Because things are not good. They're very sad. That's all I can say really.

But I'm not writing this out of fear, which is normally what I do when I write about something that hurts me. I'm writing this solely out of love, because right now my brother is being the best man I have ever seen in my life. He is being Superman.

He is being strong and caring and patient. He is remembering doctor's notes and nurse's notes and oncologist's notes and what all the jargon of terminal cancer even means. He is remembering to call family members: the distant ones, the close ones, the friends from the pub.

He is being Superman.

He is texting people back at a rate quicker than any millennial with a sense of digital malaise. He is being Superman. He is being the male role model that this big gay poof has looked for ever since his dad died of cancer ten years ago.

And, for that past decade, I have yearned so much to find one man who I could love as much as my dad and here he is. Right under my nose the whole bloody time. Clouded throughout the past decade in plumes of anger and dinner-time differences and mutual neglect and opposing Brexit votes and the fact he can actually sit through an episode of *Top Gear* without wanting to rip his ears off. Bloody weirdo.

And despite all these many differences: we are now sat on a bench together around the corner from University College Hospital on Tottenham Court Road. Beyond my fear and anxiety for him is a feeling of total pride. Pride I have never felt for another man in my life. And I know soon he will need me as much as I have always wanted to need him.

I guess I'm writing this for those of you who, at some point, may have been or will become the loved one of someone going through the worst pain imaginable. A situation of total utter bullshit where no one can do anything to take that pain away.

It's in this moment I realize that all I can do is support him throughout whatever is to come. That I must ensure he has the space and time to talk and open up and vent the anger and unfairness and pain, and for him to feel the roller coaster of emotions knowing that I'm here for him.

It's in this moment I realize that I am no longer jealous of all my mates who've got close sibling bonds, because right now I don't want anything else in the world but for him to be OK.

IT'S IN THIS MOMENT
I REALIZE WHAT IT MEANS
TO BE HIS BEST MAN.

GOODBYE, NORMAL

BY

WRITER, INFLUENCER, DESIGNER

I think that being told I was normal is one of the most obstructive things that ever happened to me. People tend to give me an odd look when I say that. Maybe it's fitting.

Everyone gets stressed sometimes.
Everyone worries.
It's totally normal.

Everyone feels down.
You need to meditate.
Take some vitamins.
What you're feeling is normal.

Does everyone struggle to sleep at night unless they stay up to the point of utter exhaustion, because just a glimpse of the smoke alarm on the bedroom ceiling can cascade into a story in your head? About the batteries not working or the sensors not working and waking up in the night to a fire or, worse, not waking up at all and what if I wake up but my partner doesn't and I'm not strong enough to drag him outside or the door lock expands in the heat so it won't open and what if the window gets stuck too and what if we didn't live on the ground floor and what if it was too late and the smoke has already suffocated our cat and our neighbour's children upstairs because they're smaller and the smoke got up there too and even if I survive or we survive how will I continue to live with this guilt and after this loss?

(That was an example of the night I tried to sleep without my phone in the bedroom because being on your phone before you sleep is 'bad'. This was worse.)

If it's normal to feel this level of anxiety, and everyone else feels it too, then why can't I cope like they can? If what I'm going through is normal, and people have it so much worse, then why do I feel so depressed? If this is normal, and I'll always feel this way, how am I going to carry on?

I went on a course once and they told us that you could comfort people who were exhibiting self-harming behaviours by saying that what they were feeling was normal, and I thought, *How is that comforting? When they feel so bad?* I said so to the other people on the course and they looked at me like I was reacting very strangely to a nice, reassuring thing. Which could well be true but then maybe that's because . . . I'm not normal?

I know that the instinct to comfort and to normalize is a very compassionate reaction. It comes from a lovely place. To try to make you feel like you're not on your own.

But when it comes to mental health I think that *normal* can be a dangerous word. Normal gets you stuck. If something is normal, you don't do anything about it – if it's not broken, then it doesn't need fixing. While I think it's very important that discussions around mental health issues become normal*ized*, suffering shouldn't be the norm.

It's complicated because then you get on to whether or not these things can be 'fixed' at all. Experiencing mental health issues isn't like having a headache. 'Head hurts? We've got some pills for that.' Done, tick, normality is restored. Fixed. If only, right?

I don't currently believe that I will ever be 'over' depression or anxiety. I do have hope – my life will change, my chemistry will change, stranger things have happened. I don't like to think of being forty years old, fifty, sixty and still having these feelings. Maybe I won't (who knows?), but maybe I will. Honestly, it's something that has caused me a great deal of pain.

Some months ago I was having one of the worst, longest depressive episodes I can remember. There was some light in the middle, to be fair – Christmas was nice – but overall it was a big, long, dark stretch of bad. I did get through fourteen seasons of *Grey's Anatomy* in about five weeks, which feels shameful to admit . . . but it might give you a good sense of the countless, rambling hours, days and weeks I spent on the sofa under a dark cloud, for the sheer lack of will to do anything else, hoping nobody would realize. At least I spent it with Shonda. I thought, *I'm going to be thirty next year* – and, more than the milestone scaring me, the thought of getting to

"

WHILE I THINK IT'S
VERY IMPORTANT THAT
DISCUSSIONS AROUND
MENTAL HEALTH ISSUES
BECOME NORMAL*IZED*,
**SUFFERING SHOULDN'T
BE THE NORM**.

"

thirty and still wallowing in the same mental mess just felt unacceptable. Or, more than that, just really sad?

The fact is, mental health problems can be mundane. For some people things happen quickly, but for others we trudge a marathon, not a sprint; suffer trundling problems, not acute crises. And the way to deal with it isn't quick or easy either. It's not a question of a hot bath and a few cups of tea, and rain on the window. What is it with all this liquid? There's nothing aesthetic or mysterious or desirable about depression. Anxiety doesn't make you a Manic Pixie Dream Girl. It's real and it's hard and it's boring.

I started going to therapy this year, which is something I've always put off, for a variety of reasons. It was a last resort before I went back on medication, because after years on and off I still felt very resentful of needing help at all. Why me? Why am I different? Why should I have to? I think there's a kind of grief that comes with accepting mental illness as a part of who you are, and it can be hard to get there alone. Having people listen and understand you and just get it feels like water in the desert. I told my therapist how I felt and she didn't say it was normal or that everyone feels the same. She knows the names for my feelings. She says things like, 'The aim of worry is laudable – but it doesn't work.' Laudable means praiseworthy, means it's a good idea. Worrying exists to try to prepare us for problems, for danger – for the sabretooth tiger lurking outside the cave, maybe? Anxiety wants to keep us safe. It's not a normal way to feel, but it makes some sense. It never made sense that I was so sad. Sense helps.

Maybe I'm talking too much about my own process. Maybe I haven't had it bad enough. Maybe I'm not being eloquent enough in describing problems or I've used the word 'normal' so many times that it's lost all meaning to you.

I do believe, though, that this is why talking about mental health is so important. Reading about it too. Just trying to understand other people, and to be understood, finding a community who have faced similar challenges – that helps. Finding small nuggets of wisdom and quotes and different thought processes that make sense can be really powerful, and that's why talking is essential – from conversations with friends to books and podcasts to social media accounts that draw cartoons that make you feel attacked and seen and heard all at the same time.

To people who've never felt these feelings, they can be unfathomable. To people who've never seriously considered the fact that not being alive is better than being alive, these feelings seem to be against human nature. Their normal isn't like ours. But we can be happy for them. There are enough of us in the club. What you're facing is not normal – but you're not the only one.

"WHAT YOU'RE FACING IS NOT NORMAL –

BUT YOU'RE NOT THE ONLY ONE.
"

BEATRICE

BY

Kate Weinberg

AUTHOR

'Sorry I'm late,' I said, as the door was opened by a small woman of around seventy with short hair and an astute gaze. 'I got lost.'

The eyes brightened even more. 'I see,' she said in a slightly amused voice. There was a pause as if she wanted my words to hang in the air. 'Well, then. Do come in.'

I walked into a narrow, Victorian-tiled hallway and turned left into a small sitting room, with a desk and chair, low bookshelves, a small glass vase of cut flowers and a potted plant in the corner. Against one wall was a single bed with a ridged purple bedspread. A clean tissue had been unfolded and carefully spread over the covered pillow. I looked at the woman, who'd introduced herself as Beatrice.

'Am I supposed to lie down?'

'If you don't feel comfortable you can sit for now,' she said, taking a seat in a chair behind the head end of the bed. 'But yes. I suggest you lie down. Tell me, why do you think you are here?'

At twenty-six years old I *had* got lost on the way. My mother had died abruptly when I was three and a half (brain tumour; coma; gone two weeks later), and my father had remarried quickly. As a young kid I had managed to navigate what you might call 'a complicated family situation' in the way that young kids – made of plasticine, built to adapt – naturally do. But in my teens I had fallen down a hole. A dark hole of eating disorders and impulsive, escapist behaviour – no fixed abode, long periods abroad – and something else, which I didn't yet know was depression. Apart from a short stint in hospital – three weeks, during which I made two friends and witnessed a girl die of anorexia – I had clambered out of the hole myself, gone to university and muddled through. This was not, I told Beatrice, the reason why I'd decided to start therapy.

'Oh?' The voice came from behind my head. 'So why, then?'

I stared up at the ceiling, off-white, a few scuff marks in the paint which I would get to know very well.

'I'm trying to write a novel. But I'm stuck. I keep rewriting the beginning.' Another pause.

'In that case, let's start at the beginning, shall we?'

For a year I saw her twice a week. And then for the next five years once a week. Each week, pretty much the same ritual. Arriving, breathless and apologetic at her door:

'I'm sorry I'm late, the damn traffic . . .'

'I'm sorry I'm late, got caught on a call . . .'

'Sorry I'm late. I got lost again. I know, I know, two years, you'd think I'd know my way by now . . .'

And at the end of each session she'd get up and walk carefully over to her desk to look through her diary, while I, leaning on the desk next to her, wrote out a cheque:

'*Please* fill in your stub,' she'd say sternly, glancing over, glasses at the end of her nose.

'But there's no point; I haven't filled in any of the others,' I'd protest, flicking through.

'Well, just do it anyway, won't you?' she'd say with an impatient sigh.

What did she do for me, this Jewish South African psychotherapist, with her gravelly, cigarette-laden voice, her frequent flashes of wit, her searing common sense?

She sat at the end of that bed every Thursday, for fifty minutes, through most weeks of the year, through almost every mood. The days when I was uncustomarily quiet, when it felt like there was metal running through my veins and my joints were stiff and puffy and my brain was numb. The sessions when I wasn't really there at all but distracted and impatient, listening to the noises of the children in the sports field across the road, keen to get out in the sunshine and live, live, live and wondering what I was doing in this old lady's home in West Hampstead after all these years: was she a con artist? There was really nothing wrong with me after all – was she in it for the money? And surely shrinks should not be so opinionated, should not let me know their feelings, and anyway – how long could I stare at those shelves with the same rows of books on attachment and loss?

She sat there, out of sight, dispensing a wisdom that seemed to come from life and people more than her books, until the voice stayed with me when I wasn't in that room. Until I began to hear her, began to predict what she would say when I wasn't there, too.

'Just wait,' she'd say, about a person or a situation. 'Don't judge or do anything now. It will emerge.'

Or, one week, when I arrived with bad news and a tearing pain in my chest:

'IT'S UNBEARABLE,' SHE SAID.
'LET IT BE UNBEARABLE.'

'I think that falls into the "Oh, Beulah, peel me a grape" category,' she'd tell me, quoting from a Mae West movie in a southern drawl – her gentle way of telling me that what I had just related was an example of me being spoilt or lazy. Though 'lazy', she went on to say, was almost never a character trait, was almost always a symptom; 'lazy' needed thinking about, too.

'Learn to shut up,' she said once, surprising me. 'When you're feeling like that, don't phone a friend immediately. Sit with it, or pick up a book. Bring it back to me next week. See if you can.'

And another time: 'Even in those three years, she must have given you something very strong, your mother. Otherwise you would have been broken. Something I can feel, deeper than the sadness, a little pilot light that hasn't gone out. Let's turn it up. Let's work out how.'

'Am I bringing you down?' I once asked anxiously, during a session in which I heard my own voice, low and flat, in which I was aware I had brought a different energy into the room, and my mind had not been quick to do the work, to make leaps, and I hadn't made her laugh at all (which I loved, more than anything else, to do).

A pause, and her voice came out a little more husky than usual.

'Whatever you're feeling, whatever day you've had, you always turn up at my door with a great big smile for me.'

And about the time when she'd just about done this – when she'd taught me to live and love better, when she'd seeded inside me the self-care I'd never learned, in the week that my husband-to-be was about to propose – Beatrice died.

'You've very thin,' I'd remarked, a little carelessly, when she'd opened the door after taking the odd week off here and there for 'health issues'. 'Are you OK?'

'Thin,' she agreed. 'It's annoying. But fine.'

Then the sessions had been suspended again.

A few weeks later, sitting in the car, I got a call from someone who introduced herself as Beatrice's daughter.

'She's in hospital,' she said quickly. 'She wanted me to tell you –' and here the voice caught on a sob – 'that she's very fond of you.'

Everything spun.

'But she's going to be OK?' I heard myself say.

'I have to go –' the daughter's voice rose even higher – 'but she wanted you to know. She said it was important that you should know.'

The funeral took place in a cemetery in north London that I knew well. I sat crying in the back row of a small, packed synagogue. *This is your therapist,* I tried to remind myself. As her friends and family took to the podium to talk about her, I looked around the grieving faces, wondering which of them had been her patients; confused and pained by the fact that although I had known all the different nuances of her voice, known when she was worried, or tired or distracted, had known her in this way so deeply – I hadn't known her at all. *This is unbearable,* I heard her say in my head. *Let it be unbearable.*

Now, ten years later, my car still slows as I drive past the street where she lived. I have missed her, with a sharp pain, at all the landmark moments of my life – my wedding, the arrival of my two children – or still, now, in those days when I get stuck, when it feels like the metal is running through my veins again. Often I hear her voice in my head, the same gravelly warmth, like the time she said goodbye to me after my first session and I agreed to come back the following week. 'If you're game, this will be quite a journey,' she warned with a smile. 'But I promise we'll be on it together.'

And sometimes I visit where her ashes were scattered in the cemetery garden. In a flower bed, about thirty feet away from a small copper beech tree where the ashes of my mother – another Jewish South African woman, who, had she lived, would have been almost the same age – were scattered twenty-nine years before.

GRIEF

BY

INFLUENCER, PRESENTER,
FASHION AMBASSADOR

GRIEF IS A PAIN THAT SUCKS YOU IN,
IT'S WHERE THEIR HANDPRINT LIVES WITHIN.

It makes your body ache inside,

That at the beginning you try to hide.

I live in faith he still exists,

that handsome face I truly miss.

I'll always wonder, rain or snow,

how you hid your pain and I wasn't to know.

Through sleepless nights I tried to conceal

that what horrid thing happened was actually real.

Trying to deal with such a loss

showed me kindness and love comes at no cost.

There aren't words to fill that hole,

but when I'm down I feel your soul.

I realized quickly there was no goodbyes

so every so often I throw a kiss to the sky.

I'll never forget, no day or night,

your memory lives on – I love you, Mike.

HELLO, MY LOVES

BY

Miranda Hart

ACTOR, WRITER, COMEDIAN

Hello to you.

Now, here's the thing – I am cross! Not cross in the British way of desperately wanting to turn round to the person kicking your chair in the cinema but instead seething with the odd 'tut' while devouring popcorn at an Olympic competitive-level speed. Nor one of those sudden bursts of crossness, unable to keep it in for a moment longer, such as, 'Oh, Marjorie, DO SHUT UP!' during an otherwise calm coffee morning. (I love witnessing those!) No, instead, it's a crossness of energy, born of compassion and mixed with frustration, for wanting to help people in a way I KNOW they can be changed. Of wanting to help YOU. You, reading this. Hello. I know you. I love you. Hello to you.

You see, I am cross if anyone has ever told you that you are 'ill'. I am cross if anyone has ever told you that you are a statistic. I am cross if anyone has ever told you that you will only be able to *manage* your anxiety and never recover. I am cross if you believe that you are not worthy of a free and adventurous life. I am cross because I care about you. And mainly I am cross because I truly believe that you don't need to suffer in the way you are. There absolutely is hope. Trust me. I know. I know because for years I have researched the universal answers by studying all therapeutic approaches from neuroscientists to spiritual teachers. The keys to holistic well-being. (And there *are* keys: keys to unlocking your pain that are less complex and mysterious than you might currently believe.) I had to research and delve deeply, because I was in a bad way. A bad way in many, many ways. (Pop the kettle on and I'll come over and tell you the story – in fact, that's impractical. I will crack on with the book and video series I am writing.) And when I found the answers, those keys – oh, the freedom that came.

There is so much that I want to say to you. For now, within this marvellous book, I will share the nuggets currently on my mind, the nuggets I wish I could have told my younger self, the nuggets I hope may help you in this very moment of your life . . . But hold on – for I am suddenly struck by the extraordinary irony, perhaps fortune, and certainly poignancy, that I happen to be writing this in a tiny, beamed cottage, which I am staying in, that's directly opposite Virginia Woolf's house in Rodmell, Sussex. As I get still and look at the house in which she was alive, breathing, looking out of the same windows I am looking into; as I get still and see the short walk she would have taken to her writing shed every day she was able, I take a deep breath, for I can sesnse her pain. It's in the air. It's as if there is no disconnection between any of us; we are all part of something much bigger, we all share suffering. I sense the imprisonment of her situation; the agony of her depression; the heaviness of thoughts within her extraordinary mind. I hope she would be proud of this book, proud of us for sharing our experiences and what we are privileged to know now that she never did, proud of the changes we are making for our sisters past and present. Our vulnerability is our greatest strength, and together we are changing culture in a way she could only have dared to imagine. As I wipe away a little tear for all the sorrow that is and has been, I shall to get back to my nuggets. For Virginia, for you, for us all . . . (By the way, good word: NUGGET.)

> Firstly, **Chicken**. *looks to camera, turning briefly in to my sitcom character* I said I was going to talk about nuggets and then said chicken, chicken nuggets, brilliant.

Joking apart, laughter aside . . . (Although laughter should never be an aside, of course – did you know that even putting a fake smile on has a positive effect on the nervous system as the brain doesn't know the difference between a real or fake smile? Look at me nuggeting away. Nuggeting is now very much a verb.)

THE CONDITION WITH WHICH YOU MIGHT HAVE CURRENTLY BEEN LABELLED IS NOT WHO YOU ARE. It will lift, but for now it is your superpower. It's your agency to change. It was mine.

It was for anyone else I know who has gone to the depths and come back out; the depths of the cave where the treasures are to be found. You are a warrior for going in. The avoidance of feelings is the coward's way out, not the other way round and reframing your suffering as your superpower might just help you realize how strong you are, and what you can and will do with the unique treasure that you find on the brave journey through the darkness.

IF YOU ARE ANXIOUS, THEN YOU ARE NOT:

Ill

Weird

Weak

Stuck with it

Mentally unstable or unstable in any way

Overemotional

Unusual

'Being silly'

Alone

A hypochondriac

Making it all up

Strange

A statistic

A lost cause

Shall I tell you what you are? You are HUMAN and ALIVE.

YOU ARE A COMPLEX HUMAN BEING WITH A STORY AND YOU'RE NEVER ALONE. Every single human being is complex and has a story. Everyone goes through trials, tribulations, disturbances, confusion and fear for a myriad different reasons. There is no category of people who do and people who don't. That is very, very important to know (and why I do not like the term mental health or the statistics around it). You are a beloved human being with a unique story. (Forget my book – I think I will come around for that cuppa and we can share stories. Let's have scones and jam too while we are it. And sandwiches. And cake. And crisps. And then go back to the sweet stuff again. Because we all need a feast day.)

LIFE IS RARELY EXEMPT FROM PAIN. ONE OF THE MAIN CAUSES OF PAIN IS TRYING TO LIVE A LIFE WITHOUT IT.

Mull on THAT for a moment. Oh, the years I spent wearing myself down to utter exhaustion trying to avoid pain, thinking it just simply shouldn't be there and believing everyone else was footloose and fancy-free.

THE FIRST KEY IS SURRENDER. Whatever you are suffering from right now, the more you try and push it away, solve it, fix it, berate it, the bigger it will grow. 'What you resist persists,' as neuroscientists say (I forget who the first one to say it was). I know it's instinctive to fight it off but if instead you greet it, befriend it, accept it and listen to it, then paradoxically things start to change and the weight of the problem can sometimes miraculously immediately start to lift. Would you shout this at a friend who was grieving or anxious or sad? 'Just SORT IT OUT, you SHOULDN'T BE FEELING LIKE THIS, you are WEIRD, THIS MUST STOP NOW, just get out and DO SOMETHING WITH YOUR LIFE!' Ummm, no. You would never say that to anyone you love. So why are you saying it to yourself? Listen, surrender, allow yourself to feel how you are feeling. It's the beginning of recovery.

DISCOVER YOUR INNER CRITIC. We all live with an inner critic. But when anxiety tips into a disorder, or stress tips into an illness, that inner critic has very likely taken over. I call mine Sandy the Sergeant Major. As I got still enough to listen to what was in my mind, I could not believe how cruel Sandy was! 'You didn't do enough today.' 'You are not feminine enough.' 'You didn't do that well enough.' 'You overshared socially again; you are, frankly, a dick.' Sandy was crude at times! What you are suffering from might be nothing more than inner-critic-itis that can manifest in some scary diagnoses. And the trick, which takes a bit of work, is to hear those thoughts and say, 'Hello, Sandy (or whatever you wish to name your inner critic), I hear you, I know you are scared, but actually that's inappropriate. We are doing our best, and what you are spewing are thoughts from the past that we don't need to listen to any more.' That's what the science behind being kind to yourself is. As you rewire away from the inner critic, your brain LITERALLY changes.

FIND OUT IF YOU ARE AN INTROVERT. By its true definition. Not whether you are shy or don't like parties. Some introverts are loud at times and love to perform (hello!) and we aren't always shy. But there are so many things about being an introvert that are HUGE light-bulb moments of 'Oh, THAT's why I hate big groups of people and must only socialize in small, quieter ways.' 'Oh, THAT's why I need to be alone so much to regain my energy.' 'Oh, THAT's why I can't read and listen to music and concentrate.' 'Oh, THAT's why I hate open-plan offices.' And on and on it goes. If there was one thing that I wish I'd known twenty-plus years ago – over almost anything, I think – it would be that I was an introvert. I believe living without this knowledge is one of the main causes of anxiety and chronic fatigue syndrome. If you like reading, read *Quiet* by Susan Cain. Or listen to her TED Talk. Consider taking a well-respected personality test like Myers–Briggs (not a quiz in a magazine!) or ask someone who you think might know. Understand if you are an introvert, because, if you are, the world is not set up for your gentle, sensitive nervous system, so you need to manage it. And don't worry – being an introvert is AWESOME. Come and join the gang. We have lots of cups of tea and deep chats and often go to bed at 9 p.m. (not all together). Extroverts are great. And we love and need them. But introverts are often the innovators, so they need protecting and supporting. There would be no theory of relativity or iPhones or most music and paintings and some comedy if it wasn't for introverts going into their quiet lives to stimulate the mind (to paraphrase Einstein).

KNOW THAT THE ULTIMATE SOLUTION TO WHERE YOU ARE NOW IS TAKING UP YOUR BIRTHRIGHT IDENTITY. By which I mean:

IF YOU KNOW THAT YOU ARE **LOVED** AND **ACCEPTED** AND **PERFECT** JUST BY BEING BORN, **THEN ANXIETY SIMPLY CANNOT FLOURISH**.

If you know you are loved, approved, unique and have a purpose on this earth just by being you (you don't need to 'do' anything), then there is no anxiety. You can admit your dreams and desires, with no worry of judgement because you are, yes, always loved and approved. You can confess weakness knowing it will only lead to deepening love, approval and connection. You can respect yourself to meet your core needs. As you respect yourself, you respect others. There are no 'ought's and 'should's and 'must's in your life. Why would there be? You are loved and accepted; you don't need to prove a thing. You can say no freely. You can stop comparing yourself to others. You know you are unique; you celebrate that, so why would you compare to others? You love others instead.

So listen up, you. If you are feeling alone or scared or confused or sad (or all of those things) because of your circumstances, then I am so, so genuinely sorry. And if you can't love and accept yourself yet, then know that I do. We all do. We are all connected – those writing in this book, and all those reading it. Our situations and suffering might look different, but scrape only a tiny bit below the surface, and actually it's all born of the same shared core fears. And you simply are, by being the only you in this world, loved. You have a unique purpose and the world needs you. Don't you go thinking otherwise. I'll only go and get cross!

Miranda xx

" YOU SIMPLY ARE, BY BEING THE ONLY YOU IN THIS WORLD, LOVED. YOU HAVE A UNIQUE PURPOSE AND THE WORLD NEEDS YOU. **DON'T YOU GO THINKING OTHERWISE.** "

I STILL
DON'T KNOW

BY

COMEDIAN, DIRECTOR, WRITER

MUSICIAN

This is a song written by James Righton and me for the film *Benjamin*. *Benjamin* is about a depressed young film-maker seeking love from an audience when what he really needs is to be vulnerable enough to experience intimacy. At the beginning of the film, Benjamin meets a beautiful singer called Noah. Benjamin desperately wants to be with Noah but can't let him in. After patiently waiting for Benjamin to let someone love him, Noah finally sings this song.

I still don't know,
I still don't know who you thought I would be.
Where did you go,
When you were trying to be here with me?

And you know that you're safe on your own
But you're lost.
Why were you lost with me too?

Are you longing to be scared forever?
Are you planning to meet somebody new?
If you're feeling something say how you feel.
You know it's safe to let someone hold you.

I want to know,
I want to know who you thought I would be.
Where did you go,
When you were trying to be here with me?

And you know that you're safe on your own
But you're lost.
Why were you lost with me too?

Are you longing to be scared forever?
Are you planning to meet somebody new?
If you're feeling something say how you feel.
You know it's safe to let someone hold you.

Let somebody make you cry.
Let somebody ache for you.
Let somebody ache for you.

Are you longing to be scared forever?
Are you planning to meet somebody new?
If you're feeling something say how you feel.
You know it's safe to let someone hold you.

"

ARE YOU LONGING TO BE
SCARED FOREVER?

ARE YOU PLANNING
TO MEET SOMEBODY NEW?

IF YOU'RE FEELING
SOMETHING
SAY HOW YOU FEEL.

**YOU KNOW IT'S SAFE
TO LET SOMEONE
HOLD YOU.**

"

HORRIBLE, WONDERFUL

BY

RESEARCHER, WRITER

BREAKING DOWN BINARIES

I'm not really sure how to start this piece of writing, but that's hardly surprising in a culture where we seldom have the spaces or vocabularies to talk about mental health. The global culture of shame and silence around the issue of mental health only serves to compound it, as people are often left unable to speak about their struggles. I am reminded of this when I find myself pulling down my sleeves to cover the scars on my wrists in social or professional settings, when I tell people I have been to the dentist rather than the psychiatrist or when I say 'I'm fine' when I'm really not.

Living with a severe mental health condition forges this kind of dual reality and an incredibly disconcerting severing of the self. My 'professional, temperate and reliable' self works to hide my 'shameful, hysterical, embarrassing' mentally ill self. These harmful understandings are underlined by socially constructed binaries of good and bad, healthy and unhealthy, normal and abnormal, which (particularly under the schema of neoliberal capitalism) force us to sanitize and manage the self, to keep it under control, to jam it into the mould of the status quo.

Deconstructing the way these binaries inform the way I think about myself is something to which I have made a concerted commitment. But this work is far from easy. I have thought about myself in these binaried terms for pretty much my entire life and it continues to plague my thinking (and feeling) today. But I am slowly, slowly starting to realize that, just like everybody else, I am far more complex than these simple and outmoded societal codes allow. I am neither wholly good nor bad, healthy nor unhealthy, normal nor abnormal. I'm not even somewhere in between. I can be all those things and more, all in one afternoon. I don't want to 'manage' or 'control' myself. I don't even really know how much I want to understand myself, if such a thing is even possible. Rather, I'm trying to learn to accept that I will never know or be able to define myself in any holistic way.

Incidentally, this realization has hugely aided my mental health. Finding some solace in the chaos of my disorder and learning to roll with the punches is an ongoing process, but simply embarking on this journey has relieved some of the pressure to 'get better', to be 'normal' and to be my 'best self'.

Diagnosis also plays into this dynamic. Being diagnosed can be both positive and negative. On the one hand, it reifies one's mental health condition as a 'problem' for which one must find a solution. On the other hand, it can provide clarity, understanding and serve as the catalyst for a plan of action. I spent my teenage years desperate for a diagnosis. I wanted to 'understand what was wrong with me' so that I could make it go away. In my early twenties, I rejected this and didn't want to become a 'problem to be solved'. In actual fact, and in my own personal experience, when I was eventually diagnosed with bipolar disorder a couple of years ago it was neither helpful nor unhelpful. I felt the same as I had before – frustrated and confused about my mental state at times, content and comfortable with it at others.

WEATHERING THE STORM

I was formally diagnosed when I was twenty-four, but I have been in the mental health services since I was thirteen and have suffered with various psychological difficulties (including psychosis, paranoia, anxiety, depression and mania) for as long as I can remember. Living with bipolar means navigating extreme highs and extreme lows, plus everything in between.

Throughout my life, I have been unmedicated and overmedicated. I have been hospitalized against my will and I have vehemently avoided help. I have sought help, been ignored and 'slipped the net'. I have self-destructed and self-loved. I have been to the darkest, most frightening parts of my mind and I have been at the sharpest, most exciting and fulfilling parts of my intellect. Sometimes I am grateful for the emotional insight, awareness and knowledge that my mental health struggles have afforded me. Other times, to be completely honest, it makes the life I have ahead of me feel too hard to bear.

One of the things I have found hardest about living with

bipolar and psychosis is feeling unable to trust myself – my feelings, my experiences and my thoughts. Constantly sifting through my reality to try to figure out what's warped or unwarped by chemical imbalance, anxiety, psychosis, paranoia, depression or mania. It's scary, exhausting and destabilizing. It feels like trying to keep sand from slipping through your fingers, or like trying to recall the last place you saw that thing you have misplaced.

I've been to absolute rock bottom – the sticky, debilitating black tar that dwells in the depths of my depression and devours me for months on end. I know it well and I've been there more than once. Another thing that I found difficult to come to terms with after my diagnosis was the realization that this is a familiar place – one that I will no doubt visit again and again throughout my life. But I'll tell you what else I know . . . Every time I slip into that place, I manage, some-amazing-how, to crawl my way back out. Every time, without fail. It doesn't feel brave. It doesn't feel empowering. And it certainly doesn't feel easy. But it makes me proud and it makes me resolute – I will always come out the other side.

In my darkest times, I recall a piece of advice given to my mother, Abigail, handed down to her from her father, Cliff (who – rather incredibly – went to university to study psychology at the age of sixty. What an inspiration!). The advice is this: in your truly darkest times, when all hope is lost and you can't see a way out, sometimes all you can do is curl up in a tiny ball and do your very best to weather the storm. Inevitably, and always, even if after hours, days, weeks, months, or years, the clouds will run out of rain and the storm will begin to settle. You will peek outside your tiny ball and slowly begin to unfurl. It may take some time to undo the damage the storm has left in its wake, but you will get there, step by step. You might even be surprised by how much you have learned and grown in the rain.

THE RAIN ALWAYS RUNS OUT. THE CLOUDS ALWAYS CLEAR. **THE SUN ALWAYS SHINES AGAIN.**

STRATEGIES FOR STRENGTH

It's hard, if not impossible, to envisage yourself ever coming back from that place. But you will – you always do. Try to look for the things that you can hook on to that will help you pull yourself up and out. Maybe it's the sun peeking through your window and warming your skin. Maybe it's a book, a podcast or a song that captures your imagination and helps you escape for a while. Maybe it's the warmth of the water on your skin under a hot shower. Maybe it's the gentle beat of your wonderful heart. Look for the small things that remind you who you are, where you are and your invaluable place in the world.

For me, one of the most powerful hooks was reading, education and my hunger for knowledge. I was never, ever an academic person growing up. In my family, I was always the 'creative one'. When I was eighteen, in the midst of a particularly difficult period of depression, I somehow came across videos about philosophy online. It sparked my interest. It was almost like I could feel my brain powering up after a period of being switched off. At this point I had dropped out of college where I had been studying for a BTEC in fashion. I decided to go back and try to finish college so that I could go on to university. I had the support of my incredible mum and an amazing tutor who had sent me gifts during a stay in a psychiatric unit. Both those incredible women helped me complete my studies. Thank you, Abigail. Thank you, Jan.

I went to study philosophy and psychology at university (I figured I had some insider knowledge on the latter) and my world completely changed. I was petrified – everyone around me had done A-levels in their subjects and I felt like they had a head start. To make up for it, I spent every day in the library reading texts and secondary texts, learning how to decipher philosophical doctrines and how to navigate online databases and the Dewey decimal system. Again, it was like I could feel my synapses rebuilding and forming new pathways in my brain. I felt excited. After feeling completely hopeless and as though my brain was nothing but a malfunctioning swamp full of pain, illness and suffering, I started to feel like it was this amazing, malleable muscle that I could flex, train and fill with knowledge, strength and useful things. Better still, nobody could take that knowledge and capability away from me. I was addicted. I continued my studies, completed two MAs and now I am finishing my PhD. Not bad for a psycho!

I realize I am incredibly privileged to have been able to study as safely and easily as I have. For many, going to school or studying is impossible. I feel incredibly lucky to have been afforded such a privilege. This is part of the reason why I have dedicated my career to democratizing the production of and access to knowledge and systems of education. Plus, it's not a journey that will work for everyone – it's all about finding what helps you survive and the strategies for strength that help you cope.

Don't get me wrong – I have had incredibly difficult periods since that time. I have had to take time out to take care of myself and curl up into my tiny ball. Alongside the support of my amazing wife, Rene, and the support of my wonderful family, knowing that my world of old and new words and ideas was waiting for me when I unfurled has helped me get through those times. It has grounded me, helped me realize my potential and helped me unlearn some of that shame and binaried thinking about my horrible, wonderful mind.

RESISTING THE CULTURE OF STIGMA, SHAME AND SILENCE

I am trying to resist the culture of stigma and shame that work both internally and externally to silence discussions about mental health. I am trying to be more open and honest about my illness by telling my colleagues or new acquaintances about my experiences. I also try to make sure I am someone who people feel comfortable talking to – someone who people can trust. Whether we experience mental health difficulties or not, we can all make these little changes.

- Think about changing the language you use. Do you find yourself using the terms 'crazy' and 'psycho' as pejoratives? Do you say 'What's wrong with you?' instead of 'How do you feel?'

- Think about tackling your own unconscious biases. Do you find yourself thinking or saying that people are 'dramatic,' 'negative' or giving 'too much information' when they share details about their mental health?

- Think about how you can support the people in your life. If you find yourself getting exhausted or annoyed with a friend or family member who is suffering, could you help them find or access the services they may need?

- Think about how you can help others. If you see someone who looks distressed in public and you feel safe and able to approach them, could you check if they need any help?

- Think about yourself. Do you check in with yourself like you would your best friend? Are you patient and understanding with yourself or are you hard on yourself for struggling psychologically?

These small, micro-level shifts make a huge impact and serve to break down some of the barriers that keep people isolated and afraid in their suffering. Not everybody knows how it feels to experience depression or psychosis, but everyone has experienced feelings of fear, loneliness and hurt. We ought to view these things on a spectrum rather than in the binaried terms of normal and abnormal so that we can encourage empathy, understanding and patience and make the world an easier place for those with mental health difficulties to navigate.

Being a psycho is confusing, humbling, terrifying and boundless. It is grounding, astounding, debilitating and dynamic. It is overwhelming, emboldening, frustrating and frightening. It is awesome, awful, enlightening and entrapping.

It is horrible, it is wonderful, and so am I.

**BEING A PSYCHO
IS CONFUSING,
HUMBLING, TERRIFYING
AND BOUNDLESS.**
IT IS GROUNDING,
ASTOUNDING, DEBILITATING
AND DYNAMIC.
IT IS OVERWHELMING,
EMBOLDENING, FRUSTRATING
AND FRIGHTENING.
IT IS AWESOME, AWFUL,
ENLIGHTENING AND
ENTRAPPING.

MENTAL HEALTH IS YOUR FRIEND. LITERALLY.

BY

Grace Beverley

ENTREPRENEUR

Things I do for friends when they're blue:

1. Ask them if they're OK.
2. Listen, whether they say they are OK or they aren't.
3. Assure them their problems are valid.
4. Never think that they're overreacting, annoying, irrelevant.
5. Never think that their problems aren't big enough.
6. Never believe they are a burden.
7. Check up on them.
8. Encourage them to put themselves first and take it easy.

Things I do for myself when I'm blue:

1. Know I'm down.
2. Maybe a face mask.
3. Or a glass of wine.
4. Or both.
5. Tell myself to get on with it.

I don't know about you, but I'm finding that to spot the difference between the above two lists is, um, not hard.

So, my confession:

I NEVER take my mental health seriously.

It doesn't matter how much I truly believe in the importance of mental well-being, or how fervent my belief is in mental health being placed alongside physical health, when it comes to my own mental health I am about as good at TLC as Matilda's Miss Trunchbull. Aka, I suck.

I'm not sure why, how, when, where or in what world my mind decided to take this stance, but I've come to learn that it's not one in which I am unique. I've also come to learn that it doesn't have to be a weakness – as much as I work to change my mindset, it has turned into a pretty useful self-care mechanism. *Taking Your Mental Health Seriously for Dummies*, if you will.

I INVITE YOU
(AND ME, TAKE NOTE, GRACE)
**TO TREAT 'BLUE YOU'
AS A BLUE FRIEND**.
IT'S AS SIMPLE AS IT SOUNDS.

You might think that I don't mean physically texting yourself when you know you're down, or going to visit yourself rather than attending that event you promised to be at, or be the host of other luxuries of understanding you offer to your friends but never to yourself when it comes to mental health – but I do. I really do. Let me explain.

The second I hear of friends' struggles, celebrities' qualms or prior generations' denial of mental health issues, I will always be the first to stand up in sympathy and solidarity. I support and argue and stand fervently on the side of understanding and embracing the severity of mental health. Then, when it comes to my own troubles, I become a closed book. A denier. The very naysayer I reject as having an outdated view of the importance of mental health. When it comes to my OWN mental health, I act as if I might as well be calling in sick because I stubbed my toe.

I don't know when this happened, when ignorance and stubbornness prevailed, but I've never taken my own mental health problems seriously, and I'm sure I'm not alone. Unless there's a physical symptom in the way, I'm 'fine'. Unless my arm is broken or I have the flu or my toe physically falls off, I'm good to go. And yet we all know that the mental health spectrum – from feeling blue to anxiety to depression to PTSD and anything in between – cannot be compared to the experience of physical pain or injury. No matter how big or small, mental health weighs on us like any physical ailment multiplied tenfold and sat inside our brains. But hey, out of sight, out of mind.

I've tried time and time again to outright change my mindset and I've definitely nudged my way closer. I've become much better at not second-guessing myself, taking myself and my mental health seriously, and this nifty trick has truly meant that, if I can't behave and turn my views around on the spot, at least I can force myself to commit to self-care. This particular method began when I'd had an awful week: I was rushing around to events and meetings and catch-ups, all in the name of 'I gave my word!', but not for one second did I wonder when I'd ever give said word to myself. I felt down, I felt anxious, I felt stressed, I felt as blue as the damn sky in summer (albeit not an English summer). I was ready to head out to what felt like my 378th commitment of the week, feeling a deep longing for home, a snuggle with my duvet and some good old TLC. I considered a liiiiiittle lie to get me home: was one of my friends sick? Did I forget to feed the dog? Until I wondered why my absence was more acceptable if it was caused by a friend's well-being crisis or by my dog's stomach pangs rather than the fact that I, the attendee, was feeling not far from mental spontaneous combustion. I did lie in the end. I lied that my friend needed help, but the friend I was referring to was myself. My friend needed me; she needed comforting and time to talk and relax. I guess my mental well-being became my blue friend.

Now, I don't think this resolves the issue of my own ignorance towards my well-being, nor do I want to trigger an epidemic of excusing emails because, well, we ALL forgot to feed our dog, but I do know that it has helped me. My friend was down, she needed me, I knew it was right to go and look after her. I afforded myself the luxury of support that I would provide for any friend. If I couldn't change my mindset, I'd physically change my treatment of the situation.

Every time I know I should be taking a step back and looking after myself, I explain my mental health needs to anyone who needs to know as those of my friend. I feel a slight guilt at not just embracing my troubles and shouting the importance of mental health from the rooftops when I do the right thing and embrace self-care but, for now at least, I put myself first, even before the importance of talking about my mental well-being. My mental health is my friend, and sometimes she needs me.

Next time you feel like forcing yourself to 'get on with it', when inside you know you truly need a break, take the position of your friend. Be your own friend: listen to yourself, look after yourself, make an effort to understand yourself. There's no shame in looking after your friend, and there's no shame in looking after yourself.

"

BE YOUR OWN FRIEND:
LISTEN TO YOURSELF,
LOOK AFTER YOURSELF,
MAKE AN EFFORT TO
UNDERSTAND YOURSELF.
THERE'S NO SHAME IN
LOOKING AFTER YOUR FRIEND,
**AND THERE'S NO SHAME IN
LOOKING AFTER YOURSELF**.

"

COURAGE

BY

Charlie Mackesy

ARTIST

To appear weak was failing, and I was scared and ashamed to do it, but in the end asking for help was the most courageous thing I ever did.

Asking for help wasn't giving up – it was *refusing* to give up.

I think that asking for help is an act of strength and extreme kindness to yourself, and you're probably the strongest you can ever be when you dare to show your weakness.

"

YOU'RE PROBABLY
THE STRONGEST
YOU CAN EVER BE
**WHEN YOU DARE
TO SHOW YOUR
WEAKNESS**.

"

"what is the bravest thing you've ever said?" asked the boy.

"Help," said the horse.

DISTRACTIONS

BY

Mona Chalabi

JOURNALIST

In the winter of 2011 I collapsed a cheap umbrella and ducked into a tower in central London. If it hadn't been raining, I probably would have noticed that Eagle House was the ugliest building in the narrow street – modern and aging terribly.

At the top of a stairwell was a room painted in a dark-cream sticky gloss and filled with about forty people on identical plastic chairs. I avoided eye contact with the man standing beside a big flipboard at the front of the room and walked in as apologetically as I could, head down, shoulders slumped, but I was still greeted with: 'Hi! Grab a seat anywhere you like!'

The man continued, 'So, in 1953, Chad decided to set up a phone line in his parish. And that was it! We've obviously grown a lot since then and now we have thousands of volunteers across the country. Are there any other questions about the history of Samaritans?'

A tanned man raised his hand. He had a white rectangle stuck to his chest that said in large white letters: KEFIR.

'Does the organization still have any religious connections?'

'No, no,' replied the man by the flipboard, waving his hand in front of his face. 'None at all.'

Kefir was the only person with a question.

Next, we introduced ourselves: a name and why we were there. About half the room said that they were psychology students looking for a little more experience before becoming therapists. The other half shrugged and confessed that they wanted to do something 'good' with their time. I wonder what I said (I can't remember), but I wonder even more what the truth was.

That meeting was just an information session. We found out about the time commitment of volunteering (in addition to a weekly shift, we had to do at least one night shift every month) and also the challenges that some of us would face.

'Any emergency phone line will receive calls of a sexual nature. About one in five of our calls comes from someone who wants to masturbate to the sound of a voice. Apparently 999 has similar rates. Some of them you can tell straight away, but some of them might begin to tell you a story while they touch themselves; those ones are harder to figure out sometimes.'

My hand rose and the volunteer nodded in my direction. 'What do you do?' I asked.

'You let the caller know that the behaviour is inappropriate and tell them to call back another time.'

One in five. I thought about those numbers for a long time afterwards.

The information hour was up. We could go home and decide whether we wanted to try to become a Samaritan. I wanted to.

After filling out an application, I was invited to a selection day and, following the selection day, I was invited to provide some references. Once I'd done that, I was invited to begin the training. Completing six modules would mean that I could move on to the phone lines for a probationary period. Completing all nine modules and a Criminal Records Bureau check would mean that I could become a Samaritan. I never made it that far.

Back at Eagle House, on a Saturday from 10 a.m. to 4 p.m., I learned how to let someone know you are listening when all you have is a phone receiver – these were the principles of 'active listening'. You know those '*mhmmm*'s and '*yeah*'s you do so instinctively? They can let someone know that you're paying attention. They can be even more effective when you're also summarizing what someone just said to you. Or asking open-ended questions. The important thing, we were told, was to be attuned to the other person's feelings.

When we huddled in groups I noticed Kefir. He didn't do much talking, but he leaned forward over his crossed legs and nodded a lot. It *looked* like active listening. I imagine that even a caller in distress would find comfort in Kefir's lean. During a biscuit break I asked him where he was from. 'Israel.' I then said, 'Did you know that your name means "unbeliever" in Arabic?' and regretted the question before it was out of my mouth. He wrinkled his nose and said, 'Yeah, I did know that.' Kefir was maybe ten years older than me. We changed the subject.

We also learned about the limits of our role. There were very few circumstances in which we were allowed to call emergency services. Back then, even if someone told us that they had cut their wrists and were bleeding to death, we would offer help but we could not arrange for an ambulance unless we were given an address and the caller's permission. (Years after I did this training, Samaritans changed these rules while still preserving the caller's privacy. As of 2017, if a caller is under thirteen, or a 'vulnerable' teenager or an adult deemed to be at significant risk, then the call can be referred to social workers or emergency services as long as the caller shared their details.)

I thought about whether I would want someone to call an ambulance for me. A few years earlier I had slowly starved myself. The malnourishment meant that for short periods of time I lost my hearing. By 2011 I thought I was doing good and so I should do some good. For what it's worth, I was twenty-four.

Modules Five and Six were an opportunity to practise what

we had learned. On this Saturday we would also have an interview with a Samaritans volunteer, who would determine whether we were competent enough to take phone calls from people who were in emotional distress.

I didn't have to travel too far to Eagle House since I was living in a flat in central London with three strangers – a loud Northerner who worked in fashion, talked incessantly about her latest diet and repeatedly told me she was 'living for the weekend'. A shy and largely absent Scot who would avert his eyes whenever you spoke to him but would bring strangers back to the flat on Friday nights after consuming large amounts of cocaine. And a passive-aggressive Frenchman. I hated eating in the kitchen, I hated watching TV in the living room, and I hated sleeping in my bedroom.

The door to the flat was a black door with a little diamond at the top containing a pane of glass. I had always thought I could see out of it. But one morning, when I opened the door, there was someone sitting on the doorstep. There was something strange about the back that was facing me, the body that hadn't turned round at the sound of my

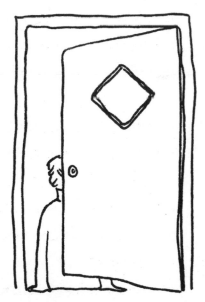

approach. I couldn't step around it either. I summoned up an 'excuse me' and audibly gasped as the body slowly revolved.

The first thing I saw was a black eyepatch, then a toothless mouth, then a scalp that was missing clumps of hair – absences all over. The head looked straight at me. Heart pounding, I closed the door. Then opened it again and darted out. I heard it slam behind me and felt bold and ashamed of myself.

At Eagle House, I was looking forward to the role plays. We split into groups of five or six people, each one allocated an experienced Samaritan. The Samaritan was holding a thin bundle of A4 sheets, stapled at the corner. The paper contained dialogues – cues that came from real phone calls from real people in real distress. The Samaritan could improvise a little, but the point was to see how each of us would respond to these real scenarios.

I watched another trainee take his turn.

'*Brrring brrring, brrring brrring, brrring brrring,*' the volunteer mimicked. (Samaritans always let the phone ring three times. This gives callers a chance to steady their nerves.)

'Samaritans, can I help you?' the trainee replied. (This too is what we had been taught to respond.)

The caller was being bullied by their boss. The next caller was a widow feeling suicidal.

I watched the others critically but also with the kindness of someone who hasn't yet taken their turn.

'*Brrring brrring, brrring brrring, brrring brrring.*'

'Samaritans, can I help you?' I replied.

'Hi.'

There was a long pause. I know that I needed to sit in this for a little while. Not panic; give the caller space to find their words.

After a while I asked, 'What made you pick up the phone today?'

'I don't know,' he said dully.

More silence. I tried to count to five before saying anything else, but when I got to four he interrupted with:

'I don't know . . . I'm just trapped.'

'Trapped?' I felt smug about my clever mirroring.

'Yeah, trapped.'

'Do you know what might be making you feel that way?'

'I just . . . I hate my life. I love my kids but I hate my life. I feel bad saying it because I really love my kids but I'm just so trapped.'

'How old are your kids?' I asked, regretting the question straight away. This was a suicide hotline, not a new colleague. We had learned to keep it about the caller – don't focus on other people's feelings; what matters is the person on the other end of the phone.

But he didn't hesitate. Or at least the Samaritan pretending to be 'Trapped Man No. 1' did not hesitate. Maybe he even had it written down in front of him on those sheets.

'They're thirteen and eleven. I really love them. They're not the problem.'

I could feel my anxiety rising as my impatience set in. The tone of the silence shifted and it sounded like maybe he was getting impatient with me too:

'How's their mum? I mean, can I ask what your relationship is like with their mother?'

'It's horrible; I want to leave. We just don't love each other any more, you know?'

'Mmm,' I say, hoping he'll go on.

He doesn't.

'You want to leave?' I try.

'Yeah, but I can't. I'm a teacher and we can barely get by as it is. See, she doesn't work.'

'Oh. That must put a lot of pressure on you.'

'It does. I worry about money all the time. I can't sleep, I worry about it so much.'

My head wants to suggest that if they separate maybe she'll get a job, but this doesn't seem right. As I'm thinking, the volunteer looks at the sheet and adds, 'Besides, it would never work.'

'What do you mean by that?'

'Well, I'm actually in love with someone else. But it will never work.' The volunteer is looking at me now.

I meet his gaze and respond, 'Why are you sure that it won't work?'

'It just won't. It can't.'

I decide to try a different strategy. 'Can you tell me a little about this other woman?'

Shit, I think. *Maybe it's not a woman.* But the volunteer doesn't seem ruffled at all and replies straight away, 'She's incredible. She's so smart and kind; I've never met anyone like her.'

I'm still thinking, *Phew*, about my gender assumption and have to catch up with the conversation.

'Erm,' I say audibly (big mistake: when you let the caller know you're nervous, you're changing the dynamics of the call). 'How did you meet?'

'At work,' he replies.

Boring, I think, and ask, 'Do you enjoy your work?'

To which the man responds, 'Listen, if you really want to know, she's one of my students but it's not . . . She's my soulmate.'

My eyes are wide even though my eyebrows have swooped down. I look around the circle with my mouth hanging open; somewhere in my brain I'm registering the name tags. Inside, I'm raising my internal voice as I think, *What the fuck? Right, Susan? You look like a mum for Christ's sake; I bet you've got a baby back home.* Mouth still open, my eyes land back at the volunteer, whose expression is neutral, waiting.

'Erm, I don't . . . Erm, how old is she?'

The volunteer pauses and says, 'I know what you're

thinking but it's not like that. She's eleven. She's in love with me too. She wants us to make a life together.'

I don't remember how the role play ended. I don't remember how the formal interview went except that it was in a small room, but I remember the volunteer saying that he had felt judged by me during the call. I don't remember going back to that flat or whether anyone was in when I came home.

Not long after, I received an 'unfortunately' email from the Samaritans. It didn't contain any explanation, and I didn't need one either.

One day back then, before I moved out of the sad flat, I bumped into Kefir on the street.

'Did you finish the training?' he asked me.

'No,' I said. 'I suppose they thought I didn't have what it takes. You got it though, didn't you?'

'No,' he replied, shrugging. 'I was sure you would have gotten it.'

In the winter of 2018 a man went out into the rain to buy me breakfast. We had been on a few dates – four, maybe six. I peeled the lid off a plastic tub he had brought back containing eggs and bread and labneh, and as I was shovelling the food into my mouth I noticed the way that he slowly put his phone down on the kitchen counter.

'What's wrong?' I asked.

He told me that his ex-girlfriend lived in France. X was sick; she was dying, actually. Would soon be dead.

I felt bad for the man and promised him empathy. A few days later he met with X when she visited New York. And a few days after that he told me that, not only was her brain cancer getting worse, X was pregnant with his child.

I am not quite sure why I stuck around. I was beside him when he discovered that X was admitted to hospital. We were eating dinner when he received an email from X's sister to say she wouldn't make it through the night. And I was lying next to him one night when it occurred to me that X might not be telling the truth.

He called the hospital and they had no patient there with her name. X had gone through the man's bins, discovered some condoms and then went through the man's phone and discovered my name. She messaged me asking if I was dating the man. X's sister was never able to speak on the phone and had spelled her own name wrong in the emails. Twice. X told the man that she had performed an abortion on herself by stabbing herself in the stomach. Then X said she was still pregnant. Then X said that, actually, she was not. As X's messages became more erratic, my attention turned from the screen to the man looking at it.

The man who brought me breakfast was adamant that X was telling the truth. Even when X had claimed for the twelfth day running that she only had twenty-four hours left. Even when a Google search result revealed that, despite claiming to be bedridden, X was still working. As a dancer. Even when she sent an ultrasound scan of a foetus with the name of the mother conveniently snipped off. He believed her.

As I watched him scroll through the text messages he had sent X and ignore the pile of work on his desk, I started to think about my training for the Samaritans.

I used to think empathy was a great thing, a human thing. Feeling a fraction of someone else's pain or happiness had always seemed like it was a reassuring counterbalance to all the pettier, nastier traits that lived in me. I want to understand where other people are coming from (it's part of the reason why, the year after I failed my Samaritans training, I went into journalism). But I think that empathy works best if the other person believes that I can understand their experiences. And it seems to me unlikely that I'd be able to do so. Each person sits in the middle of their own Venn diagram that consists of a thousand different hoops of experience. What are the chances that someone's concentric circles are the same as mine?

Caller no. 1 and dancer X made me question whether empathy is always even what is needed. Sometimes an effort to understand someone else's reality might dangerously endorse it. And sometimes it's an impossible exercise that might distract you from your own problems.

In the winter of 2011 I was still grieving the slow and painful death of a loved one; as well as that, I was looking for a job, any job, and I had been dumped (by email). I despised myself.

RECOGNIZING THE LIMITS OF MY OWN EMPATHY MIGHT HAVE MEANT THAT I COULD HAVE SHOWED UP IN A MORE MEANINGFUL WAY FOR THOSE WHO REALLY NEEDED SUPPORT.

I don't think the man sitting on my doorstep needed me to try to imagine his life, let alone attempt to feel it. Maybe, all he needed was a 'Hiya, how are you?' and a genuine willingness to listen to his answer.

THE RIGHT THING TO SAY

BY

Mathew Kollamkulam

SHOUT VOLUNTEER

I distinctly remember the first time a friend told me about his struggle with mental health. It was at a party. I hadn't seen him in a while, so I popped out to the balcony to catch up with him. That's when he told me he was going through depression. Nodding slowly, with a concerned expression on my face (or at least that's what I thought), I managed to mask the fact that my mind had gone into overdrive. *Oh shit! I think I really need to say something now. Please DON'T say anything that sounds stupid. Or insensitive. Or condescending.* 'Umm . . . That's . . . I . . .' I stammered. 'I'm really sorry to hear that. I hope everything becomes OK.'

Since last June I've been a volunteer for Shout, a UK service where people text in when they're in psychological crisis – suicidal, stressed, anxious, particularly low or needing support immediately. I realize now that there was so much more I could have done to support my friend that night on the balcony, but I had absolutely no idea what.

A survey by the NHS back in 2009 estimated that approximately 25% of people in the UK (one in four) will experience a mental health problem each year[1]. The odds have been favourable for me so far – as of today, I lie in the 75%. I've had my ups and downs but haven't yet struggled with my mental health as some have.

Never having gone through something like that myself, I didn't know how living with a mental illness felt, and assumed

[1] McManus, S., Meltzer, H., Brugha, T. S., Bebbington, P. E., & Jenkins, R. (2009). *Adult Psychiatric Morbidity in England, 2007: Results of a household survey.* The NHS Information Centre for health and social care.

I couldn't help someone who was dealing with it. Not true. We have no difficulty empathizing with someone with a physical illness like cancer or even suffering pain from a broken limb.

WE DON'T HAVE TO EXPERIENCE MENTAL ILLNESS IN ORDER TO **SUPPORT SOMEONE WHO IS SEEKING HELP**.

I sense that there may be many more people who feel like I did on the balcony – nervous, quite clueless and fumbling for the 'right' thing to say. To them I'd like to say, first, being worried about saying the right thing shows that you care. Second, as a heads-up for a future moment when someone bravely tells you something about their struggle with mental health, I asked my 'massive' Instagram following of 526 and a few of my colleagues at Shout what they wished others knew about their mental health when they were at their lowest point:

'I wish they'd known that it was real and happening – I wasn't trying to be dramatic or attention-seeking.' Jason

'I want people to realize that, at least for me, mental health is a "work-in-progress" – there's no end goal and no "one-size-fits-all".' Trevor

'That it doesn't look or feel the same for everybody and it can happen to anybody.'

'I want people to know that having a mental illness doesn't mean I'm any less intelligent.' Lee

'It's not as simple as taking a pill and it's cured.' Alice

'I wish they'd noticed everything was not "OK", even though that's what I kept telling them.'

'I want people to know that it's not because I'm shy or don't feel like doing something; it's because I can't.' Susanna

'I wish they knew that "It's going to be all right" isn't helpful and is frustrating.' Natalia

'I had good days and bad days – and that doesn't mean it's any less real.'

'I wish I'd told her how much her support helped me get through it and that an "OK" meant a "Thank you" from the bottom of my heart.'

'Just because everything looks fine on the outside doesn't mean everything is fine on the inside.'
Adam

VOLUNTEERING WITH SHOUT, I REALIZE THAT WHEN SOMEONE DECIDES TO OPEN UP AND TELL ME WHAT THEY'RE GOING THROUGH, **THEY'RE SHOWING ENORMOUS COURAGE**.

They are deciding to risk being judged as weak, unintelligent, needy, fake (and every other misconception mentioned above) in order to ask for help, or maybe just for someone to listen. That is a sign of strength, not weakness.

It's a humbling experience to be the person someone decides to confide in. Today, when volunteering for Shout, I listen. I listen intently and then try to acknowledge how they feel, understanding that, regardless of how I think I would feel in their situation, their struggle is real. Solving their problem for them is not the important bit. Even though we have a veritable treasure chest of resources for our volunteer texters, loads of the most helpful conversations we have on the platform don't reach the problem-solving stage. Sometimes the best help I can offer is just to listen and acknowledge the feelings they are experiencing.

My experience on Shout has taught me that people are remarkably strong and resilient. Texters I've chatted to have endured the most devastating situations, and get through each day with a fight in them that pushes them to keep going. It gives me hope. Hope that, no matter how difficult things may get in my own life, with some support I too can make it. Volunteering for Shout makes my day. If you're in the UK and feel that you need some support to get through the day, text us. If you think you'd like to support the amazing work Shout does, volunteer with us. Either way, it's a life-changing experience.

THE DAD, THE NURSE, THE FRIEND, THE SON, THE WASHING MACHINE

BY

MENTAL HEALTH NURSE, SHOUT VOLUNTEER

The Then

I remember asking my mum if I would EVER feel anything other than sad again . . .

My bed became my best friend.

Wearing a 'Daddy's OK' mask was exhausting, constantly pretending I could be arsed when it was the furthest thing from the truth.

Being a mental health nurse made me feel worse . . . How am I allowed to feel like I do when I know the signs, the symptoms and the positive ways to manage it?

Knowing that I had a responsible job made no difference whatsoever to how I felt, and work just went out of the window.

I was embarrassed to see my GP (although he was fantastic), and again this was because of my job and professional training – the shame was overwhelming.

SEEING MY BEST FRIEND BECAME NOTHING BUT 'BEIGE', WHEN IT USED TO BE **A RAINBOW-FILLED, UNICORN-DANCING EXTRAVAGANZA**.

My brain felt like an overstuffed washing machine going round and round; all I wanted was for someone to stop the machine, take some laundry out and give my head a bit more room to process (or wash) what was going on.

Even now, I'm embarrassed to say I used to wish (a lot) that something would happen on the motorway so I could be involved in a crash which would remove all this 'thought-laundry' and just give me a break. (I'm glad it never did.)

I felt so alone, it was tangible.

The Now

Time has been a MASSIVE help (to underestimate this is foolish).

Medication worked for me, and so did seeking professional counselling (despite the shame I felt accessing these things).

I couldn't have got this far without my mum, my best friend and my children – they were tolerant, supportive; listeners, carers, comedians, confidants, fun-enhancers and sometimes pains in the arse too.

The washing machine is now well maintained and happily running on a normal load (mostly). Sometimes it's necessary to pause and take some laundry out but, on the whole, all is manageable.

WAR

BY

Khalil Aldabbas

WRITER, ENGINEER, ARTIST

WAR, death and escaping . . . The beginning of the war will remain secret while the beginning of my problems with my mental health won't. It all started when I was in Damascus, Syria, aged thirteen years old, with the breaking news on the large TV screen in my home. It told us, 'People have been asking for freedom!' The government was shooting at the sky to separate the crowds, and two men were killed. Were these just stray bullets? This planted the fear inside me and with the first shock of my life, my first grey hair appeared. Shock by shock, more grey streaks grew in my chestnut hair.

Weeks after the first shock, at home with my tutor, I heard the sound of strong thunder on the sunniest morning ever. My tutor stood up with wild eyes, saying it was an explosion. She was right – it was an explosion in the centre of Damascus. Not long after this, I actually experienced an explosion while in a class to support my studies at school. My class was taking place in the basement of the building – I remember it had small windows – when suddenly everyone was flipped from their chairs, flying from the bomb explosion. Dust came through the small windows but the sun was still shining. I called my mum; she knew I had been in the attack and was crying, but I told her I was fine. I told her being underground had saved my life and everyone above was killed or injured. I had been lucky.

I have experienced a lot of traumatic situations (I can't

write them all here) and here I am in England, surviving. Death has kept its distance, with timing playing its role, and seconds have made a difference in my survival. Here I am, safe – but even once I'd come to England my mental health was not, after all the tough situations I had been through. I didn't want to talk to anyone about my feelings. During three years at college doing my BTEC Level 3 in Applied Science, I kept all my thoughts and feelings inside. My chemistry teacher began to notice there was something wrong and she asked if I needed help. She told me it was important to see a therapist. My answer was 'No, thank you', as back in our country seeing a doctor for your mental health meant that you were called 'crazy', and I didn't want that.

I had flashback after flashback – it was PTSD. I was weak, frozen, I couldn't eat, until I was forced to see a doctor. I thought *I am the only one*; I thought *I am crazy*, as I was not who I was before, overthinking and creating things in my head that were not actually true. My doctor told me, 'You are not the only one. You will get better.' She said she'd had PTSD from a gunshot sound, and I started to get treatment.

It is really important to see a doctor and share your feelings with the right people, as keeping everything inside is a WAR.

" MY DOCTOR
TOLD ME,
'**YOU ARE NOT
THE ONLY ONE**.
**YOU WILL
GET BETTER**.'
"

IT WILL
BE OK

FEMINISM AS A FORM OF SELF-HELP

BY

Scarlett Curtis

JOURNALIST, ACTIVIST

According to a lot of scholars who are far more intelligent than me, my great, great grandpa kind of invented the idea of 'the self'. Sigmund Freud argued that he had discovered primitive, sexual and aggressive forces hidden deep inside the minds of all human beings. He believed that inside us all were dangerous instinctual drives and that we were fundamentally instinct-driven individuals who were all at the mercy of our inner fears and desires, and he devised a method he called 'psychoanalysis' as a way to control these desires.

I'm not a Sigmund Freud scholar – in fact, I've spent a large portion of my life trying to make up for the sins of a man who believed that clitoral orgasms were 'immature' and female masturbation was a symptom of hysteria – but I've recently become quite obsessed with thinking about the ways in which this one man revolutionized how we think about the self.

Freud's theories have been written about more often than just one man's ramblings ever should have been, but it's hard to deny that his theory of the all consuming self dominates our world today. The concept of the self led to the rise of advertising, the nature of politics as we see it in the Western world today, the concept of hyper-individualism, and it fuelled many of the ideas that are still used to this day by therapists, psychologists and self-help books.

This book is many things, but one thing it is not is a self-help book. I've read a lot of self-help books in my life (a kind of worrying, mildly obsessive amount of self-help books) and, while they still line my bookshelves with covers promising a 'NEW YOU', the old me sits here today, bruised, battered, keeping the books around only so they can fill in the gaps in my colour-coordinated book collection.

During my years of self-help mania I would write myself a to-do list every night: a collection of self-chastizing wishes and commands. There were two hundred things that I felt I 'should' be doing and only two things I felt I actually had the ability to do: cry and sleep. The list would always begin with 'wake up, get out of bed, brush teeth, breathe, put on clothes, deodorant'; it would continue to encompass a collection of activities that my self-help books had promised would help me feel better: meditate, yoga, mood board, visualize your future. Each day I failed and each day I would try again; I made all the mood boards, I formulated all the mantras, one night I even burned everything in my house that reminded me of my past. None of it helped. None of it made me feel any better. My mum is still angry about the fire.

After a long time spent wondering why no amount of meditation or self-actualization could pull me out of the void, I realized that the problem was that I didn't want to get better for myself. My self-worth was so abysmally low that the idea of getting happier or better for Scarlett Kate Freud Curtis's sake just didn't seem appealing any more. I wasn't interested in the self, I wasn't interested in getting better for me, I wasn't really all that interested in being alive any more.

I was a broken girl sitting in a bookshop searching for some way out of the darkness. After years of therapy and yoga and massage and crystals and acupuncture and self-help book after self-help book, on a rainy, cold day in the dusty back room of a London bookshop I finally discovered this one self-help book that changed my entire life. It was called *Women, Race & Class* by Angela Davis and I'm pretty sure it wasn't actually a self-help book.

Within the pages I found something to try for. Unwilling to fight for my own life I had found something else to fight for. For the first time in my life I had found something bigger and louder than the voices in my head. This beguiling force was called feminism and, like the most alluring of lovers, it made me want to recover, so that I could be a part of its world.

I threw away my to-do lists and vowed to get stronger for the sole purpose of joining this movement, this beautiful movement that didn't really have anything to do with me, that didn't really care all that much about middle-class white girls, but that was all about joining together with other people on this planet to make our world a better place for everyone, regardless of gender. I had something to fight for. It wasn't my life or my brain or my sense of self; it was a collective self that I could join and for the first time in seven very lonely years I felt like I was a part of something.

Like a small, straggly cat on a mission to catch an eagle, I began to override my fears in the pursuit of my mission. I moved to New York and, after seven years of breaking out in a cold sweat every time I had a conversation with someone who wasn't in my family, I joined an activist collective in a living room in Harlem. I made friends, beautiful friends, friends who showed me that this movement looks different for everyone and sometimes the only way to fight is to listen and learn. I took a seven-hour bus ride from New York to D.C. for the Women's March and felt my body pressed up against the thousands of other bodies of women demanding change. I read and I read and I studied and I learned and I revised everything I had ever known about the true meaning of privilege and equality and liberation.

Depression tells you that you are alone and that you will always be alone. It convinces you that your mind is a prison and makes you believe that to bring anyone into your life is to lock them inside with you so it's probably just easier to push everyone away.

Feminism made me feel like I was a part of something, a small part of something huge and historical. Feminism gave me friends and enemies and a better understanding of my place in this world than I ever even dreamed of having.

Feminism is my self-help. And it has nothing to do with the self. I don't actually believe that human beings are as selfish as we like to make out. We do a lot of selfish things, but we also do a lot of fucking amazing, seriously unselfish things. We join movements that are advocating for the rights of others, we sign petitions, we stand on picket lines, and we meet in the living rooms and basements of each other's houses and come up with plans to change laws and save the world.

Sigmund Freud may have believed that we are all governed by selfish ideals and selfish desires, but I also think he never quite understood what Audre Lorde so perfectly articulated almost a century after he died:

NO WOMAN IS FREE WHILE ANY WOMAN IS UNFREE EVEN WHEN HER SHACKLES ARE DIFFERENT FROM OUR OWN.

I don't believe that the only thing that drives humans is our desires or a wish to possess an actualized, individualistic self. When I read the essays and pieces within this book I see a group of people who are motivated by a collective identity and a collective understanding that to be a human is to be a single dot in a web of people who all possess a right to the fundamental freedoms of humanity.

In 1659, philosopher John Locke wrote that 'the necessity of pursuing happiness [is] the foundation of liberty'. I do not believe human beings have the right to be happy. Happiness is a fleeting state of being, a transient moment to celebrate but not expect. We do not have the right to happiness, but we do have the right to purpose. We have the right to community. We have the right to not feel like life isn't worth living any more. We have the right to be OK.

Feminism gave me something to get better for. It's as simple as that. It didn't cure my PTSD or calm my anxious thoughts, but it lit a match at the door of the tunnel I had been stuck in for seven years and showed me how to find my way out.

"FEMINISM . . . LIT A MATCH AT THE DOOR OF THE TUNNEL I HAD BEEN STUCK IN FOR SEVEN YEARS AND **SHOWED ME HOW TO FIND MY WAY OUT**."

TOOLS TO HELP YOU CO-HABIT WITH YOUR SUFFERING

BY

Davina McCall

PRESENTER

Low self-esteem. That was my thing. That's what I used drugs for, that's what drove my desire for fame, that's what plagued me in my youth.

I still have moments now. Flashes. But, for the most part, I can say that I like myself. Warts and all.

The other day there was an international happiness day. I am certain that, like all the other 'days' created to indulge us, the International Day of Happiness came from a good place. A place of kindness and well meaning. So why is it that when I read about it I felt really pissed off? Annoyed and belligerent, defiant even. *Right,* I thought. *I'm going to be sullen all day . . .*

I spend an inordinate amount of time self-analysing – so why did I feel so strongly about this day?

I believe that Life is suffering. It's hard. People are dealing with terrible hardships every day. Addiction, abandonment, bereavement, infertility, divorce, poverty, phobias, abuse.

However, we are living in the most privileged time in history. So many of us have our health and longevity. We as a society have low infant mortality, vaccines, convenience – everything! Coffee shops, restaurants, gyms, better working conditions, holidays abroad. In fact, holidays at all; one hundred years ago, that would have seemed ludicrous. And yet our suffering doesn't go away.

But sprinkled throughout our lives are moments of utter, unbridled joy. The birth of a child, love, food with friends,

puppies and kittens; that moment when the lights go on in the
club at the end of the night and the DJ drops a total BANGER.

We have to find a way of living with the suffering.
Co-habiting with it, while we wait for our moments of joy.

So this idea of choosing a day when we are all ordered to
be happy is ridiculous. What we need is a Tools to Help You
Co-habit With Your Suffering Day.

I don't think that's going to happen any time soon. In the
meantime, though, here are my tools. Share. They might help
others.

Talk. Don't keep it to yourself. There's a great saying
in Narcotics Anonymous: an addict alone is in bad
company.

Let people in. It's scary and sometimes it can go
wrong, but when you manage to connect with people,
it's magic.

Let people go. (The toxic ones.) They don't need to
know – just gently withdraw.

Learn to say no. I struggled so much with this, but
when I started to do it, it was one of the most liberating
things that ever happened to me.

Learn to say yes. As I've got older, I've become quite 'safe'. I am trying more and more to take myself out of my comfort zone.

Find purpose. It can be anything – a charity, volunteering . . .

Accept that Life is a roller coaster. Ups and downs.

Accept yourself. Even the bits you really don't like – you can work on those. No one is perfect.

Try not to judge. If I'm judging people, it says more about where I am than about them. It's at that point that I probably need to talk to someone . . .

Music is a mood-altering drug. Some songs can make you cry, but some can make you really euphoric. I choose to mostly listen to the latter.

Exercise. There is science to back me up here. Exercise is a no-brainer for mood enhancement.

Look after something. Let something need you for its survival. It doesn't have to be kids. It can be an animal, a houseplant, anything.

And last but not least . . .

Faith. I'm not sure what I believe in, but I do feel that when I pray, my prayers are being heard. Not always answered, but heard. And that's enough.

"
WE HAVE TO
FIND A WAY OF
LIVING WITH
THE SUFFERING.
CO-HABITING
WITH IT, WHILE
**WE WAIT FOR
OUR MOMENTS
OF JOY**.
"

HAPPY, NOT PERFECT

BY

Poppy Jamie

FOUNDER OF HAPPY NOT PERFECT

Since I was a young girl, people have often said to me, 'You're the happiest person I know,' and, 'You have so much energy.' While sometimes this is true, it often isn't the case. Along with the great highs I experience, I also have low lows, some that drag on for days or weeks, or perhaps pass in minutes or hours. That's the thing with our mental health: it's sensitive, delicate, unpredictable and irrational. Some days, what I project in a meeting, social setting or online is far from my internal reality, and when I began my research a few years ago I quickly realized that I wasn't alone. It is practically impossible to understand another person's mental health journey. The age-old quote couldn't ring more true: 'Everyone you meet is fighting a battle you know nothing about.'

Here are some of my diary entries, to share the unfiltered thoughts I've had over the past two years.

1st Jan 2017

We are trapped by identities
Formed many years ago
That took seconds to be placed on us,
Years to take off.
I wonder what life would be like if we had no fear
To be ourselves for a whole year.

I hit rock bottom around the age of twenty-five. When I unpack why it happened, it's not particularly surprising. I lived with anxiety, worry and extreme perfectionism that was like a room-mate who wouldn't shut up. My negative self-talk was a broken record on constant play and my need to please others was on steroids. In my eyes, nothing I did was good enough, I never looked good enough, I was a walking embarrassment, and thus my self-esteem was nowhere to be seen and I craved external validation as if it was oxygen. I then started working with a person who triggered my darkest fears. They were someone I deeply respected but they had a tendency to be extremely negative, and it became very clear that I was not good enough for them. This was heart-shattering because, in knowing this, all my negative self-beliefs weren't just a part of my internal reality; they stared me in the face. Every day I was faced with my great fear: that I was not wanted or thought to be good enough.

29th Sept 2017

Wanted to cry throughout my meetings today.

After about six months of traumatically trying to seek validation from my new work colleague, desperate for them to say 'Good job' or 'Well done', which never came, I broke. I know this may sound trivial but, at the root of all humans, we have the desire to be accepted and loved. This paralysing rejection coupled with chronic stress, anxiety and lack of sleep led me to rock bottom. I lay in bed one morning with no energy, unable to move, and my stomach was so bloated it looked like I was pregnant. I was about to learn one of the most important lessons of my life: *there is no health without mental health*. I had hit a stop sign; my mind and body had given up – and, looking back, I couldn't be more grateful. Emotions are energetic signals of information and I had gone too long trying to ignore my worry, anxiety and lack of self-compassion – they had turned into deep sadness. This was a clear message, telling me that things needed to change.

22nd June 2017

I feel anxious but I don't know why. I have a horrible feeling in my chest and stomach and dreading going to this music festival tomorrow. I have this horrendous fear that I'm going to feel like such a loser and be a bit of a social outcast. It brings up horrible past memories of feeling like a 3rd wheel / 7th wheel. Urgh it's horrible. I have been hibernating so much lately and forget I have anything to say to anyone. Literally I can only talk about work, work and more work, which everyone finds really boring. I feel, like, so boring.

The breakdown kickstarted my journey into exploring mental health in new ways. I decided to dedicate my life to understanding the brain better in the hope that I could prevent others from suffering like I had. The world of Happy Not Perfect officially began . . . and we developed an app and products full of information, tools and techniques to help everyone with their mental health.

The Happiness Workout on the Happy Not Perfect app has been my saviour, and it's a non-negotiable daily ritual I do upon waking and before I sleep. It helps me to relax and focus on establishing a positive mindset, regardless of what is happening.

The daily breathing exercise, journalling moment, grateful diary entry, self-compassion exercise and short meditation are my coping strategies to maintain mindful balance.

Spending a moment to reflect, process and reframe with the app has taught me to develop better reactions throughout the day and to learn to avoid that feeling of paralysing, overwhelming chaos.

Just as our physical health is a lifelong commitment, so is our mental health; I treat my mental health as a priority and I reallllly notice when I stop.

Entrepreneurship is like being in a daily thunderstorm. And on the days when I wonder why I ever chose this career path, I remind myself that what we are building is for everyone. For everyone to have the tools to look after their mind. For everyone to manage the blue days and sustain the bright ones.

AND IF WE CAN HELP ONE PERSON TURN A BLUE DAY BRIGHT, IT'S ALL WORTH IT. THIS ALONE GIVES ME THE STRENGTH I NEED TO GET THROUGH.

WHAT I WISH I COULD HAVE SAID

BY

Ripley Parker

WRITER, ARTIST, STUDENT

You have just been born, with tiny fingernails and straight black hair. You have just been born when, really, you never should have been. You don't know this yet, but the chances of your father meeting your mother would have been roughly one in 20,000. Multiply that by the chances of them forming a long-term relationship, getting married, deciding to have kids (one in 2,000), and this overall number goes up to 40,000,000. Then consider the number of eggs and sperm produced by your parents throughout their lifetimes (not that you're even nearly old enough to know about that sort of thing). The chances of that one egg meeting that one sperm to form you after your parents met, got together, got married is one in 400,000,000,000,000,000. That's a 4 followed by seventeen zeros. But now cast your little mind back to all the previous generations of the last 4 billion years for whom this exact same process would have had to occur, the likelihood becoming increasingly minute, until they culminated in the mash of cells and numbers that is you, this tiny little living, breathing, perfect thing. These are the odds that a child will be born and go on to reproduce every generation for 150,000 generations. This number is one in 10-to-the-power-of-45,000. This number is greater than the number of all particles in the universe if each particle was in itself its own universe. But the right sperm had to find the right egg in each of those unions resulting in reproduction for 150,000 generations. The odds of this happening are one in 10-to-the-power-of-2,640,000. Now, we can add all this up to get . . . non-existent. Nothing. Such a tiny chirp into the void that no one in a trillion trillion trillion years would hear it or care. In conclusion, there was no chance at all that your parents would look down and see those big brown eyes, which just opened for the first time.

You are four and a sister now. She has just been born, with tiny fingernails and no hair and cries which raise the goddamn roof. She is so beautiful. All 26,000,000,000 cells of her. She will always be beautiful.

You are eight and have just discovered that school is bullshit. End of.

You are eleven and you can't breathe. You are standing outside the classroom you just ran out of when you felt your lungs take flight and your limbs are on fire as your chest rattles and your mind swims and your mouth tries to wordlessly form the right combination of syllables to ask for help. All of you feels wrong, so wrong. The blood in your veins has grown startled and rejected the harbourage of your heart; your insides feel in danger of turning outside. You don't get it. Eleven-year-olds aren't supposed to have heart attacks. You're sure you must've heard that somewhere. No one has ever told you what a panic attack is.

You are fourteen and drowning. You are drowning while all those around you breathe calmly, and you don't have enough breath left over to ask them how they do it. People worriedly smile and tell you that, someday, *things* will get better. Always *things*; never you. And you don't understand this because *things* have not changed; *you* have. There are, as there have always been, rainbows in your clouds. But the problem is, once you are no longer underneath the cloud but inside it, those rainbows grow less visible. Less visible, in part, due to the immediacy of this feeling, this Wrong, this overwhelming vagueness haunting your dreams. But they are less visible primarily because you don't want them any more. Every one of those rainbows (be they people, places or things) has become just another blow to your target-practice heart when you recognize that none of them can be the thing to save you. You have stopped wanting their beauty and their magic and their loveliness.

You want to die. You want to die because no one ever tells you exactly how far *someday* is. You're starting to think they made it up.

You are fifteen and barely able to come up for air. There are more good moments now, many more. Some days you can almost fill your lungs entirely before that Wrong inside you pulls you back down into yourself. And this is worse, much worse, because it is at those moments when you can feel it only slightly out of reach. The fruit-bearing vines graze your cracked lips, but retreat the second you open them to take the first bite. The boulder nearly crests the hill before rolling back down, taking you with it. You'd never noticed quite how heavy gravity can be.

But you are not ungrateful, you never have been. Always, you could see the whirling constellation of wonders that makes up your life. God, there is just so much to love. Dust motes lit up by stage lights, the creak of a book's binding when it's opened for the first time, the ache in the back of your throat from singing too loud, the whirring noise of a light bulb as it's flicked on, a warm blanket in a cold room, a kiss when you didn't know you needed one, dark pencils, the wet snuffle of a dog's nose, strangers who say 'Bless you' when you sneeze, mahogany, the dusty silk of flower petals, good lines in bad poems, the watercolour mess of sunset, snow, liquid-ink pens and more. So much more. So much more that you couldn't in a thousand and one lifetimes even begin to count them. The world is so heartbreakingly crammed with minuscule miracles that you want to scream and to cry and to dance, and to love each and every one of them until you burst. And that is exactly the problem. Darling, you have so much love, such excruciating amounts of love and rapture and boundless tenderness, and the weight of your world warring against it. *If only they knew*, you think.

IF ONLY THEY COULD
SEE HOW MUCH
I WANT TO GIVE BACK,
HOW MUCH I LONG
TO TELL THEM THAT,
WHILE ALL OF ME LONGS
TO STOP BREATHING,
**I CAN STILL
ACKNOWLEDGE MY
EVERY BREATH AS
MIRACULOUS**.

You are sixteen and in love. Totally. Irretrievably. Unendurably. She makes you want to play the guitar, or speak Spanish, or prove the Riemann Hypothesis. Her wrists are a crosshatching of fairy tales and her voice is venom with a smile. You fall in love with her scars almost as much as her skin. But, of course, no one can know. No one can know about the lie of her lips or the forgiveness of her palms. No one can know that her heart is the beat around which the melody of your breath conducts itself, or that, if the sound of her laugh down the phone was your alarm, you'd bound out of bed every morning. No one can know because every time you try to tell the story of her, none of your words come close to that moment in 'Sally Cinnamon' when the drums kick in. And it doesn't matter that she doesn't love you back or that you're hurting or that you know you are only there to be her stepping stone, because love doesn't need to have a point, and neither do you. Because she makes you feel lucky to be alive. Because the universe has a point, as long as she's in it. So you'll trace those words *it felt right* across your teeth ten thousand times and hate every smile you see for not being hers. You'll stretch out your circulatory system, wrap it around the world, and still it won't be enough. Because it doesn't take more than a smile from her to envelop yours. Your world won't ever be enough.

You are seventeen and scared of the mirror. It is big, omnipresent and unforgiving. Over in the corner, the cyclopean spotlight of its gaze is always on you. This is because you have recently realized the following: you are not very good at being a girl. Of course you would try harder if you knew how, but you seem to have been sick that day in school when they taught you how to be beautiful. You feel you are missing something that reaches far deeper than long hair and delicate hands and poise and elegance and ovaries and oestrogen. It is base and fundamental, yet your bones don't know how to do it. Your bones do not feel quite alive enough; they are stacked and locked in the wrong order. There is no fun, femininity, sex, sparkle or that angry, electrifying grace. Grace. That's what you're missing. That grace of hair and rolling hips and damp thighs and scuffed soles and clacking teeth hiding sharp tongues and straining necks and trembling hands.

And the secret, one which you would never dream of admitting, is that you really, truly, desperately want to be beautiful. You want to be beautiful more than anything in this world, and you hate yourself for wanting it. You want to be beautiful because you know that nothing ugly will ever be worth protecting, and you have never felt so unsafe. But I know that what you really want, all you have ever really wanted, is a voice that someone will care about. A voice that will make anyone, anywhere, pause what they're doing and turn up the volume. You want to be larger than life and realer too, far realer. You want to scale the Empire State Building and have the fighter jets give a damn about shooting you down. But you know that your hands are not strong enough to pull you up those 1,454 feet, so you will settle for being small, smaller than small. Small enough to slip through the floorboards of those rooms full of strangers with smiles like snared wire, or the pages of the diary you pour your toxins into, or the brittle spokes of the ribcage you wish to God was more visible.

And to do that, food has to go. Because you are not yet small enough, you can still see yourself in that mirror. Your feet still make that ugly noise when they hit the ground, that sound of aching consequence. You keep your sins close like beads on a string, run them through your fingers so as not to forget. They are the weight of the sky, and you know your body must make room for them. Your hands are milk-pale spiders, knuckles like pulled teeth, every third thought now lodged in your stomach. The number on the scale grows steadily smaller, but the mirror remembers. Even in minus numbers, it would still remember. You want to be a minus number. So when you get scared, which is a lot these days, you trace patterns against the back of your throat. But soon your body stops wanting to let the food go. Your body is so fucking selfish sometimes.

You are eighteen and have fallen in love with life. With softness. With warmth. With the crackle of the needle on a record before the first note chimes, and the syrupy thickness of music as you dance, and the vibrations in your palms after cheering for an encore, and with her smile. With a smile that turns every minute into a moment. With the smile that could make forever feel like an instant. With all the beauty and the magic and the loveliness of breathing. With the power of young girls with strong convictions and a hummingbird's beat in their chest. With the peace you have not yet found within your bones, but know you someday will. Because when you are trying to turn yourself bulletproof, trying to corrugate the softest parts of yourself, to freeze your exoskeleton, you can't let in that which makes you melt. You have started melting, my love. Still a little rough at the edges, some of your curves still sharp to the touch, but survival shouldn't ever be entirely easy. You are softness. You are warmth. Breathe in the mythology of your continuance, let your lungs know they are not relics. You will punish yourself for many things, but don't ever let your survival be one of them.

You are eighteen and the mirror still scares you. It always will. But then again, so does the ocean, and that doesn't stop you from swimming.

You are eighteen and wish you were older. Maybe then you'd have it all figured out.

You are eighteen and wish you were younger. Maybe then you wouldn't care that you haven't.

"YOU WILL PUNISH
YOURSELF FOR
MANY THINGS,
**BUT DON'T EVER
LET YOUR SURVIVAL
BE ONE OF THEM**.
"

You are eighteen and there are still days when all you can do to survive is ghost your fingertips over the faded scores the razor left on your skin and tell yourself over and over again, 'These do not make you less.' Those days aren't going away any time soon, but that is OK, because you are still here. All 37 trillion cells of you. All 37 trillion minuscule miracles.

You are seventeen and you are beautiful. Your arms don't need to be matchsticks when there's already a fuse in your fingertips and a world soaked in sulphur.

You are sixteen and she will not be the only one. You are not a stepping stone, not another mile of the journey. You are a destination.

You are fifteen and I'm sorry I don't talk to you more nowadays. Perhaps I healed too whole to still feel the part of me that is you. You hated the fact that, all these weeks and months and years away, I would still be here, but I am so achingly grateful for you every day. I promise, the surface is not as far as it feels.

You are fourteen and I'm afraid *someday* is still not tomorrow. It may not be tomorrow for quite a while but, trust me, whenever it comes, it's worth sticking around for.

"

YOU ARE NOT A STEPPING STONE, NOT ANOTHER MILE OF THE JOURNEY. **YOU ARE A DESTINATION.**

"

You are eleven and you are not having a heart attack. This happens. Not enough people talk about it perhaps, but it does happen.

You are eight and you're right: school is bullshit. But whoever said bullshit had to be a bad thing? After all, it helps plants grow.

You are four and don't let go of this feeling. She looks at you as though you encompass the whole world. Keep that world safe. She needs it. Tell her how proud you are that she made it here. Tell her that of all the frillions upon frillions of people she could have been, you are glad she's her.

You have just been born, and I love you.

THE LIST

BY

Emma Thompson

ACTOR, SCREENWRITER,
ACTIVIST, AUTHOR, COMEDIAN

I'm sure there will be many harrowing stories in this book. Depression has so many faces, and some of them are positively demonic. My depression isn't one of those. It is ironically undramatic. A simple, common-or-garden anhedonia, like being wrapped in a cold, wet blanket.

Shakespeare puts it best. He generally does, I find. Here's Hamlet:

> *I have of late – but wherefore I know not – lost all my mirth, forgone all custom of exercises. And indeed it goes so heavily with my disposition that this goodly frame the earth seems to me a sterile promontory. This most excellent canopy, the air, look you, this brave o'erhanging firmament, this majestical roof fretted with golden fire – why, it appeareth nothing to me but a foul and pestilent congregation of vapours.*

Yup.

The operative word, for me, is *sterile*.

TO BE ALIVE IS TRULY AN **EXTRAORDINARY GIFT**

and when all seems sterile and empty one simply has no access to it. One of the recipes I have used over the years is a list of recommendations by another dead bloke called Sydney Smith. He calls his state 'low spirits' – a catch-all phrase used in the eighteenth and nineteenth centuries to describe all manner of mental conditions. Herewith, and with the greatest possible respect to Sydney, is my reworking of that marvellous list.

1. Live as enjoyably as you can within financial reason.

2. If you have a bath, draw an inch or two of cold water and splash about in it. A cold shower will have the same uplifting effect.

3. Never stay up all night watching Netflix Originals about serial killers.

4.

DON'T THINK TOO FAR AHEAD. EVENING IS FINE, **BUT TOMORROW CAN LOOK AFTER ITSELF**.

5. Keep reasonably busy.

6. See as much as you can of the friends who like you, support you and make you laugh. See as little as you can of the friends who judge you, compare you to others and tire you (and don't pretend you don't know who they are).

7. Apply the same rules to casual acquaintances. If your instincts tell you they are toxic, walk away and don't look back.

8. If you are low in the water, do not pretend that you aren't. It makes it so much worse, and

A STIFF UPPER LIP
ONLY GIVES YOU
A SORE JAW.

9. Good coffee and tea are a genuine help.

10.

DO NOT
UNDER ANY CIRCUMSTANCES
OR FOR ANY REASON
AT ANY TIME
COMPARE YOURSELF
TO ANYONE ELSE.

11. Cultivate a gentle, healthy pessimism. It can result in more nice surprises.

12. Avoid drama about what is wrong with the world (unless it is funny), emotionally powerful music, other sad people, and anything likely to make you feel anxious or that you are not doing enough.

13.

RANDOM ACTS OF KINDNESS ARE
HUMAN ANTIDEPRESSANTS.

14. Form a close bond with a local tree.

15. Make the room you most like sitting in as much of a comfy nest as you can.

16. Listen to David Attenborough.

17.

STOP JUDGING YOURSELF. STOP PUNISHING YOURSELF.
IT'S NOT YOUR FAULT.

18. Keep warm.

19. Think as much as you can about space, infinity and the beyond. Anything that much bigger than you can be very relaxing.

20. Trust me.

WHAT MY LIFE IS LIKE

BY

Saba Asif

YOUTH MP, ACTIVIST, TEENAGE ICON

I'd be lying if I told you it was easy. I'd be lying if I told you it wasn't fun, sometimes. And I am telling you the truth when I say I am in love. This tragic, triumphant and terrifying love I have – I have it for you, everyone, the things that hurt me, the people who brush past me on my way to college, my nephew, that single, brilliant pink wire that goes through the tunnels on the Metropolitan line, which no one else seems to see but me.

That silly, stupid little pink wire doesn't know how it has cheered me up on my way home after long, dreary meetings about things I want to change but can't seem to. My nephew doesn't know how his toothless smile engulfed every edge of my existence; for him I do everything with a stupidly hopeful spirit.

And to the people who brush past me every day: I will never know who you are, where you've been, where you're going or who you dream to be, but I am in awe that you are living and breathing around me; it means a great deal to me.

TO THE THINGS THAT HURT ME, YOU ARE NOT EASY TO LOVE, **BUT I HAVE LEARNED TO REGARDLESS**.

Now I have learned that, as we get older, our problems become more frequent and more complex, but we will not let those complexities consume us. The ugly beauty of life cannot and will never devour our diamond minds.

My heart has been broken many times by words, actions, events and even a person. So, in good spirit, I commend to you heartbreak, for making me write better, feel more deeply, think harder – and mostly for making me appreciate romance when it was there and graciously wait for its eventual reappearance one day.

As for the crucial components that orchestrate this society – the politics – I thank you for being harsh and cold; if you were not, I wouldn't be fighting you to change. For this fight has made me stronger, kinder, and intolerant of your wrongdoing and deceit. Politics will not get away with the pain it has caused. And those fighting the war for us – with respect and integral dignity I thank you a thousand times over.

Years ago I wouldn't have, but now I thank my identity for making life more challenging. Being a female, Muslim, British Pakistani, working-class person has given me a unique take on life and a deeper understanding of how ugly people can be. So the path I walk is like no other: bumpy and battering, it is a difficult one, but day by day I am learning to enjoy every step of it. I understand I can't fight the things I cannot control, but I simply make the best of who I am born to be – and the truth is, *I was not born to be successful*; in fact everything I had as a child gave me the exact opposite, *so now I fight to be successful*. That means being strong and unrelenting to those who try to use my wearing of the hijab, my culture, my religion and my socio-economic deprivation against me. This means I push harder, chase faster, read more, listen more, question all authority and never give up on the impossible. Like a brazen bull with no remnants of weakness, just a pure iron will, I will never let anyone ever make me feel ashamed of myself again.

So, when I feel that unrelenting, overwhelming wave of sadness, and I am being driven insane or feeling much too sane . . . I think of these little things that I love: everyone, the things that hurt me, the busy, beautiful motion of you and me somehow going through our lives, my nephew, and that single, solemn, stupid little pink wire taking me through the tunnel of my wonderful little life.

Your friend always,
Saba ☺

WHEN IT'S NOT THE BRIGHTEST DAY

BY

AUTHOR

Today is not the brightest day. And I think that's OK. I think it's all right that everything feels a little bit grey and cloud-covered. I think it's fine that I'm having moments of wishing that I could just feel a little less. I think it's perfectly acceptable that I'm sat here, wanting to write something inspiring about mental health, and realizing that actually I feel a little empty. I've felt like this before. And I've figured out a few things about how to weather days like today as well. I'm going to write them here, in case you need to hold on to them too.

What Not To Do on Days Like Today:

- Try not to fall down the 'Why am I like this?' spiral. You've never found an answer there that made you feel more whole.

- Don't listen to the voice that minimizes, dismisses or belittles. Keep reading this next part until you believe it: *You are allowed to feel how you feel. You are allowed to feel how you feel. You are allowed to feel how you feel.*

- Never stumble into the trap of blaming your body. Yes, you would still feel these things if you were smaller. No, even that number of pounds won't make every bit of grey disappear. You don't have to love your body right now; just try to see that it's carrying you the best it can, and that alone makes it worthy of your kindness.

- Refuse to equate your productivity with your worth. Maybe some days it's more important to just *be* than to constantly *do*.

What To Do on Days Like Today:

- Be as gentle with yourself as you would be with the most precious thing in the world. Then be more gentle.

- Remember the relationships that make you feel like your truest self – nourish them.

- Do that thing that brings you the tiniest bit of joy, and don't give a fuck about whether you're good at it or what it's worth to someone else.

- Remind yourself that this feeling won't live here forever. You don't need to kick and scream at it to get out; it will leave in its own time.

- Recall that every day like today has added something to who you are.

- Reframe the 'Why do I have to feel so much?' as 'How extraordinary that I get to feel so much'.

- Give yourself permission to just exist.

Maybe tomorrow will be brighter. Maybe not. But since I've survived 100% of my most grey days so far, I have no reason to believe that I won't weather this one too.

THE LIGHT WILL SHOW UP SOON.
SEE YOU THERE.

BEFORE THE BALL

BY

WRITER, ACTOR, PRODUCER, DIRECTOR

I found painting during the hardest month of my life. Or rather, painting found me.

As a child I was an obsessive painter: before I could write, it was the only way I knew how to tell stories, and my parents (both artists, both working at home) loved the way it distracted me and kept me from being a neurotic gnat, always buzzing in their busy faces. I would paint portraits: of my mother and her belly, pregnant under her Yohji Yamamoto tunic. Of my father, gangly legs emerging from worn tennis shorts. Of my dad's best friend John who had Coke-bottle glasses and a bald head with wispy hairs growing from the sides. I also loved to paint fairies, mermaids and 'fashion girls'. I felt sick a lot as a kid and so the couch became a theme park, toys buried between the cushions, pencils scattered on the floor, a leather pillow that felt cool against my back when I read in the August heat.

Once I found writing, I gave up making pictures. The two causes seemed at odds. I wrote every day from the time I was six until I turned thirty-one. It was my escape, my play, my flirtation and ultimately my job. Then, one day, it stopped.

I had never experienced writer's block before. But, honestly, this wasn't just writer's block; I had lost all my words. I was sick, skinny and addicted to pills. Even texts intimidated me. And so I went off to treatment to face my pain. All day, therapy. All night, a blank computer screen.

Then my adopted brother Spike came to see me. He showed up right at eleven in the morning, when visiting hours started. I awkwardly introduced him to my new friends, staring at my feet like a fourth-grader. He was carrying his trusty dog, Wolf Pack, and a Strand bookstore bag full of supplies. It didn't contain food, or underpants, or condoms. In the only private space we could find (the yoga studio) he presented me with books (*The Little Prince*, Rilke) and toys (a harmonica) and a pad of paper accompanied by a mess of coloured pencils.

'If you can't write it,' he said, 'draw it.'

And so I did: shitty, jangly portraits of my fellow inmates. The girl who was recovering from years of bullying was rendered in purple pen, with extra care taken to capture the way her frayed jeans brushed against her Converse. A dreamy sketch of the guy with a borderline personality disorder standing over his keyboard (I had to sit in the hall while he posed inside his room, a barrier we weren't allowed to cross). I drew two angles of one of our SAs (sober assistants) with her blunt bob and her myriad nose rings. On my overnight with my boyfriend at a local inn, I drew him sleeping on the bed after the final time we had sex, and as I sketched I realized I would drown alive if he didn't let go of me.

In the outside world I forgot about the notebook. I forgot about the peace I felt while finding the curve of a nostril or drawing individual strands of hair. Then one day I found it in a bag of things I wanted to forget and decided I might try painting again, expanding to a simple child's watercolour palette.

A year later my home is full of colours; in palettes, tubes, on plates. I mix my own. I use brushes of all sizes. I paint little ones and big ones, realist and fantastical. But they're always of people, usually women.

I WANT TO CAPTURE THEM ON THE PRECIPICE OF CHANGE, **IN THE PROCESS OF HEALING**, AS I WAS WHEN I FELL IN LOVE WITH MAKING (THIS KIND OF) ART.

This is a painting of a selfie I took before I attended a massive ball. I was just a little high, shaky from not eating, breasts deflated, hair patchy. The picture informed me of my condition, and now the painting reminds me of a place I'll never return to, yet somehow I'm glad I went.

A CONVERSATION WITH MYSELF

BY

Scarlett Moffatt

TELEVISION PRESENTER

'I don't want to do this. I don't think I can face her, not today.'

'But you have to at some point – you can't hide forever. Stop pacing back and forth – you can't just live in your bedroom. You can't sit in that oversized jumper for eternity. One day you will have to be surgically removed from that bloody jumper.'

'I've got a better idea. Let's turn our mobiles off, lie in bed all day, eat carbs and watch *The Young Ones*, then when I'm feeling more up to it tomorrow I will face her, I promise.'

'No, because you know then you will cry all day tomorrow feeling angry at yourself for having a day of eating carbs – I mean, even though you need them to survive – and you will mentally punish yourself all day for ignoring your friends, the people who love you, like me. I love you.'

'I don't know why you love me – all I do is moan constantly.'

'That's not true! You always put other people before yourself. You are kind, funny, caring! Stop this, stop this now and get ready – you can do this. Today is your day!'

'I suppose you're right. I can't hide forever. Help me pick

something nice to wear. What about my favourite monochrome co-ord? And I'll highlight my cheeks to the gods and wear my matte red lipstick. She won't be able to say one bad thing about me if I look this confident.'

'That's the attitude! Now hurry up – we're going to be late.'

TWO HOURS LATER . . .

'Ha ha ha! OH MY GOD, have you seen yourself? Do you realize what you look like? This is laughable, honestly. Why don't you post a picture online? I'm sure people will agree you look an absolute fat mess.'

'See, I knew this would happen. I told you I wasn't ready to face her.'

'Five-foot, overweight mess! Look at the size of those hips, man. What makes you think you could wear an outfit like that? You're meant to be on the television – look at the state of you. How do you have the job you have? Do you not realize how much of a fat mess you look like compared to everybody else? No amount of hair extensions or make-up is going to improve that face. I can't believe you would even dare go out of the house with a body that shape. How saggy are your

boobs? You haven't even had kids! Your boobs should not look like that – you're only twenty-eight. I think people only hang around with you because they feel sorry for you. Think about it logically – why else would anybody want to be your boyfriend or your friend? You cry all the time, you overthink everythi–'

STOP
STOP
STOP!

'You can't do this to me any more. Not everyday at least – I won't let you. I spoke to my family and friends, I've spoken to my GP – I'm getting help and I'm speaking to someone who has introduced me to cognitive behavioural therapy.

'All these people have made me see I can fight these thoughts, taking little steps every day.

'And I going to start by telling you, MIRROR and BRAIN, that this conversation I've had with myself all afternoon is ridiculous. I have to stop being my own worst enemy. I have to stop bullying myself with the name-calling. I need to be my best friend and love myself!

'So today I can face you, Mirror – I can look right at you

and I like what I see! That's right, little mean voice in my head. Do you hear that you can't stop me from having a good night? Now excuse me and do one for the night, Anxiety – I'm off out for tea with my friends wearing this fit outfit and to fill my face with carbs.'

"

I HAVE TO STOP
BEING MY OWN
WORST ENEMY.
I HAVE TO STOP
BULLYING MYSELF
WITH THE
NAME-CALLING.
**I NEED TO BE
MY BEST FRIEND
AND LOVE MYSELF!**

"

THE NIGHTMARE OF THE BLACK DOG

BY

JOURNALIST, AUTHOR

A reimagining of Henry Fuseli's 1781 painting *The Nightmare*.

This version depicts the piece's illustrator, Yomi Adegoke, after an encounter with the Black Dog (i.e. during a depressive episode).

LOSING PERSPECTIVE

BY

Elizabeth Uviebinené

AUTHOR

I have a really bad memory. I made a joke to a friend that I only remember life from age eighteen. The day I fled to university.

At that moment I realized I had the opportunity to take charge of my life and create a new one. All those years of plotting in my bedroom – scribbling in my journal, Destiny's Child ballads in the background, feeling alone and depressed – would pay off.

Even though I was part of a big family, I always felt alone and misunderstood. Growing up, I began to shut out all my bad memories that had caused me anxiety and hope-lessness. One by one, I simply started to file those bad memories away. I convinced myself I didn't need them. Years went by and, just like an up-and-coming high street in south London, a process of gentrification took place.

It was my way of coping, I guess: out with the old, in with the new. It was a simple yet effective plan and it served me well for some time.

But it also robbed me of some of my best memories growing up, which until recently I struggled to remember.

By shutting down a lot of my bad memories, I began to also shut down the good ones. I had forgotten parts of who I was and what made Elizabeth. I wasn't a product in a shiny new box with millennial pink and rose-gold packaging and a twenty-eight-day return policy.

That's the thing – by tricking my mind into thinking that I'd magically landed on earth at age eighteen with no back story, no roots, no good or bad, I had exposed myself to an even worse spiral of loneliness in my early twenties. It made me lose perspective and struggle to live in the moment.

And, boy, when this happens, I am driven by fear and insecurity. Not love and hope.

When I feel like this, I spend time listening to nineties R&B and pop playlists in the hope of triggering my memories; I make an effort to meet up with old childhood friends and I go to the area I grew up in and sit there for a while, refamiliarize myself with what I once knew.

Reconnecting with and remembering parts of my identity that I had buried under ambition and success helps me gain perspective, and gives me hope. I've learned that there's no point in suppressing them any more; instead I need to face them head on and use them to propel myself forward.

" RECONNECTING WITH AND REMEMBERING PARTS OF MY IDENTITY THAT I HAD BURIED UNDER AMBITION AND SUCCESS **HELPS ME GAIN PERSPECTIVE, AND GIVES ME HOPE**. "

EVER BEEN IN A PLACE

BY

WRITER, SILVERSMITH

Ever been in a place where you suddenly for once feel happy; life feels great – all rainbows and butterflies – and for a moment everything is so wonderful you are overwhelmed? Colours are electrically heightened and saturated to the point where all you can see is white, as if you are staring directly at the sun on a clear summer day. And then you are overtaken by the panic of your heartbeat because happiness, which is meant to be normal, desirable even, feels alien; for so long all you've known is sadness and misery. You have to yank yourself out of happiness to a place that feels more familiar because, as painful as it is, it feels more comfortable. It's then that you know you are more accustomed to being in pain than at peace, because you feel you don't deserve to be happy. It seems unfair to feel happiness while you know what you know and have seen what you have seen. That's when you know that, more than comfort and serenity, suffering and torture for you feel like home.

*

I am five years old, on the back of an elderly bicycle bumping over the dimly lit, ancient cobbled streets of Aleppo, my arms round the waist of my uncle, on the way to his workshop. 'He should be in bed!' I can hear my mother say as we leave for our midnight excursion, but we are away and bed will have to wait. This uncle makes floor-to-ceiling aquariums where fish can swim like a thousand coloured stars in the foyers of fancy hotels and showy lobbies. The people who order them are very wealthy and important so they haggle aggressively on time and price. My uncle is firm. He can do it, but it will be expensive and it will take a long time. He enjoys telling people no. All the other children are frightened of him. Just his name makes them scurry theatrically behind furniture. He and I understand each other. We are made of the same stuff. We like to feel wood beneath our fingers and imagine what it might become with enough patience and nurturing. I am the only one invited to his midnight crafting sessions. It makes me feel special. I watch. I copy. I learn. I make. I admire the old city of Aleppo after dark on our journey home. I have heard the grown-ups say it is the world's oldest inhabited city – except for Damascus, which is my city. Aleppo has been here as long as anyone can imagine and it will be here long after we have gone, we think. We cannot envisage anything else. The saw meets the wood with its metal grooves. To you it might look like a violent collision, but really it is the imagination meeting the possible, and that's where creation lives.

When two extreme emotions such as euphoria and agony collide in a moment of impact, while the sound of it is absent, it echoes very loudly, like being in a chamber of deafening silence.

*

I am twenty-three years old. I am building a temporary living shelter in Calais, France, for a refugee. I am at the top of a ladder with a circular saw and I am wearing no protective clothing. There are no health and safety regulations in the refugee camp or, if there are, no one seems to care whether they are followed. I am not special any more. I am the opposite of special. I am one of a large number of unwanted. The only state where I am entitled to live is one where I shall surely die. I can face death but I cannot face killing, and I am of age to be a soldier. You think becoming a refugee is something that happens to someone else, but here I am in this camp with the others who have no country to call their own. Now we are more like the fish in the tank, circling round, looking for an exit and jostling past each other, waiting for food to be dispensed from above by a generous volunteer. Some of us are in brightly coloured donated hoodies that say 'I ♥ London' shiny like goldfish. I think of my uncle and his craft that I have brought across the world, smuggled in my fingertips.

As I build shelters, bombs rain on old Aleppo like an angry saw meeting wood, but only for destruction – to chip the wood into a million useless bits. I hear news that my uncle dodges the explosions in the dead of night to rescue what he can from his workshop before the very oldest part of the second oldest inhabited city in the world is gone. He enjoys telling people no. He even enjoys telling bombs, 'Not tonight.'

TRAUMA DOESN'T SEEM TO HAVE A SENSE OF WHEN MIGHT BE A GOOD TIME OR PLACE TO VISIT. **IT CAN STRIKE IN THE MOST UNEXPECTED WAYS.**

Sometimes even in the middle of a euphoric and intimate moment with someone else. Someone who knows nothing of such events. Flashbacks from childhood and adolescence that you never thought you could remember so vividly play before your eyes like a slow-motion movie at times – and like a lightning bolt at others. The sound of the bicycle wheels on the cobbles twinned with the shells exploding like fireworks across the Damascus skyline, the face of someone you loved – lost in a moment.

Why would such a vague memory of innocence paired with a vivid memory of evading an instant death accompany a moment of pure happiness in this way? Perhaps my brain is in ecstasy and opening filing cabinets at random, throwing things in the air, rock-'n'-roll style.

You escape the deafening boom of a nightclub and go to a loo stall, sit on the floor behind the door and block your ears with your fingers to have a moment of silence, only to realize that the noise in your own head is far more raucously frightening. Words start rushing into your mind with such speed that you can't even distinguish what they are, only how they make you feel. You understand that being alone, which seemed so necessary, is actually a big mistake, and that you have to go back to that loud party outside and pretend everything is fine and normal and nice; otherwise you will lose your mind. You go back out, but you stand in the corner and look at everyone, feeling like a freak. You want to be normal and engage in conversation so you don't make all this obvious, but it feels impossible because of the million thoughts rushing through your head that aren't letting you focus. You try to cut out the static and walk towards someone outside; you don't even smoke but you ask for a cigarette and start talking.

*

In truth, I don't know what the consequence is for my mental health, nor for that of my friends who lived in a war zone, haven't seen their families in a long time and are now displaced. It's hard to assess the impact of not being able to process trauma, because of one 'once-in-a-lifetime traumatic event' coming immediately after another. All this leaves the brain no time or energy to process.

I HAVE READ THAT THE BRAIN HAS A SHELVING MECHANISM.

I KNOW I'VE COMPARTMENTALIZED A LOT BECAUSE I'VE HAD TO, AND THAT'S BEEN USEFUL FOR MY SURVIVAL, BUT AT SOME POINT I'LL HAVE TO SORT THROUGH IT.

I'll need to start taking things off shelves, examining them, processing them and putting them back. Things far too terrible to tell you about, or even think about yet.

*

When British volunteers came to help in the Calais Jungle refugee camp, they always said, 'It's just like Glastonbury without the bands.' Now I've been to Glastonbury I know that's not true. The Portaloos in Calais were nowhere near as bad.

In a moment of joy, watching The Killers perform on the pyramid stage, I notice someone in the crowd waving a British flag and I remember that I am safe and happy. I remember where I will never be again – a place I once called home. It was home because of the people who were there, who made home mean what it meant then – people with whom I shared love, bread and salt and tears, and all the beauty and ugliness of the years of my life that shaped me into who I am. People who are not there any more, who weren't lucky enough to make it out of the hell of that country that was once called heaven on earth. People who deserved, if not more, then no less than me to survive and be safe and happy in a new place and a new life. Feeling happiness in this moment here feels wrong; letting go of the pain of the past in this moment of joy feels like letting go of those souls I left behind. The jokes and the innocent smiles, the marbles and the card games, the hikes and the horse rides in the green of the forests that turned into arid fields of torture and blinding dust. Moving on is what is needed for a new life, to be able to create something good with the pain rather than be stuck in the dark – but moving on to the light feels like a sin. It feels like betrayal . . . I'm Mr Brightside.

*

How do you know you're triggered? What is the feeling you get when you hear a loud siren in a DJ set in a late-night basement party and you don't know if you need to leave immediately because your heart is suddenly beating out of your ribcage? Is that what being triggered feels like or am I being dramatic? I don't want to leave because if I do the people I'm with might notice what's happened and that might ruin the fun of the night. Do I just stay, tell myself not to overreact? 'You're safe and sound in a party in London! Come on! Get it together!' How do I know when I'm being dramatic and when I'm truly being affected by the past? What is the right way to react? I stay in there and let whatever the feeling is doing to me do what it does. I let it be. I don't know what it is. I don't react. In order to survive, I keep calm and quiet and I observe.

*

'Do you miss it?' he asked me when he found out I was from Damascus. We were a group of ten, my friends and his friends, having dinner at a nice Indian restaurant in north London. My mind had been preoccupied the whole day after a phone call I received from my dad that morning. Things aren't good back home. The whole day I was feeling on edge and agitated. I couldn't do any of the things I was planning on doing. I just sat in my room wondering what to do and trying to understand my feelings and work out what was causing my anxiety.

I wanted to cancel the dinner but I couldn't, so I had to block those thoughts and pull myself out of this state, which is what I often do. I wasn't feeling very sociable, but my friends having a good time started to brush off on me and, as orders were taken, drinks were poured and starters spread across the table, I started getting in the mood and joining in the chat.

The chicken biryani was really good. I looked around and thought, *This feels nice.*

'What do you do for a crust, Steve? How do you survive?' he said.

'I wing it,' I said as I had a sip of water, dodging the question.

A friend leaned across the table and cut in: 'Steve makes silver jewellery. He used to be an architecture student, but he stopped because he is a refugee from Syria.'

'Oh god,' he said. 'You must have seen horrible things. I mean, I can't imagine. You must have a lot of trauma. All the horrors of that country, right?'

'Yeah, well, it's certainly nice to be here, having a lovely time in this restaurant,' I replied, putting up a wall to his line of questioning.

'You must have quite a story – I'd like to hear it,' he shot back. 'Where in Syria are you from?'

'Damascus,' I said.

'Do you miss it?'

'Yes.' I smiled, returning pointedly to my chicken biryani and my former conversation. I didn't want to eat any more. I didn't want to talk any more. But I didn't want to ruin the night for everyone else either.

He didn't mean anything by it. He just meant to show an interest.

On the way back, while people were chatting in the car, I suddenly felt overwhelmed and shoved my fingers in my ears for a moment of silence to try to understand what I was feeling. When I got home, I tried to put those feelings into writing, but didn't find the words.

If someone's mother had just died, would you ask, 'Do you miss her?'

*

Sometimes I feel like my mind is back in my uncle's workshop. A block of wood, waiting to be shaped. I like to feel this wood beneath my fingers and imagine what it might become with enough patience and nurturing.

Sometimes to shape our narrative and understand our darkest crevices, we need to take a saw to the wood. It might look like a violent collision, but really it is the imagination meeting the possible, and that's where creation lives. You can hear the scary, anxious voices in your head and enjoy telling them, 'No.' If it helps, you can say it in my uncle's voice. You already know how it sounds.

Peace lives somewhere deep inside us, but it can be frightening to go there when unhappiness feels like home.

SOMETIMES WE NEED TO BUILD OURSELVES A TEMPORARY SHELTER OF COMPASSION BECAUSE WE ARE REFUGEES FROM JOY, LOOKING ALL THE TIME FOR A LAND OF SELF-LOVE AND UNDERSTANDING THAT WILL OFFER US A PASSPORT.

Ever been in a place where you suddenly for once feel happy; life feels great – all rainbows and butterflies – and for a moment everything is so wonderful you are overwhelmed?

KIND

BY

WRITER

As kids, some of us were punished for having feelings, and it shows. Through abandonment issues, self-sabotage and malfunctional attachment styles, we try our best to express the very same thing we have been expressing since childhood:

I JUST WANT
TO BE LOVED.

Learning that love is something you earn rather than something you deserve means that you process and understand each mistake, struggle and rejection as 'I am unlovable', instead of thinking, 'I am allowed to make mistakes because we only learn from being wrong and it's important to always keep in mind that my mistakes do not reflect my capacity to love, bring warmth to the world and inspire people.'

We internalize every projection imposed on us but prioritize absorbing the most untrue and hurtful ones because we are conditioned to repeat the pattern of linking our mistakes to our morality. Morality is a concept that, when explored further, is pretty fascinating.

'Goodpersonhood' is a requirement of every human being as a general social rule, but, as the world evolves and we all start to realize the individual role we play within it, it seems like we have less kindness to spare for each other. Imagine what our lives would look like if we stopped trying to be good and started trying to be kind. 'Good' is arbitrary, subjective and nebulous. But 'kind' is universal, gentle and pure. I would rather be remembered as kind than be remembered as good.

"

'GOOD' IS
ARBITRARY,
SUBJECTIVE
AND NEBULOUS.
**BUT 'KIND' IS
UNIVERSAL,
GENTLE
AND PURE.**

"

INSIDE VOICE

BY

Gabby Edlin

CEO AND FOUNDER OF
BLOODY GOOD PERIOD

I don't know if he silenced her, or if I ignored her. Either way, I just stopped hearing her for those two long years. When I needed her most, I lost my inside voice, my voice inside. She did try to call to me at first, to tell me, *This relationship is not right any more. It's damaging you and it's crushing you.* But I'll admit that I didn't want to hear, because she frightened me with the things she could tell me about myself and about him.

And before I lost her, before she was quiet, neglected, it's not like I listened to her much anyway. So, what do you do when you don't even know how to listen to yourself, to the voice inside, but your relationship has become a farce and the only person who knows it is you?

Should you leave? Yank yourself out of something cosy but claustrophobic? The fear of being alone in the world is too strong. Your inside voice tries to speak up, to tell you to leave, but you're scared of being alone. So you tell yourself that the precious knowledge of your unhappiness brewing in your gut is just anxiety messing with you. It's amazing what you're capable of believing.

ANXIETY IS WHAT YOU NAME THINGS YOU **CAN'T OR WON'T PROCESS**.

Things are fine at home. Every couple has problems. So typical of you to sabotage your own happiness. You learn to ignore the voice inside, and you imagine those feelings are just anxiety, because what makes you think you could do any better? And because you know not to value anxiety, it's not so hard to learn to disregard the inside voice. It's really not so hard to drown out that voice inside with a much louder one, his outside voice, telling you that you're overreacting. Even louder are the faceless, nameless voices transmitted through screen and page that say you're only validated in a couple, that you must visibly show you are worthy of love.

So.

So you take a deep breath and you do what anyone would do, and you google *Anxiety in my relationship*. You search for *Obsessive thoughts about leaving my partner*. You ask your mum, 'How do I actually know if I've found the one?'

Google spits up *Relationship Obsessive Compulsive Disorder*. And, by the way, your mum says, 'Do what's right for you.' But you don't know what's right; that's why you're in this mess.

ROCD, in which sufferers are consumed with doubts about their relationship.

Sounds about right. You breathe out. The inside voice takes her chance, and opens her mouth to speak, but you can't hear her over the clacking of the keyboard. She would've told you, *You might love him but he's not good for you, to you. The two can co-exist. He can be kind, but he makes you cry more than he makes you laugh, and yet you stay with him.* The voice goes quiet again.

Sure, you've trusted your inside voice before, but she got you into trouble: you were impulsive, selfish, indecisive. She created an upheaval and it was scary. Anxiety shrieked so loudly at the same time that you don't remember she was also insightful and perceptive, and that you were quietly right.

*

And oh my god it's the year of the weddings. Not *your* wedding. All your friends marry wonderful people. The tears gush forth all summer and will not stop. Nobody believes you're just happy for the bride and groom. It's 11 p.m. And he won't look at you. Because your ex is there and he's taller than him or something. You feel anxious and furious but your inside voice won't say a word.

At the seventh wedding, he's worse than ever.

But before the anxiety can stake a claim and take the blame for his bad behaviour, all of a sudden the inside voice is an outside voice and she screams *GET OUT* and you cry and cry and cry in the hotel toilets and you cannot, in all good faith, not listen to her this time. You make him leave.

But then he's back a week later with promises of therapy, and it might be OK and you can't, you just *can't* be single again, not when you're almost thirty, not when everyone is coupled up. You smother the voice with his vows to change. You know now that your inside voice would've looked after you if you'd been stronger, alone, but she seems to have got lost and she's not coming back.

So you decide to try with him, without her. You try with the might of a thousand armies to make him happy. You apologize constantly for your anxiety and doubt. The dizzy spells start and you apologize for them too. You learn to live with the fatigue, the dizziness, the tingling fingers, the tears, the crippling doubts. The inside voice is gone.

And then one day. One day, you hear a murmur. You don't know why. She whispers when you're watching Suranne Jones ache over her husband's infidelity in *Doctor Foster*. She sighs at a women's festival when you learn the word *gaslighting*. And then over a bagel in the museum cafe, over a chat in which a casual acquaintance says to you, 'You know, someone else will eventually get to know you the way he knows you now. It's not a reason to stay,' the voice calmly and quietly makes herself known. She wasn't lost, she was biding her time. *This is not the end of you.*

And then you get the bus home from Brixton, like you do

every day. She speaks to you again, more calmly than you've ever heard, and tells you, *There's a plan and you'll be OK.*

And you put your keys in the lock and you open the front door of your flat and oh my god she suddenly ROARS. It is so deafening you can't hear him telling you 'You're being ridiculous, let's sort this out.' She packs the bag and she calls the taxi. She oozes into every part of your form and screams and screams and screams and will not stop until you promise her and promise him that this place will never be your home again. No, no, no, you're not going back, you are destined for more than this life. She bursts forth from the cellar of your stomach where you made her hide. She's thunderous and you're finally listening. She is more powerful than you ever knew. You are more powerful than you ever knew. You know you are powerful. You gasp for air and suddenly realize you are no longer drowning. You didn't know you were drowning. You assumed you were on dry land. Now you are.

*

You don't know what's ahead of you but you never go back. You no longer noiselessly trudge through treacle and silently gulp down sobs in bed. OK you do but the bed's all yours now and you cry as loudly as you want. You start to thrive. You continue to roar. You are the inside voice and the outside voice and she is you and you learn to listen to each other. You're alone and you amaze yourself and you're absolutely fine and really bloody great.

" SHE'S THUNDEROUS
AND YOU'RE
FINALLY LISTENING.
SHE IS MORE POWERFUL
THAN YOU EVER KNEW.
**YOU ARE MORE
POWERFUL THAN
YOU EVER KNEW.**
"

WHEN YOU ASK HOW I AM

BY

COMEDIAN, ACTOR, WRITER

LAST WORDS

THE
'IT'S OK'
LIST
BY
Scarlett Curtis
JOURNALIST, ACTIVIST

I first wrote this list when I was nineteen. A manifesto of sorts. I stuck it on my wall and tried to look at it every day when the dark, twisted voices in my head inevitably came calling. I'm a lot more OK now than I was then. The thick, unrelenting depression that plagued me for almost a decade started to dissolve in my early twenties and for the last few years I've been doing everything I can to slowly but surely remind my brain that everything really is OK.

Recovery, like most things in life, has looked nothing like I thought it would. I spent years pinning all my hopes on this magical day when I would be 'BETTER', cured, fixed, not broken any more. That day never came and I'm pretty sure now that it's never going to come. My brain is my brain in all its beautiful, painful madness.

YOU CAN'T FIX SOMETHING
THAT WAS NEVER TRULY BROKEN.

It's taken me a long time to realize that.

We talk a lot in this book about the days when the depression and anxiety hits but it's also worth taking a moment to talk about the days when it doesn't. When life was really dark I used to imagine all the HUGE and EXCITING things I would do once I recovered: climb mountains, run marathons, go clubbing till 6 a.m. It took me about five years to realize that I didn't actually want to do any of those things. At all. Ever.

Today I woke up and I could feel my breath in my lungs. I was groggy and tired but not anxious or depressed. I made tea, stroked my cat, sat on the sofa, called a friend, went for a walk, did some emails, did some yoga, had dinner with my family, fell asleep. To sit on a sofa with a mug of tea and a group of friends is perhaps the most huge or exciting thing I could ever dream of. It's something that at one point in my life I thought I'd never be able to do. It's something magical.

Sometimes I miss it. That's a hard thing to write. Sometimes I miss how bad it used to be. I'd built my 'self' around a wound and as the wound started to heal I lost the only version of me that I knew how to be. I don't really know who I am without mental illness. Sometimes that scares me. Sometimes it feels exciting. Sometimes I try not to think about it.

If this book makes you feel anything, I really hope that it makes you feel like you're OK just as you are. Some of the things you've been through are not OK. Some of the things your brain tells you aren't OK.

BUT YOU, MY DEAR, DEAR FRIEND, ARE NOT ALONE. YOU NEVER HAVE BEEN AND YOU NEVER WILL BE.

WE ARE AN ARMY.
AN ARMY OF STRANGERS, STANDING BEHIND YOU WITHOUT JUDGEMENT OR SHAME.

We are here to tell you that how you feel is normal, who you are is wonderful. One day you'll be sitting on a sofa and you'll find yourself laughing; for a second it won't hurt, for a second you will just be there, in that moment, and, for a second, life will feel OK. Hold on for that second. If you don't do it for you, then do it for me. I promise, I promise, I promise: it's worth it.

THE 'IT'S OK' LIST

- **It's OK** to wake up feeling like the world's about to end. Like you want to cancel every single plan that's ever been made for the future and crawl back into bed.
- **It's OK** to think that this feeling is never going to end.
- **It's OK** that the feeling's almost always gone half an hour later.
- **It's OK** that sometimes it doesn't go.
- **It's OK** that some days are still very dark. That some weeks are still dark. That not everything in your brain is quite as perfect as you'd hope it to be.
- **It's OK** to cancel plans.
- And then cancel again.
- And then cancel again.
- **It's OK** to show up at a party and leave five minutes after you arrive. People usually don't mind. And if they do mind it's OK not to care. It's OK if some people don't like you. You don't have to please everyone. Only yourself, and maybe your cat.
- **It's OK** to stumble home at 6 a.m.
- **It's OK** to try to drown out the thoughts.
- **It's OK** to stay in bed all day.
- **It's OK** to need half an hour to mentally get ready for any social interaction.
- **It's OK** to be alone.

- **It's OK** to be a bit quiet.
- **It's OK** to feel scared.
- **It's OK** to hate that you feel scared.
- **It's OK** to worry that no one will like you.
- **It's OK** to feel insanely happy when it turns out they do like you.
- **It's OK** to need time to calm down. To need time on your own. To need to take your time.
- **It's OK** to take pride in the little things, to smile for an hour every time you manage to have a real conversation. To celebrate a day without panic.
- **It's OK** to like watching *The Kardashians*. It's OK to be very invested in their problems. It's OK to care when celebrities get haircuts.
- **It's OK** to have conversations with your dog.
- **It's OK** if you hate your body. It's OK if you hate your mind.
- **It's OK** to think things that aren't real. It's OK to hear voices. It's OK to ignore them.
- **It's OK** to talk about it.
- **It's OK** to not talk about it.
- **It's OK** to try.
- **It's OK** to fail.
- **It's OK** to go to therapy.
- **It's OK** to take medication.
- **It's OK** to go to hospital.

- **It's OK** to take the time you need to heal.
- **It's OK** to think that day is never going to come.
- **It's OK** to succeed, and to tell people when you succeed. It's OK to brag.
- **It's OK** to hate art galleries. It's OK to hate foreign movies. It's OK to have not read a novel since Harry Potter.
- **It's OK** if your parents are your best friends.
- **It's OK** if your family doesn't get it.
- **It's OK** to procrastinate. It's OK to not finish. It's OK to give up.
- **It's OK** to feel like none of it's OK. To feel like it's over every time you fail, every time you stumble. To not understand why it's not better than OK by now.
- **It's OK** to keep trying.
- **It's all OK.**

ACKNOWLEDGEMENTS

Thank you to Holly Harris, my editor and my best friend. Thank you to the entire team at Penguin for believing in this book and believing that mental health is a topic worthy of conversation.

Thank you to Shout for the incredible work that you do and for partnering with us on this book.

Thank you to every single one of the writers in this book. I want to be every single one of you when I grow up.

Thank you to Shonda Rhimes for creating *Grey's Anatomy* and getting me through some of the worst days.

Finally thank you to Mum, Dad, Jake, Char and Spike for never once making me feel ashamed and for holding my hand while my brain went dark, and for leading me slowly out the other side.

This book is for Belinda. I wish she could have read it.

WHAT IS SHOUT?

- Shout is the UK's first free 24/7 text service for anyone, anytime, anywhere. It's a place to go if you are struggling to cope and you need immediate help.
- Shout is powered by a team of Crisis Volunteers, who are at the heart of this service. We take people from crisis to calm every single day.
- Shout exists in the US as Crisis Text Line, but this is the first time this tried-and-tested technology has come to the UK. It was developed by The Royal Foundation, as a legacy of the Heads Together campaign.
- The anonymized data we collate gives us unique insights into mental health trends to help improve people's lives.

GET SUPPORT NOW

Anyone who needs some immediate support can connect with this service by texting the word **BlueBook** to 85258. We can help with a range of issues, including anxiety, bullying, stress, relationship challenges and suicidal thoughts. This service is delivered by Shout and powered by Crisis Text Line.

IF A LIFE IS AT IMMINENT RISK
CALL 999 FOR EMERGENCY HELP

HOW IT WORKS?

Shout is designed to be as easy to access as possible – there is no app or data required, no registration process, no fee. It is silent, free on the major UK networks, confidential and anonymous – anyone can send a text message any time of day or night wherever they happen to be in the UK.

- Connect by sending an SMS text message with the word BlueBook to 85258.
- You will receive an automated response explaining how the service works.
- You will be connected to a trained Crisis Volunteer.
- The Crisis Volunteer will listen and you will chat back and forth by text, sharing what is comfortable.
- You will need to work with the Crisis Volunteer to address your immediate issues and agree an action plan to help with next steps.
- You might be provided with information about other specialized charities and services to continue to get support.

EVERY CONVERSATION IS WITH A HUMAN BEING . . .

There are three levels of assessment operating across the service:

- **An algorithm:** Reviews the initial text and places urgent cases at the top of the queue.
- **Crisis Volunteers:** Over 18, have gone through application, reference checks and crisis-response training. These highly trained volunteers converse with texters and are the foundation of Shout.
- **Supervisors:** Full-time paid staff. They are qualified clinicians and work alongside the Crisis Volunteers to monitor conversations 24/7.

SHOUT IS:

- A 24/7 text service
- Support to take you from a hot moment to a calmer place
- A safe space where you're listened to by a trained Crisis Volunteer
- Our service is based on a tried-and-tested model of crisis support
- Shout Clinical Supervisors work alongside our Crisis Volunteers and monitor conversations 24/7
- An anonymous, free conversation that won't show on your phone bill
- Professional support creating a simple plan of action to manage your crisis

SHOUT IS NOT:

- Shout is not the emergency services
- We will contact emergency services if we believe you to be a harm to yourself or others, BUT it is then the judgement of the emergency services as to how and when they respond, once contacted
- Our Crisis Volunteers don't provide clinical advice
- It is not a one-way process; you won't be told what to do. You will need to work with the Crisis Volunteer to form your plan
- Shout does not provide therapy or long-term support

For further information on the different organizations offering help and support, please visit: www.headstogether.org.uk/get-support

YOUR 'IT'S OK' LIST